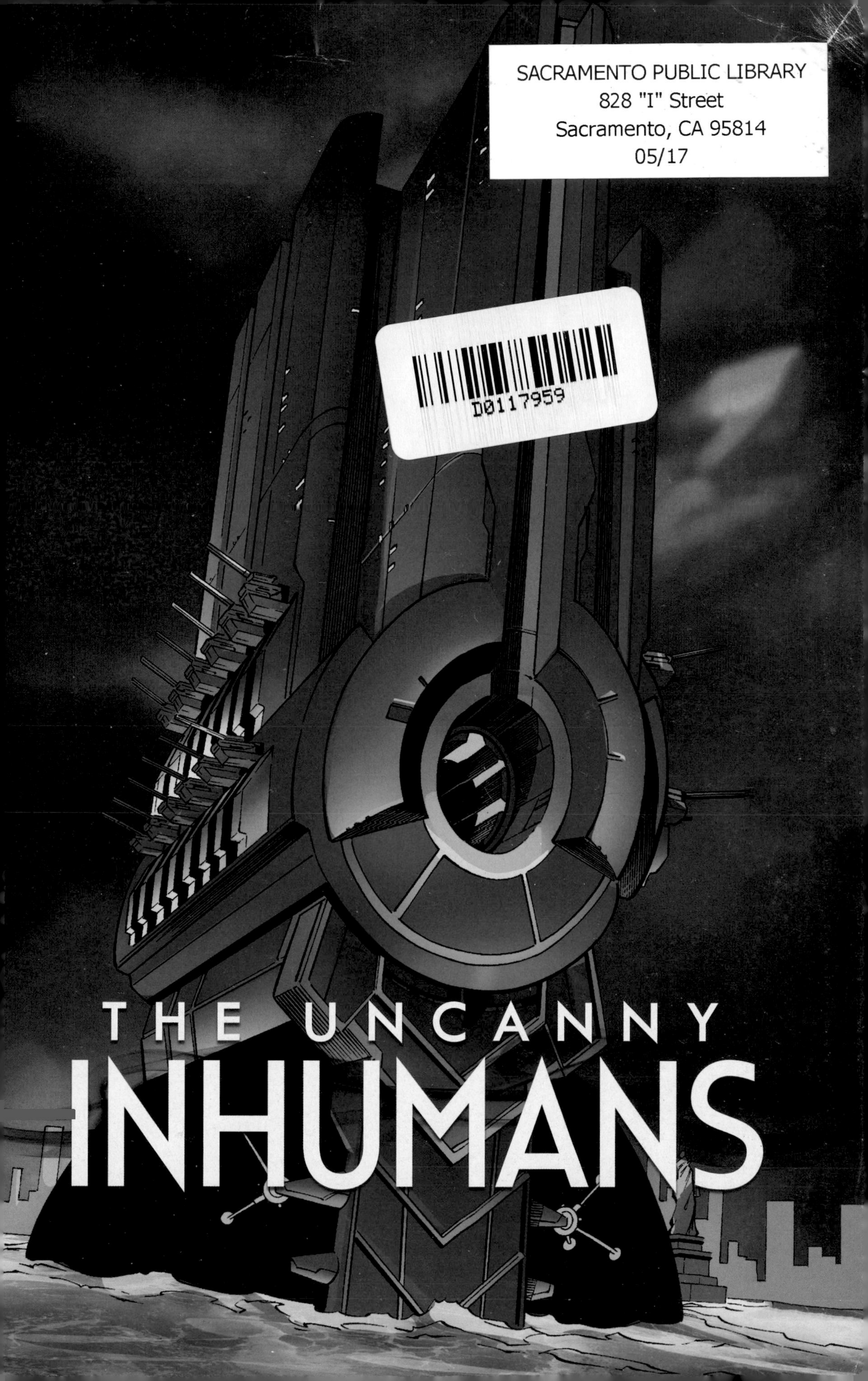
THE UNCANNY
INHUMANS

A young Inhuman named Ulysses seems to have the power to see events from the future. Using one of his predictions, the world's greatest heroes teamed up and stopped a being of cosmic power from destroying the Earth. Using another of his predictions, a mission to defeat Thanos went terribly wrong. Already suspicious of Ulysses' powers, the fallout from this second mission pushed Tony Stark, A.K.A. Iron Man, over the edge: he invaded New Attilan and kidnapped Ulysses. Everyone is watching the leader of the Inhumans to see how she'll respond — her reaction could spark a war.

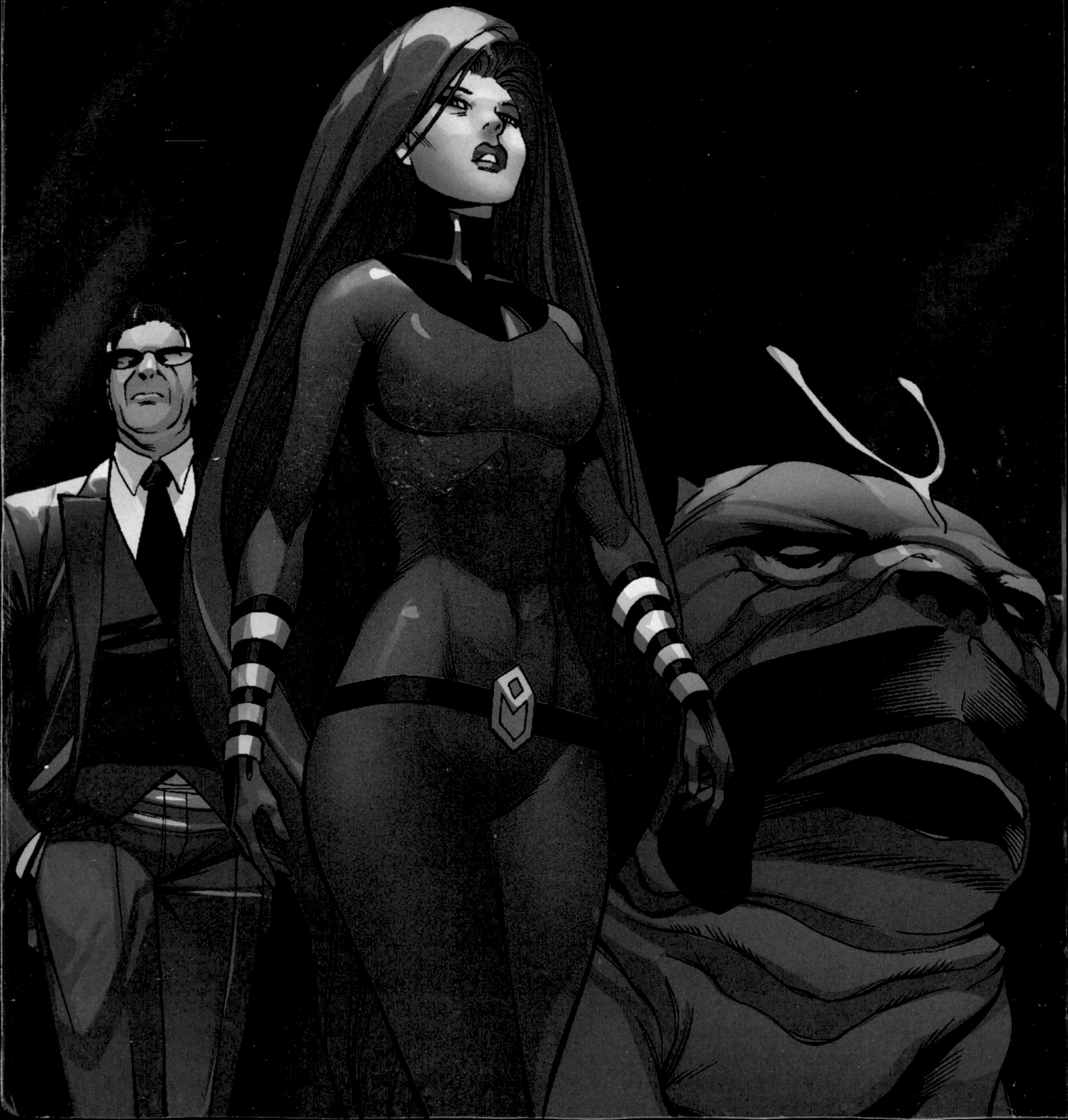

Thousands of years ago aliens experimented on cavemen, super-charging their evolution, and then mysteriously left their experiments behind. These men and women built the city of Attilan and discovered a chemical called Terrigen that unlocked secret super-powers in their modified DNA, making them...

THE UNCANNY INHUMANS

—— CIVIL WAR II ——

CHARLES SOULE
WRITER

CARLOS PACHECO (#11-13), KIM JACINTO (#13-14) & KEV WALKER (ANNUAL #1)
PENCILERS

ANDY OWENS (#11-13), KIM JACINTO (#13-14) & SCOTT HANNA (ANNUAL #1)
INKERS

DAVID CURIEL (#11-12), ANTONIO FABELA (#13-14) & DAN BROWN (ANNUAL #1)
COLORISTS

VC'S CLAYTON COWLES
LETTERER

CARLOS PACHECO & JAVA TARTAGLIA (#11), RYAN STEGMAN & RILEY ROSSMO (#12), RYAN STEGMAN & RICHARD ISANOVE (#13-14) AND JAMAL CAMPBELL (ANNUAL #1)
COVER ART

CHARLES BEACHAM
ASSISTANT EDITOR

DARREN SHAN
ASSOCIATE EDITOR

NICK LOWE
EDITOR

INHUMANS CREATED BY STAN LEE & JACK KIRBY

COLLECTION EDITOR: JENNIFER GRÜNWALD
ASSOCIATE MANAGING EDITOR: KATERI WOODY
ASSOCIATE EDITOR: SARAH BRUNSTAD
EDITOR, SPECIAL PROJECTS: MARK D. BEAZLEY

VP PRODUCTION & SPECIAL PROJECTS: JEFF YOUNGQUIST
SVP PRINT, SALES & MARKETING: DAVID GABRIEL
BOOK DESIGN: JAY BOWEN

EDITOR IN CHIEF: AXEL ALONSO
CHIEF CREATIVE OFFICER: JOE QUESADA
PUBLISHER: DAN BUCKLEY
EXECUTIVE PRODUCER: ALAN FINE

UNCANNY INHUMANS VOL. 3: CIVIL WAR II. Contains material originally published in magazine form as UNCANNY INHUMANS #11-14 and ANNUAL #1. First printing 2016. ISBN# 978-0-7851-9991-5. Published by MARVEL WORLDWIDE, INC., a subsidiary of MARVEL ENTERTAINMENT, LLC. OFFICE OF PUBLICATION: 135 West 50th Street, New York, NY 10020. Copyright © 2016 MARVEL No similarity between any of the names, characters, persons, and/or institutions in this magazine with those of any living or dead person or institution is intended, and any such similarity which may exist is purely coincidental. Printed in Canada. ALAN FINE, President, Marvel Entertainment; DAN BUCKLEY, President, TV, Publishing & Brand Management; JOE QUESADA, Chief Creative Officer; TOM BREVOORT, SVP of Publishing; DAVID BOGART, SVP of Business Affairs & Operations, Publishing & Partnership; C.B. CEBULSKI, VP of Brand Management & Development, Asia; DAVID GABRIEL, SVP of Sales & Marketing, Publishing; JEFF YOUNGQUIST, VP of Production & Special Projects; DAN CARR, Executive Director of Publishing Technology; ALEX MORALES, Director of Publishing Operations; SUSAN CRESPI, Production Manager; STAN LEE, Chairman Emeritus. For information regarding advertising in Marvel Comics or on Marvel.com, please contact Vit DeBellis, Integrated Sales Manager, at vdebellis@marvel.com. For Marvel subscription inquiries, please call 888-511-5480. Manufactured between 10/21/2016 and 11/28/2016 by SOLISCO PRINTERS, SCOTT, QC, CANADA.

10 9 8 7 6 5 4 3 2 1

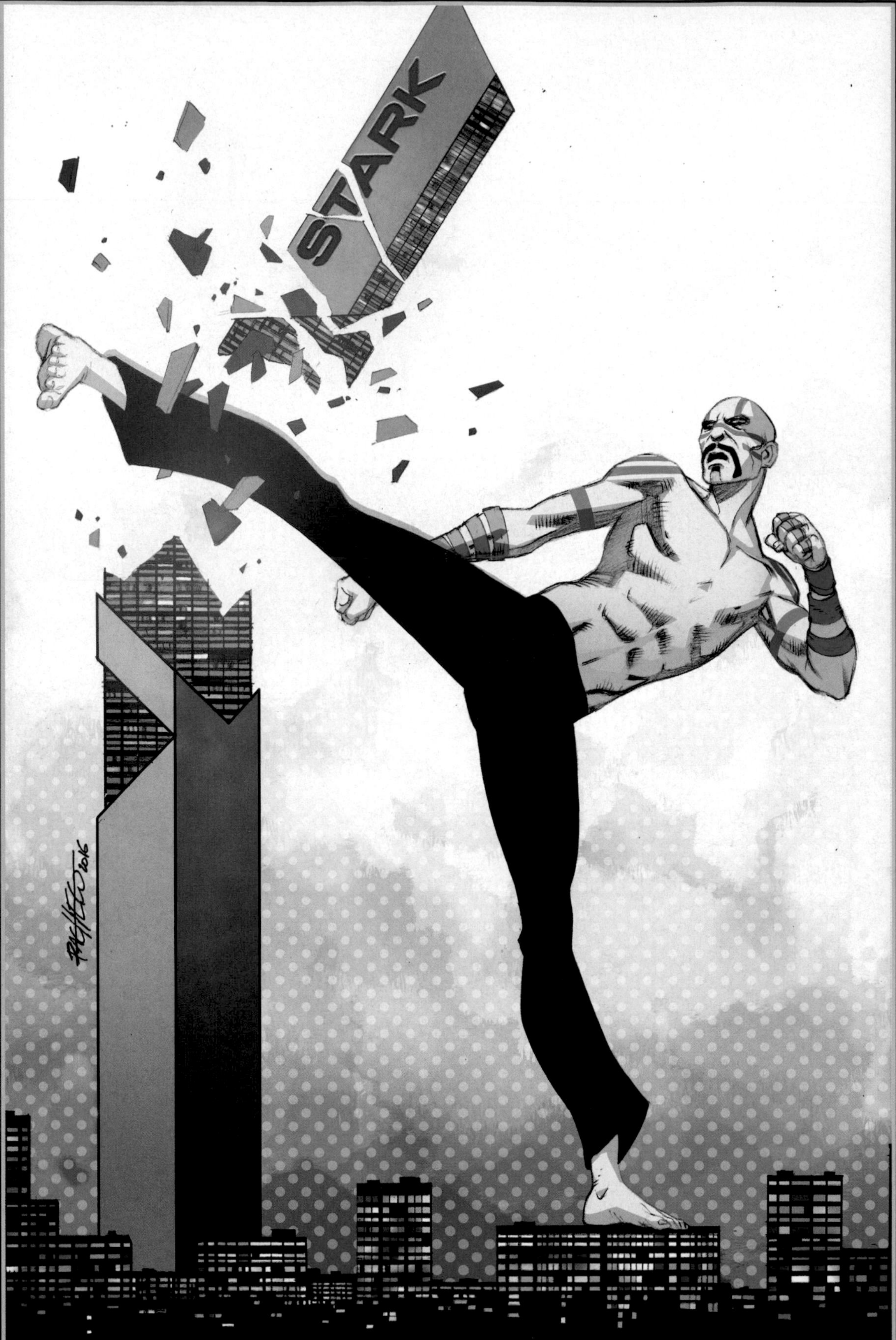
STARK

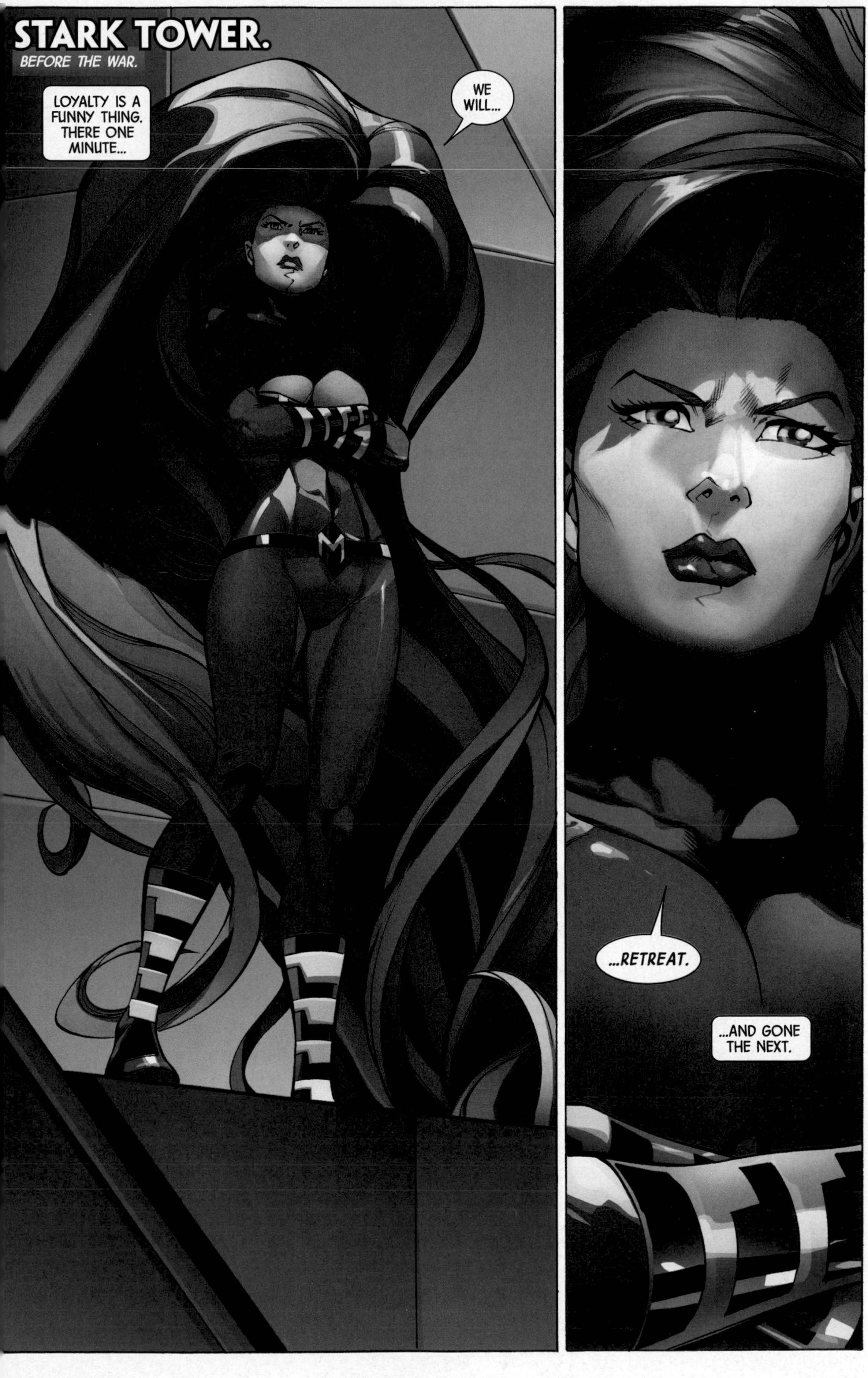
STARK TOWER.
BEFORE THE WAR.
LOYALTY IS A FUNNY THING. THERE ONE MINUTE...
WE WILL...
...RETREAT.
...AND GONE THE NEXT.

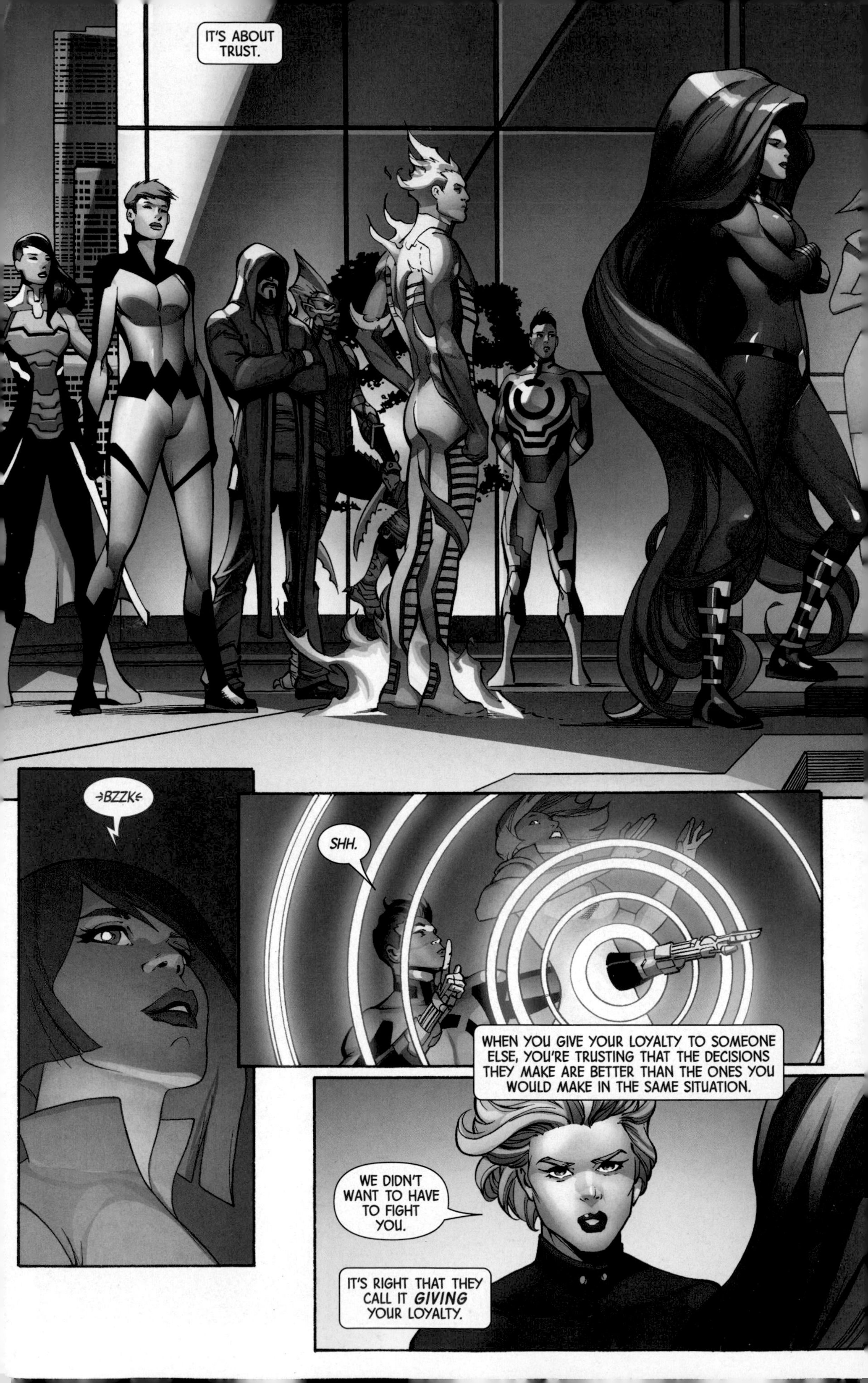
IT'S ABOUT TRUST.
BZZK
SHH.
WHEN YOU GIVE YOUR LOYALTY TO SOMEONE ELSE, YOU'RE TRUSTING THAT THE DECISIONS THEY MAKE ARE BETTER THAN THE ONES YOU WOULD MAKE IN THE SAME SITUATION.
WE DIDN'T WANT TO HAVE TO FIGHT YOU.
IT'S RIGHT THAT THEY CALL IT *GIVING* YOUR LOYALTY.

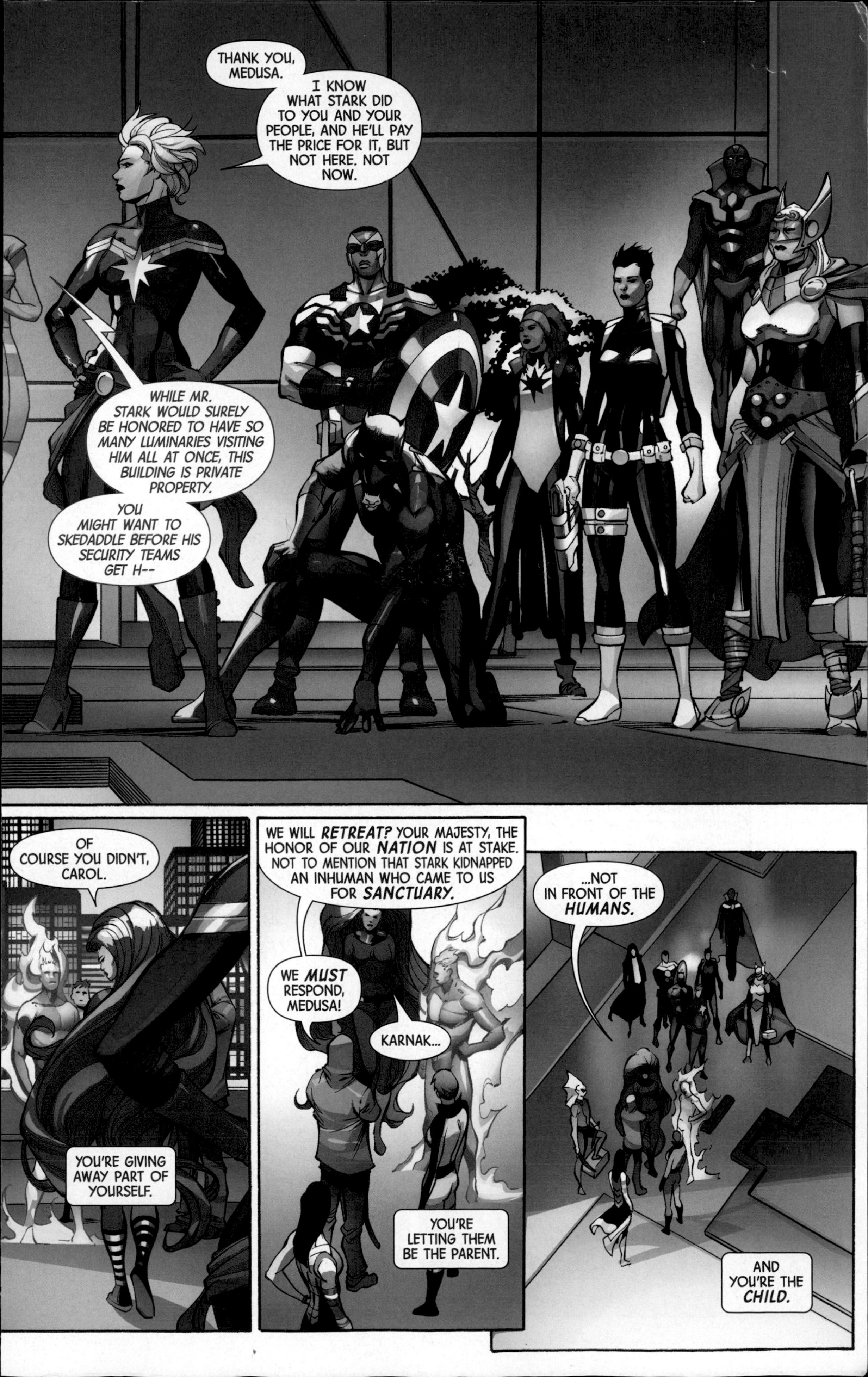
THANK YOU, MEDUSA.
I KNOW WHAT STARK DID TO YOU AND YOUR PEOPLE, AND HE'LL PAY THE PRICE FOR IT, BUT NOT HERE. NOT NOW.
WHILE MR. STARK WOULD SURELY BE HONORED TO HAVE SO MANY LUMINARIES VISITING HIM ALL AT ONCE, THIS BUILDING IS PRIVATE PROPERTY.
YOU MIGHT WANT TO SKEDADDLE BEFORE HIS SECURITY TEAMS GET H--
OF COURSE YOU DIDN'T, CAROL.
YOU'RE GIVING AWAY PART OF YOURSELF.
WE WILL RETREAT? YOUR MAJESTY, THE HONOR OF OUR NATION IS AT STAKE. NOT TO MENTION THAT STARK KIDNAPPED AN INHUMAN WHO CAME TO US FOR SANCTUARY.
WE MUST RESPOND, MEDUSA!
KARNAK...
YOU'RE LETTING THEM BE THE PARENT.
...NOT IN FRONT OF THE HUMANS.
AND YOU'RE THE CHILD.

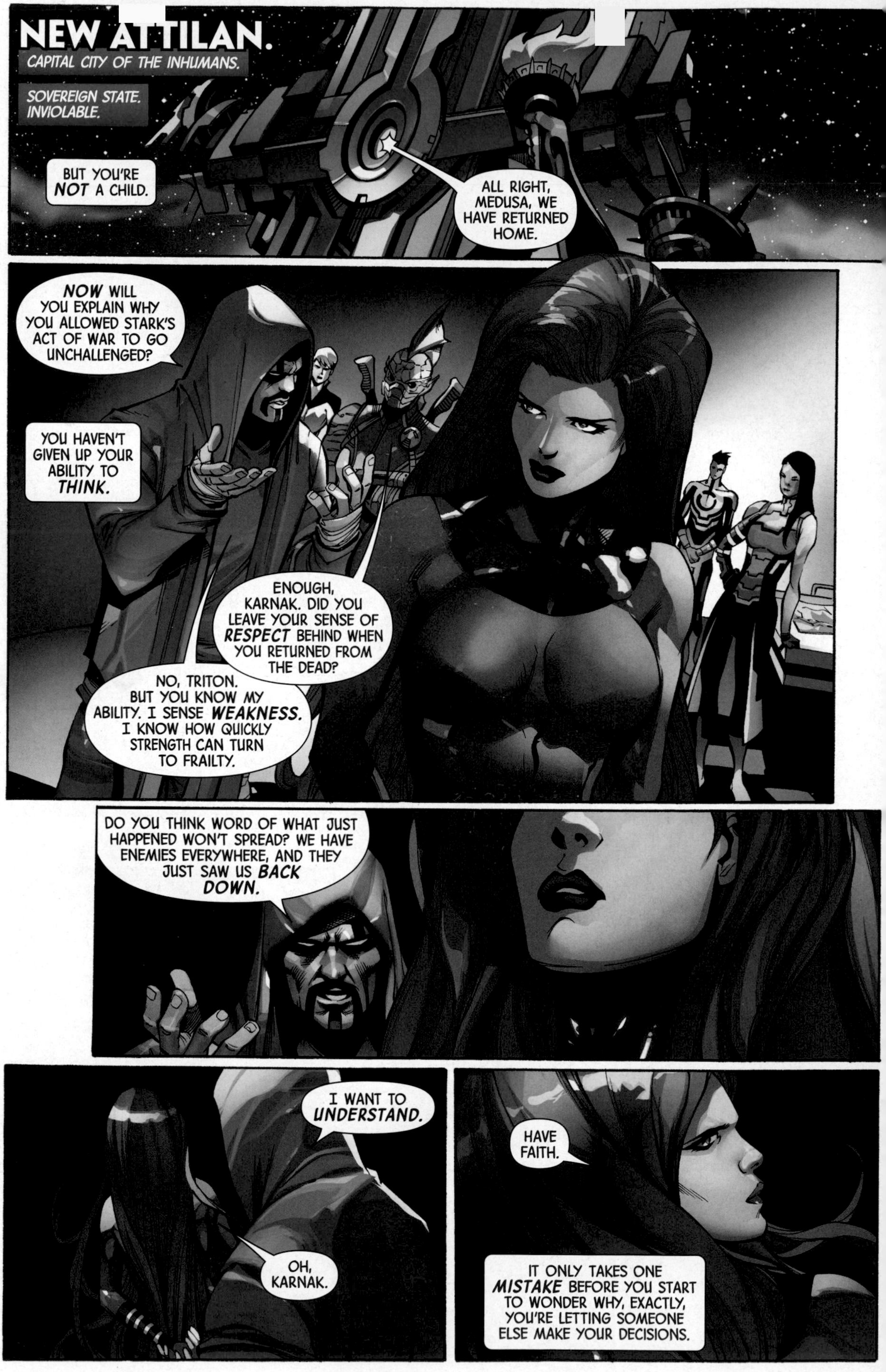

NEW ATTILAN.
CAPITAL CITY OF THE INHUMANS.
SOVEREIGN STATE. INVIOLABLE.
BUT YOU'RE NOT A CHILD.
ALL RIGHT, MEDUSA, WE HAVE RETURNED HOME.
NOW WILL YOU EXPLAIN WHY YOU ALLOWED STARK'S ACT OF WAR TO GO UNCHALLENGED?
YOU HAVEN'T GIVEN UP YOUR ABILITY TO THINK.
ENOUGH, KARNAK. DID YOU LEAVE YOUR SENSE OF RESPECT BEHIND WHEN YOU RETURNED FROM THE DEAD?
NO, TRITON. BUT YOU KNOW MY ABILITY. I SENSE WEAKNESS. I KNOW HOW QUICKLY STRENGTH CAN TURN TO FRAILTY.
DO YOU THINK WORD OF WHAT JUST HAPPENED WON'T SPREAD? WE HAVE ENEMIES EVERYWHERE, AND THEY JUST SAW US BACK DOWN.
I WANT TO UNDERSTAND.
OH, KARNAK.
HAVE FAITH.
IT ONLY TAKES ONE MISTAKE BEFORE YOU START TO WONDER WHY, EXACTLY, YOU'RE LETTING SOMEONE ELSE MAKE YOUR DECISIONS.

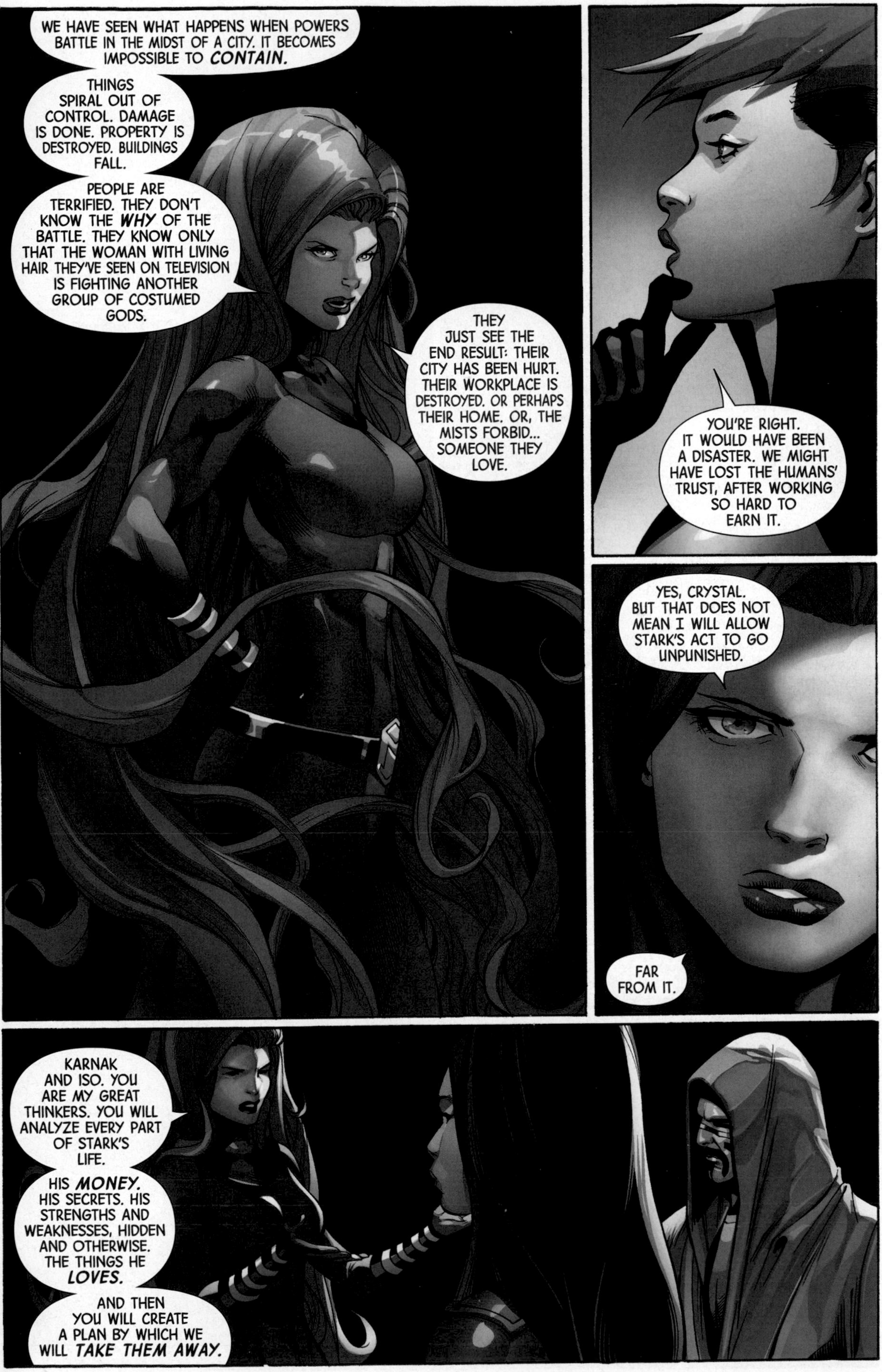
WE HAVE SEEN WHAT HAPPENS WHEN POWERS BATTLE IN THE MIDST OF A CITY. IT BECOMES IMPOSSIBLE TO CONTAIN.
THINGS SPIRAL OUT OF CONTROL. DAMAGE IS DONE. PROPERTY IS DESTROYED. BUILDINGS FALL.
PEOPLE ARE TERRIFIED. THEY DON'T KNOW THE WHY OF THE BATTLE. THEY KNOW ONLY THAT THE WOMAN WITH LIVING HAIR THEY'VE SEEN ON TELEVISION IS FIGHTING ANOTHER GROUP OF COSTUMED GODS.
THEY JUST SEE THE END RESULT: THEIR CITY HAS BEEN HURT. THEIR WORKPLACE IS DESTROYED. OR PERHAPS THEIR HOME. OR, THE MISTS FORBID... SOMEONE THEY LOVE.
YOU'RE RIGHT. IT WOULD HAVE BEEN A DISASTER. WE MIGHT HAVE LOST THE HUMANS' TRUST, AFTER WORKING SO HARD TO EARN IT.
YES, CRYSTAL. BUT THAT DOES NOT MEAN I WILL ALLOW STARK'S ACT TO GO UNPUNISHED.
FAR FROM IT.
KARNAK AND ISO. YOU ARE MY GREAT THINKERS. YOU WILL ANALYZE EVERY PART OF STARK'S LIFE.
HIS MONEY. HIS SECRETS. HIS STRENGTHS AND WEAKNESSES, HIDDEN AND OTHERWISE. THE THINGS HE LOVES.
AND THEN YOU WILL CREATE A PLAN BY WHICH WE WILL TAKE THEM AWAY.

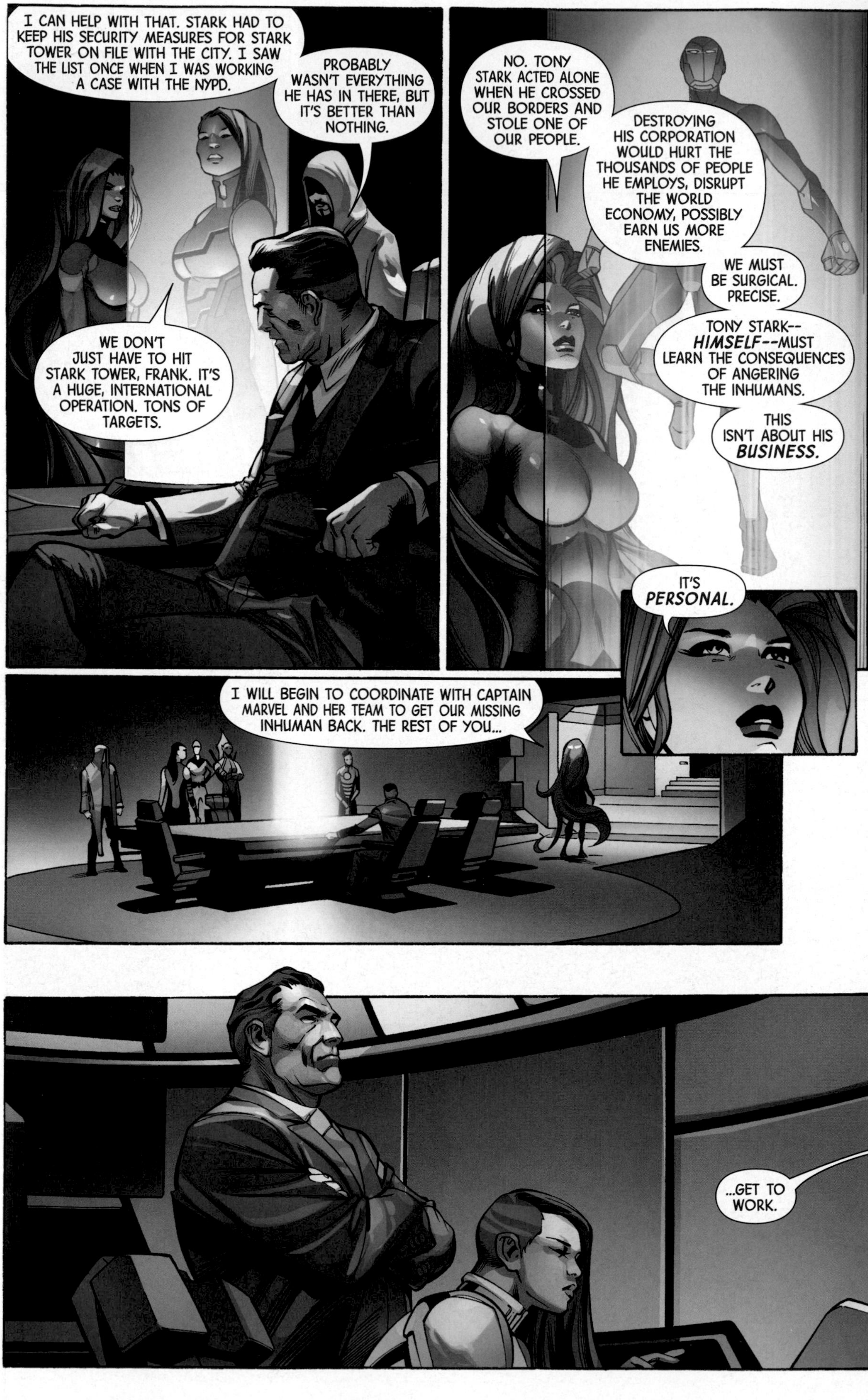
I CAN HELP WITH THAT. STARK HAD TO KEEP HIS SECURITY MEASURES FOR STARK TOWER ON FILE WITH THE CITY. I SAW THE LIST ONCE WHEN I WAS WORKING A CASE WITH THE NYPD.
PROBABLY WASN'T EVERYTHING HE HAS IN THERE, BUT IT'S BETTER THAN NOTHING.
WE DON'T JUST HAVE TO HIT STARK TOWER, FRANK. IT'S A HUGE, INTERNATIONAL OPERATION. TONS OF TARGETS.
NO. TONY STARK ACTED ALONE WHEN HE CROSSED OUR BORDERS AND STOLE ONE OF OUR PEOPLE.
DESTROYING HIS CORPORATION WOULD HURT THE THOUSANDS OF PEOPLE HE EMPLOYS, DISRUPT THE WORLD ECONOMY, POSSIBLY EARN US MORE ENEMIES.
WE MUST BE SURGICAL. PRECISE.
TONY STARK-- *HIMSELF*--MUST LEARN THE CONSEQUENCES OF ANGERING THE INHUMANS.
THIS ISN'T ABOUT HIS *BUSINESS.*
IT'S *PERSONAL.*
I WILL BEGIN TO COORDINATE WITH CAPTAIN MARVEL AND HER TEAM TO GET OUR MISSING INHUMAN BACK. THE REST OF YOU...
...GET TO WORK.

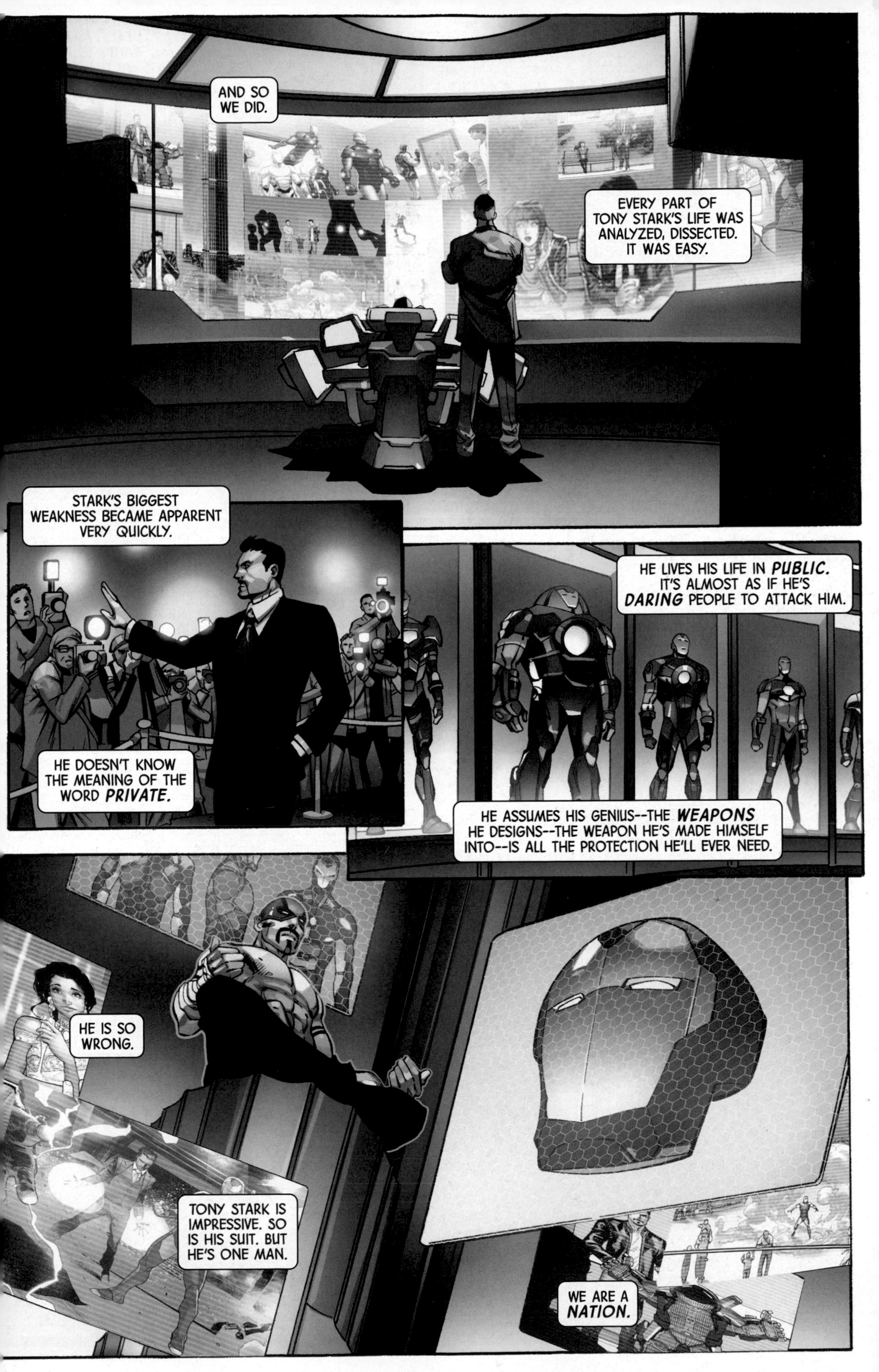
AND SO WE DID.
EVERY PART OF TONY STARK'S LIFE WAS ANALYZED, DISSECTED. IT WAS EASY.
STARK'S BIGGEST WEAKNESS BECAME APPARENT VERY QUICKLY.
HE DOESN'T KNOW THE MEANING OF THE WORD PRIVATE.
HE LIVES HIS LIFE IN PUBLIC. IT'S ALMOST AS IF HE'S DARING PEOPLE TO ATTACK HIM.
HE ASSUMES HIS GENIUS--THE WEAPONS HE DESIGNS--THE WEAPON HE'S MADE HIMSELF INTO--IS ALL THE PROTECTION HE'LL EVER NEED.
HE IS SO WRONG.
TONY STARK IS IMPRESSIVE. SO IS HIS SUIT. BUT HE'S ONE MAN.
WE ARE A NATION.

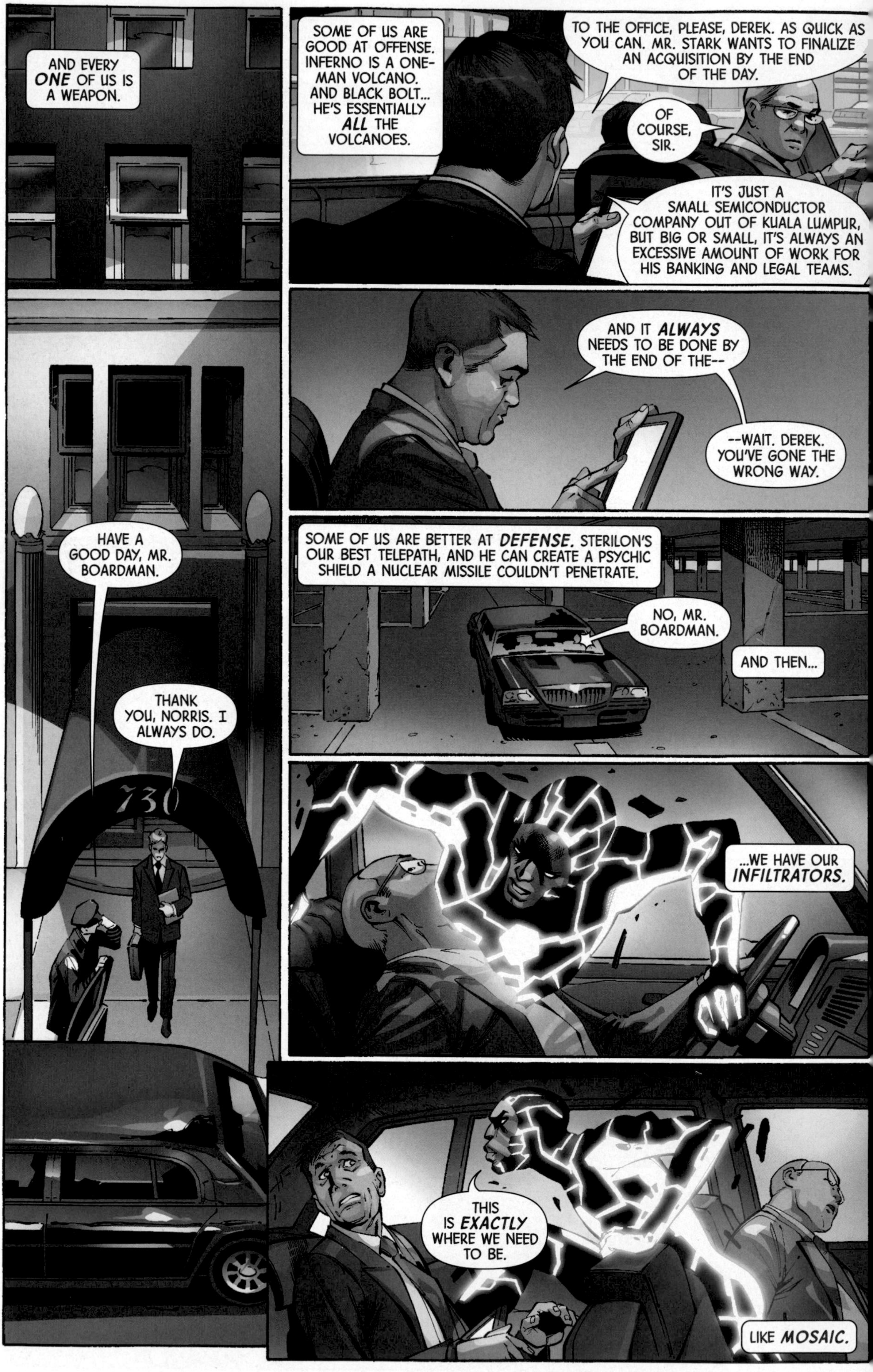
AND EVERY ONE OF US IS A WEAPON.
SOME OF US ARE GOOD AT OFFENSE. INFERNO IS A ONE-MAN VOLCANO. AND BLACK BOLT... HE'S ESSENTIALLY ALL THE VOLCANOES.
TO THE OFFICE, PLEASE, DEREK. AS QUICK AS YOU CAN. MR. STARK WANTS TO FINALIZE AN ACQUISITION BY THE END OF THE DAY.
OF COURSE, SIR.
IT'S JUST A SMALL SEMICONDUCTOR COMPANY OUT OF KUALA LUMPUR, BUT BIG OR SMALL, IT'S ALWAYS AN EXCESSIVE AMOUNT OF WORK FOR HIS BANKING AND LEGAL TEAMS.
HAVE A GOOD DAY, MR. BOARDMAN.
THANK YOU, NORRIS. I ALWAYS DO.
730
AND IT ALWAYS NEEDS TO BE DONE BY THE END OF THE--
--WAIT. DEREK. YOU'VE GONE THE WRONG WAY.
SOME OF US ARE BETTER AT DEFENSE. STERILON'S OUR BEST TELEPATH, AND HE CAN CREATE A PSYCHIC SHIELD A NUCLEAR MISSILE COULDN'T PENETRATE.
NO, MR. BOARDMAN.
AND THEN...
...WE HAVE OUR INFILTRATORS.
THIS IS EXACTLY WHERE WE NEED TO BE.
LIKE MOSAIC.

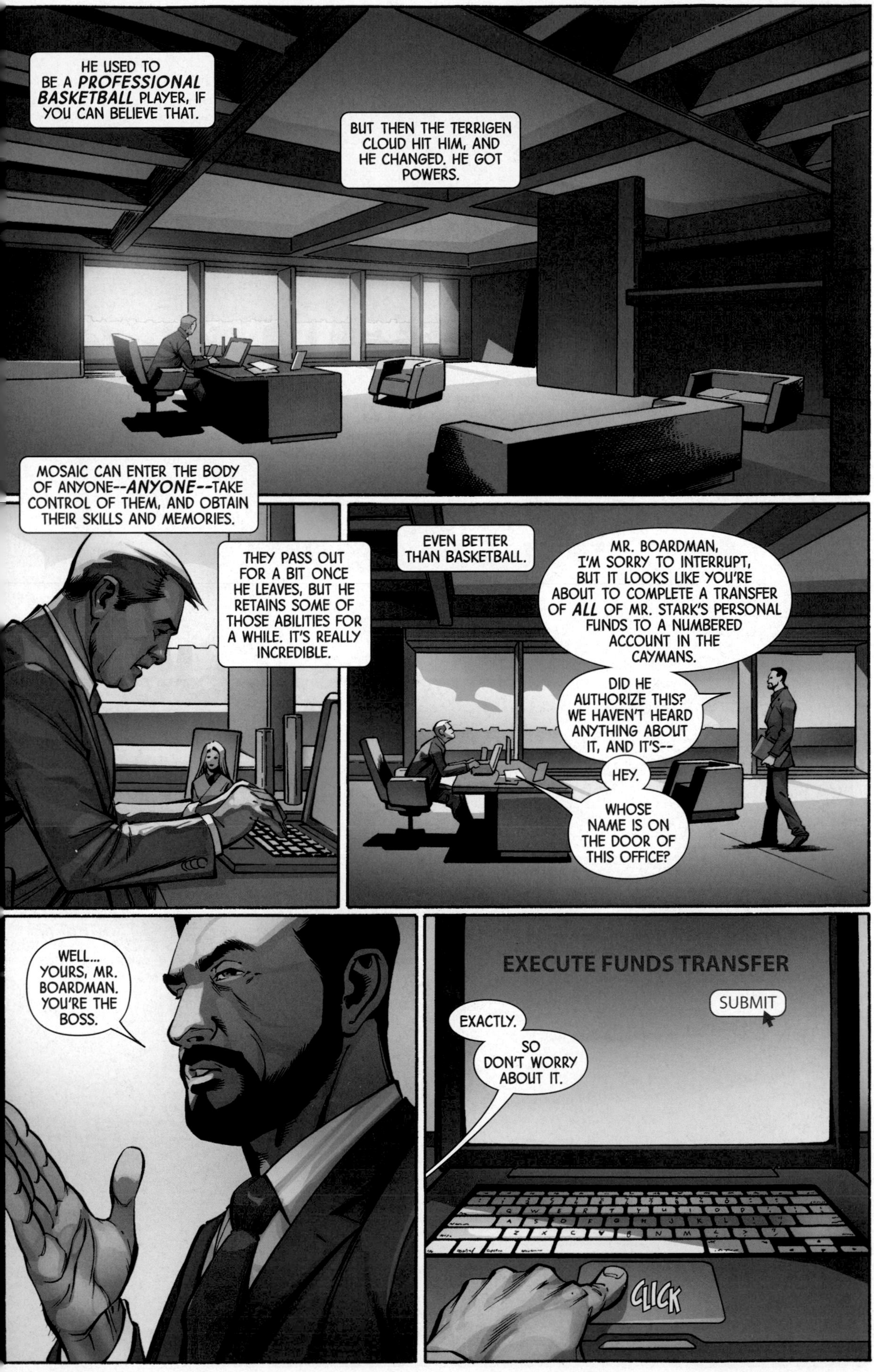
HE USED TO BE A PROFESSIONAL BASKETBALL PLAYER, IF YOU CAN BELIEVE THAT.
BUT THEN THE TERRIGEN CLOUD HIT HIM, AND HE CHANGED. HE GOT POWERS.
MOSAIC CAN ENTER THE BODY OF ANYONE--ANYONE--TAKE CONTROL OF THEM, AND OBTAIN THEIR SKILLS AND MEMORIES.
THEY PASS OUT FOR A BIT ONCE HE LEAVES, BUT HE RETAINS SOME OF THOSE ABILITIES FOR A WHILE. IT'S REALLY INCREDIBLE.
EVEN BETTER THAN BASKETBALL.
MR. BOARDMAN, I'M SORRY TO INTERRUPT, BUT IT LOOKS LIKE YOU'RE ABOUT TO COMPLETE A TRANSFER OF ALL OF MR. STARK'S PERSONAL FUNDS TO A NUMBERED ACCOUNT IN THE CAYMANS.
DID HE AUTHORIZE THIS? WE HAVEN'T HEARD ANYTHING ABOUT IT, AND IT'S--
HEY.
WHOSE NAME IS ON THE DOOR OF THIS OFFICE?
WELL... YOURS, MR. BOARDMAN. YOU'RE THE BOSS.
EXECUTE FUNDS TRANSFER
SUBMIT
EXACTLY.
SO DON'T WORRY ABOUT IT.
CLICK

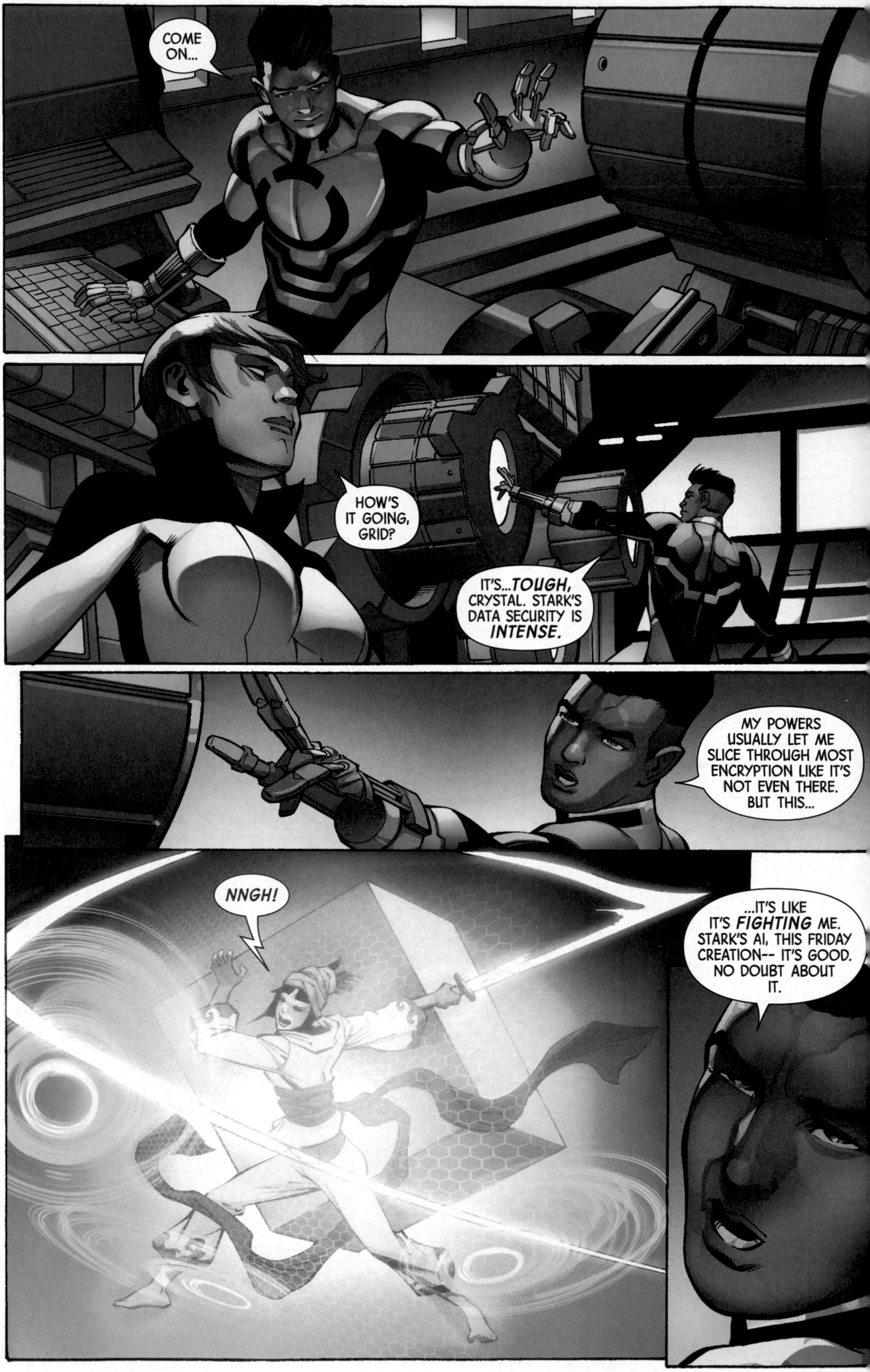
COME ON...
HOW'S IT GOING, GRID?
IT'S...TOUGH, CRYSTAL. STARK'S DATA SECURITY IS INTENSE.
MY POWERS USUALLY LET ME SLICE THROUGH MOST ENCRYPTION LIKE IT'S NOT EVEN THERE. BUT THIS...
NNGH!
...IT'S LIKE IT'S FIGHTING ME. STARK'S AI, THIS FRIDAY CREATION-- IT'S GOOD. NO DOUBT ABOUT IT.

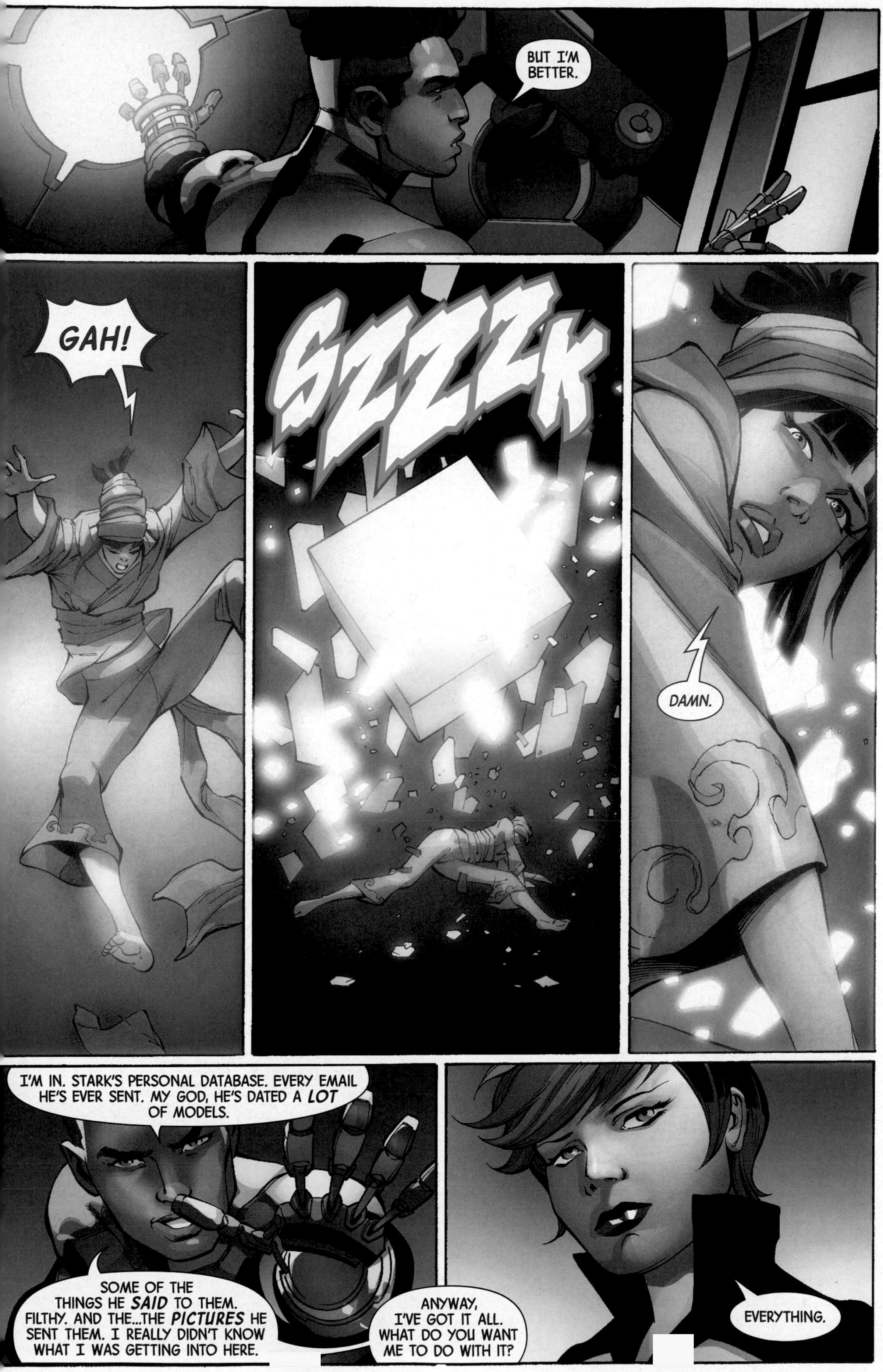
BUT I'M BETTER.
GAH!
SZZZK
DAMN.
I'M IN. STARK'S PERSONAL DATABASE. EVERY EMAIL HE'S EVER SENT. MY GOD, HE'S DATED A LOT OF MODELS.
SOME OF THE THINGS HE SAID TO THEM. FILTHY. AND THE...THE PICTURES HE SENT THEM. I REALLY DIDN'T KNOW WHAT I WAS GETTING INTO HERE.
ANYWAY, I'VE GOT IT ALL. WHAT DO YOU WANT ME TO DO WITH IT?
EVERYTHING.

STARK VEHICLE STORAGE WAREHOUSE #9.

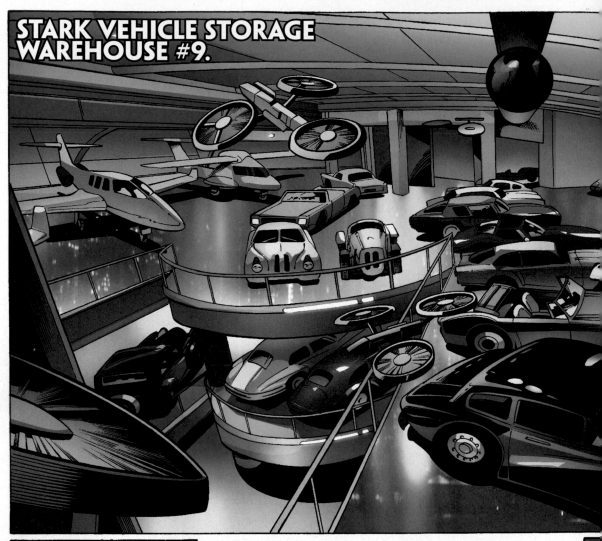

UNAUTHORIZED INCURSION!

SZZZACK

ANALYZING THREAT LEVEL.

INTRUDER IDENTIFIED AS LOCKJAW. AFFILIATION: INHUMANS.

TELEPORTATION ABILITIES.

SUBJECT HAS ARRIVED ALONE. THREAT ASSESSMENT-- MINIMAL.

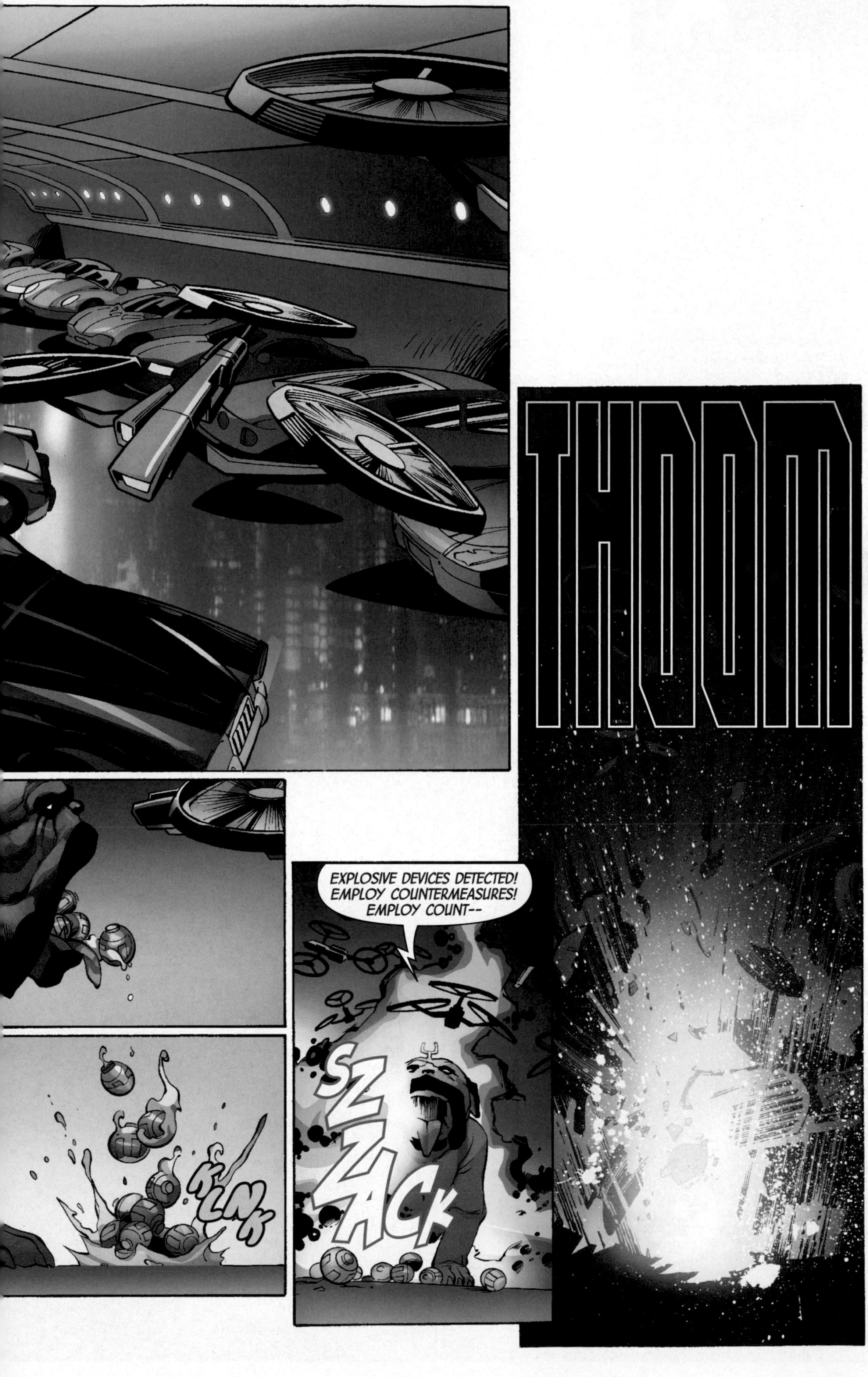
EXPLOSIVE DEVICES DETECTED! EMPLOY COUNTERMEASURES! EMPLOY COUNT--
KLNK
SZZACK
THOOM

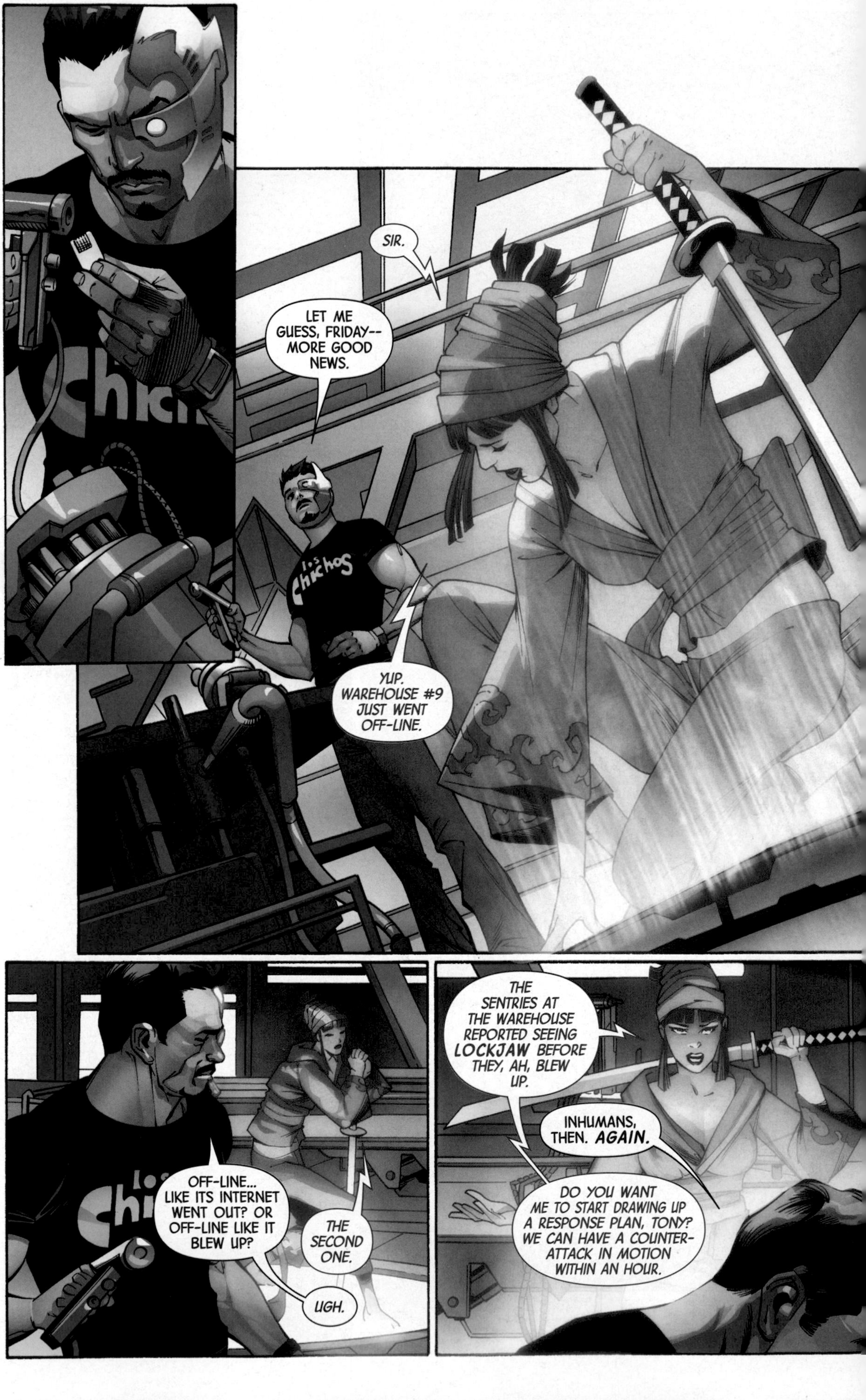
SIR.
LET ME GUESS, FRIDAY-- MORE GOOD NEWS.
YUP. WAREHOUSE #9 JUST WENT OFF-LINE.
OFF-LINE... LIKE ITS INTERNET WENT OUT? OR OFF-LINE LIKE IT BLEW UP?
THE SECOND ONE.
UGH.
THE SENTRIES AT THE WAREHOUSE REPORTED SEEING LOCKJAW BEFORE THEY, AH, BLEW UP.
INHUMANS, THEN. AGAIN.
DO YOU WANT ME TO START DRAWING UP A RESPONSE PLAN, TONY? WE CAN HAVE A COUNTER-ATTACK IN MOTION WITHIN AN HOUR.

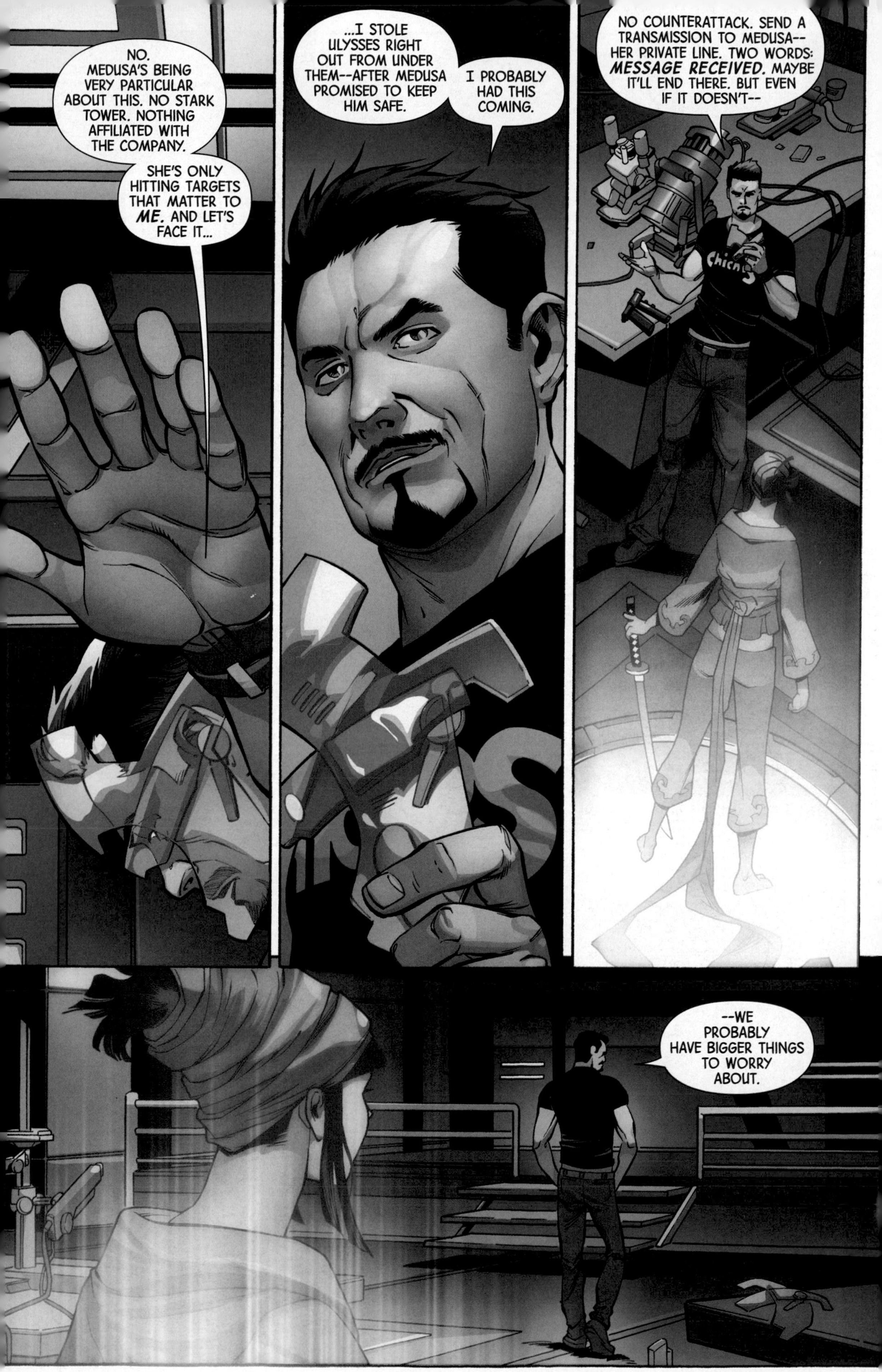
NO. MEDUSA'S BEING VERY PARTICULAR ABOUT THIS. NO STARK TOWER. NOTHING AFFILIATED WITH THE COMPANY.
SHE'S ONLY HITTING TARGETS THAT MATTER TO ME. AND LET'S FACE IT...
...I STOLE ULYSSES RIGHT OUT FROM UNDER THEM--AFTER MEDUSA PROMISED TO KEEP HIM SAFE.
I PROBABLY HAD THIS COMING.
NO COUNTERATTACK. SEND A TRANSMISSION TO MEDUSA--HER PRIVATE LINE. TWO WORDS: MESSAGE RECEIVED. MAYBE IT'LL END THERE. BUT EVEN IF IT DOESN'T--
--WE PROBABLY HAVE BIGGER THINGS TO WORRY ABOUT.

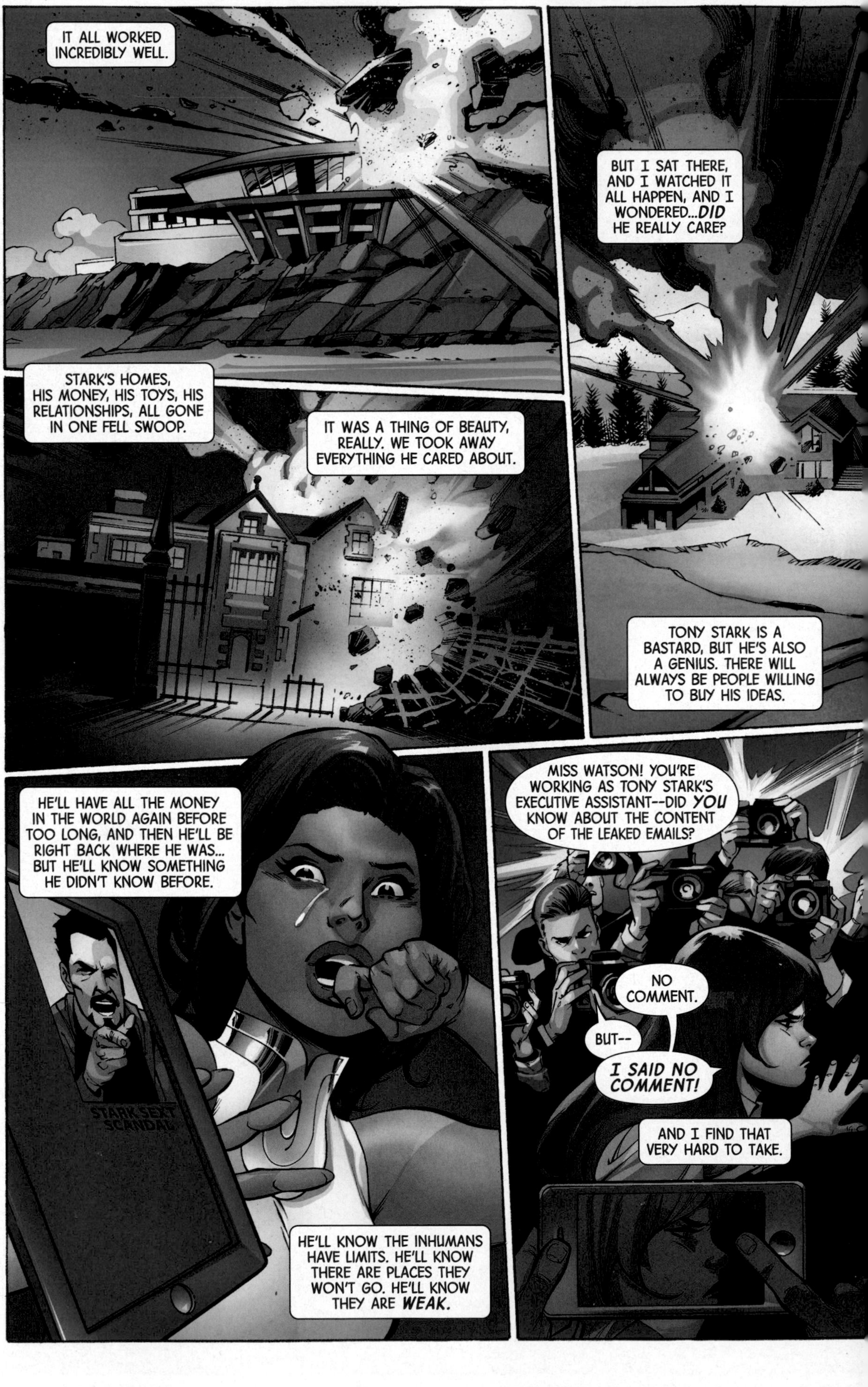
IT ALL WORKED INCREDIBLY WELL.
BUT I SAT THERE, AND I WATCHED IT ALL HAPPEN, AND I WONDERED...DID HE REALLY CARE?
STARK'S HOMES, HIS MONEY, HIS TOYS, HIS RELATIONSHIPS, ALL GONE IN ONE FELL SWOOP.
IT WAS A THING OF BEAUTY, REALLY. WE TOOK AWAY EVERYTHING HE CARED ABOUT.
TONY STARK IS A BASTARD, BUT HE'S ALSO A GENIUS. THERE WILL ALWAYS BE PEOPLE WILLING TO BUY HIS IDEAS.
HE'LL HAVE ALL THE MONEY IN THE WORLD AGAIN BEFORE TOO LONG, AND THEN HE'LL BE RIGHT BACK WHERE HE WAS... BUT HE'LL KNOW SOMETHING HE DIDN'T KNOW BEFORE.
STARK SEXT SCANDAL
HE'LL KNOW THE INHUMANS HAVE LIMITS. HE'LL KNOW THERE ARE PLACES THEY WON'T GO. HE'LL KNOW THEY ARE WEAK.
MISS WATSON! YOU'RE WORKING AS TONY STARK'S EXECUTIVE ASSISTANT--DID YOU KNOW ABOUT THE CONTENT OF THE LEAKED EMAILS?
NO COMMENT.
BUT--
I SAID NO COMMENT!
AND I FIND THAT VERY HARD TO TAKE.

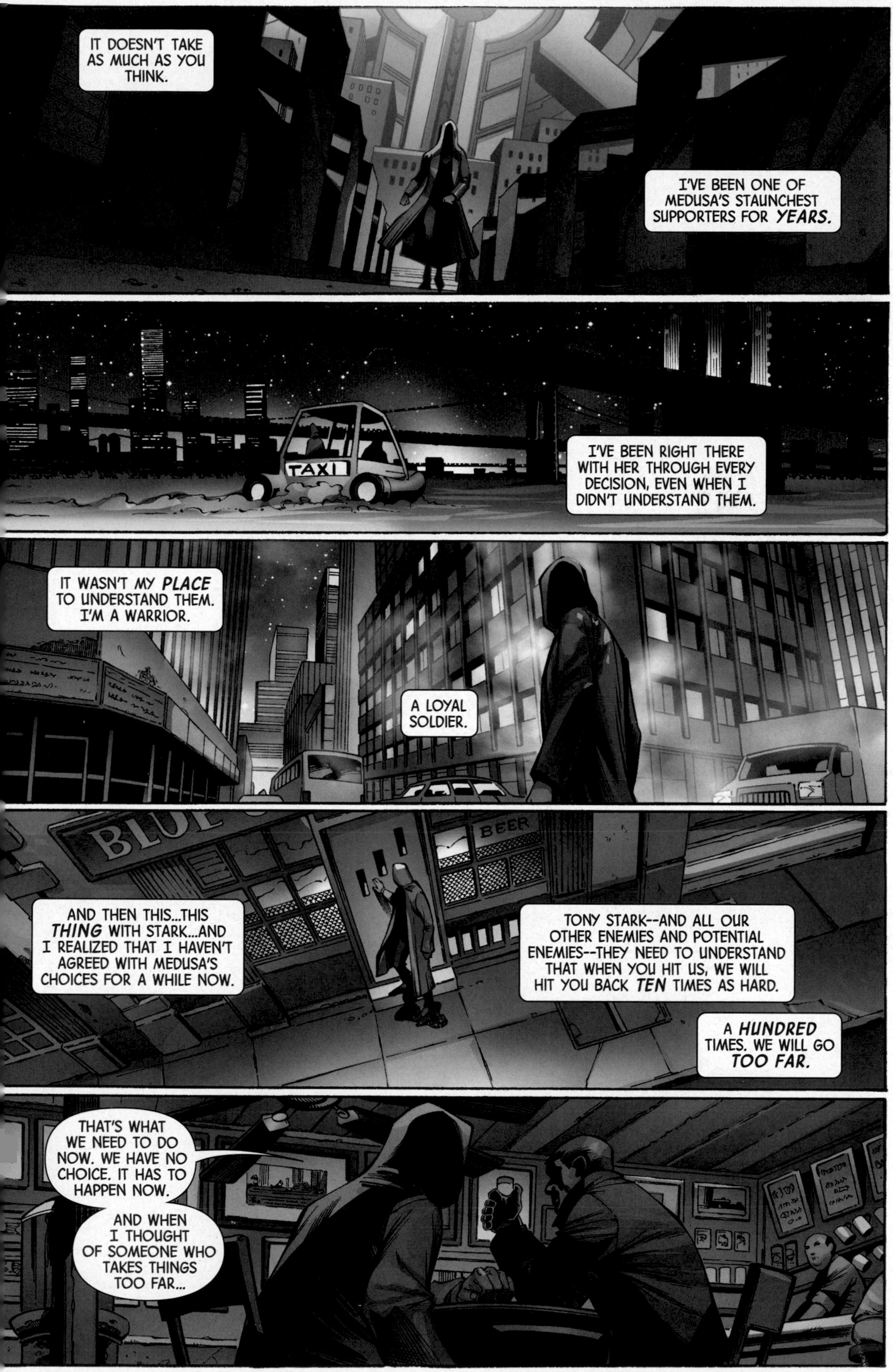
IT DOESN'T TAKE AS MUCH AS YOU THINK.
I'VE BEEN ONE OF MEDUSA'S STAUNCHEST SUPPORTERS FOR YEARS.
TAXI
I'VE BEEN RIGHT THERE WITH HER THROUGH EVERY DECISION, EVEN WHEN I DIDN'T UNDERSTAND THEM.
IT WASN'T MY PLACE TO UNDERSTAND THEM. I'M A WARRIOR.
A LOYAL SOLDIER.
BLUE
BEER
AND THEN THIS...THIS THING WITH STARK...AND I REALIZED THAT I HAVEN'T AGREED WITH MEDUSA'S CHOICES FOR A WHILE NOW.
TONY STARK--AND ALL OUR OTHER ENEMIES AND POTENTIAL ENEMIES--THEY NEED TO UNDERSTAND THAT WHEN YOU HIT US, WE WILL HIT YOU BACK TEN TIMES AS HARD.
A HUNDRED TIMES. WE WILL GO TOO FAR.
THAT'S WHAT WE NEED TO DO NOW. WE HAVE NO CHOICE. IT HAS TO HAPPEN NOW.
AND WHEN I THOUGHT OF SOMEONE WHO TAKES THINGS TOO FAR...

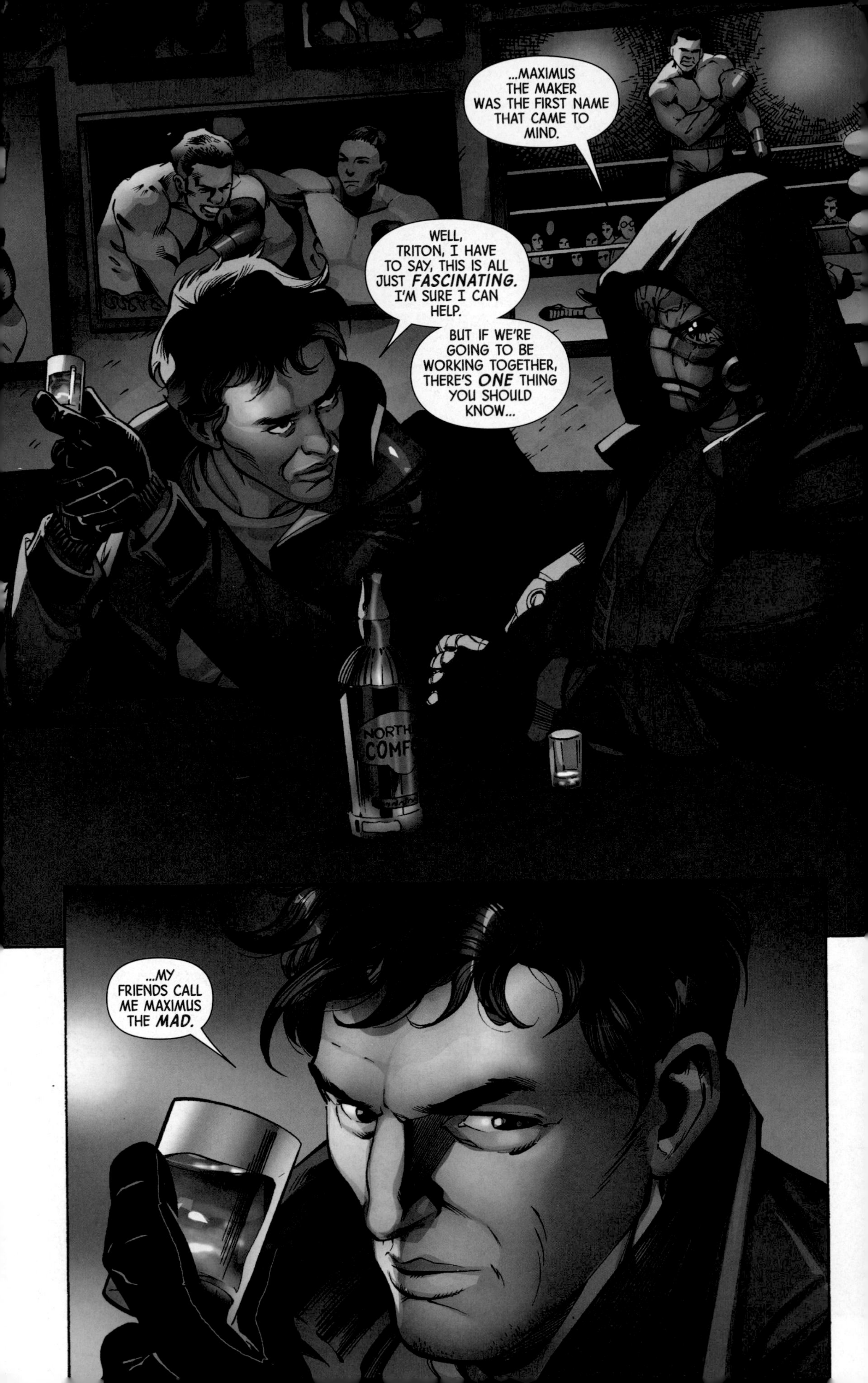
...MAXIMUS THE MAKER WAS THE FIRST NAME THAT CAME TO MIND.
WELL, TRITON, I HAVE TO SAY, THIS IS ALL JUST FASCINATING. I'M SURE I CAN HELP.
BUT IF WE'RE GOING TO BE WORKING TOGETHER, THERE'S ONE THING YOU SHOULD KNOW...
NORTH
COMF
...MY FRIENDS CALL ME MAXIMUS THE MAD.

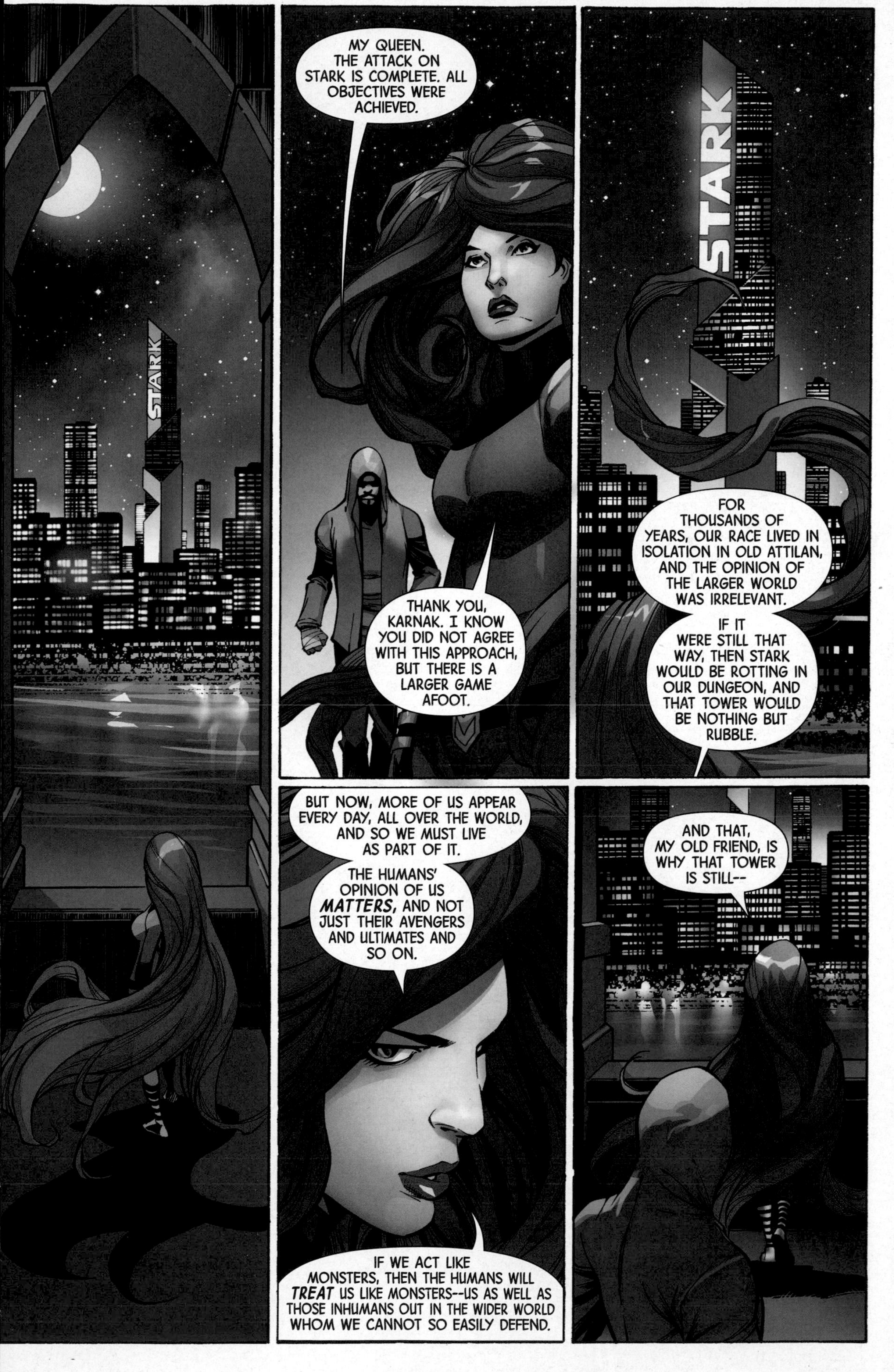
MY QUEEN. THE ATTACK ON STARK IS COMPLETE. ALL OBJECTIVES WERE ACHIEVED.
THANK YOU, KARNAK. I KNOW YOU DID NOT AGREE WITH THIS APPROACH, BUT THERE IS A LARGER GAME AFOOT.
STARK
FOR THOUSANDS OF YEARS, OUR RACE LIVED IN ISOLATION IN OLD ATTILAN, AND THE OPINION OF THE LARGER WORLD WAS IRRELEVANT.
IF IT WERE STILL THAT WAY, THEN STARK WOULD BE ROTTING IN OUR DUNGEON, AND THAT TOWER WOULD BE NOTHING BUT RUBBLE.
BUT NOW, MORE OF US APPEAR EVERY DAY, ALL OVER THE WORLD, AND SO WE MUST LIVE AS PART OF IT.
THE HUMANS' OPINION OF US *MATTERS*, AND NOT JUST THEIR AVENGERS AND ULTIMATES AND SO ON.
IF WE ACT LIKE MONSTERS, THEN THE HUMANS WILL *TREAT* US LIKE MONSTERS--US AS WELL AS THOSE INHUMANS OUT IN THE WIDER WORLD WHOM WE CANNOT SO EASILY DEFEND.
AND THAT, MY OLD FRIEND, IS WHY THAT TOWER IS STILL--

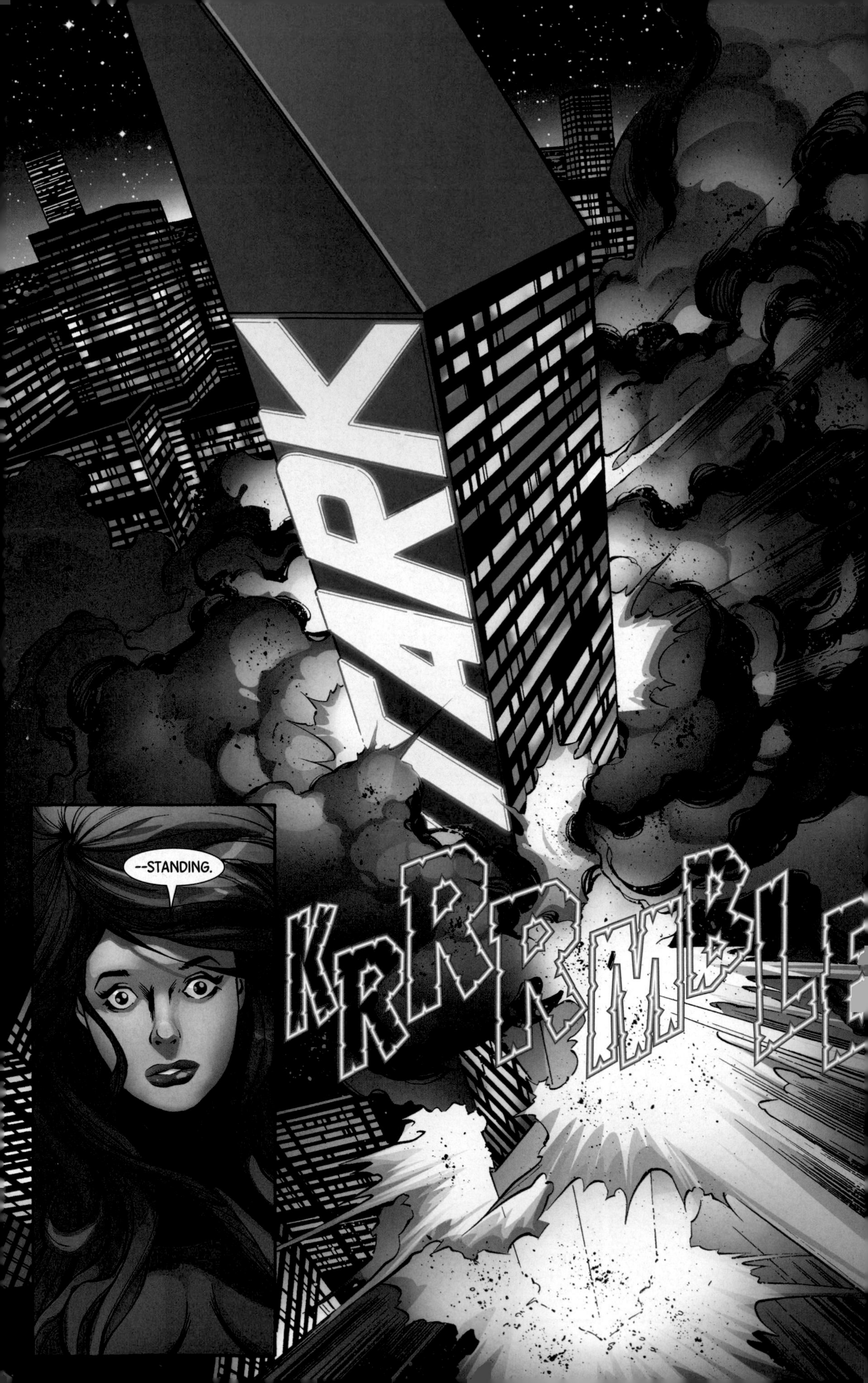
--STANDING.
KRRRMBLE

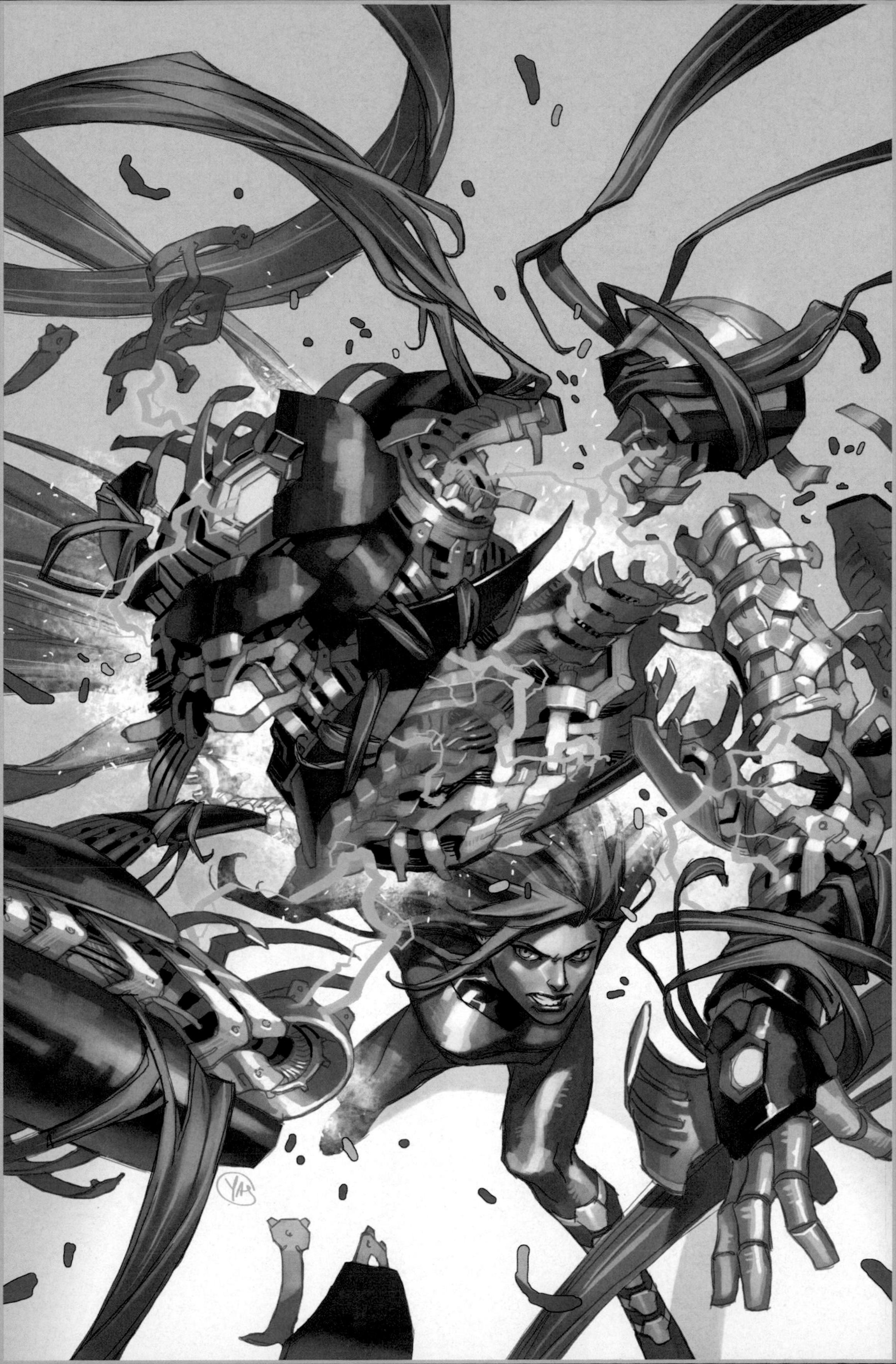

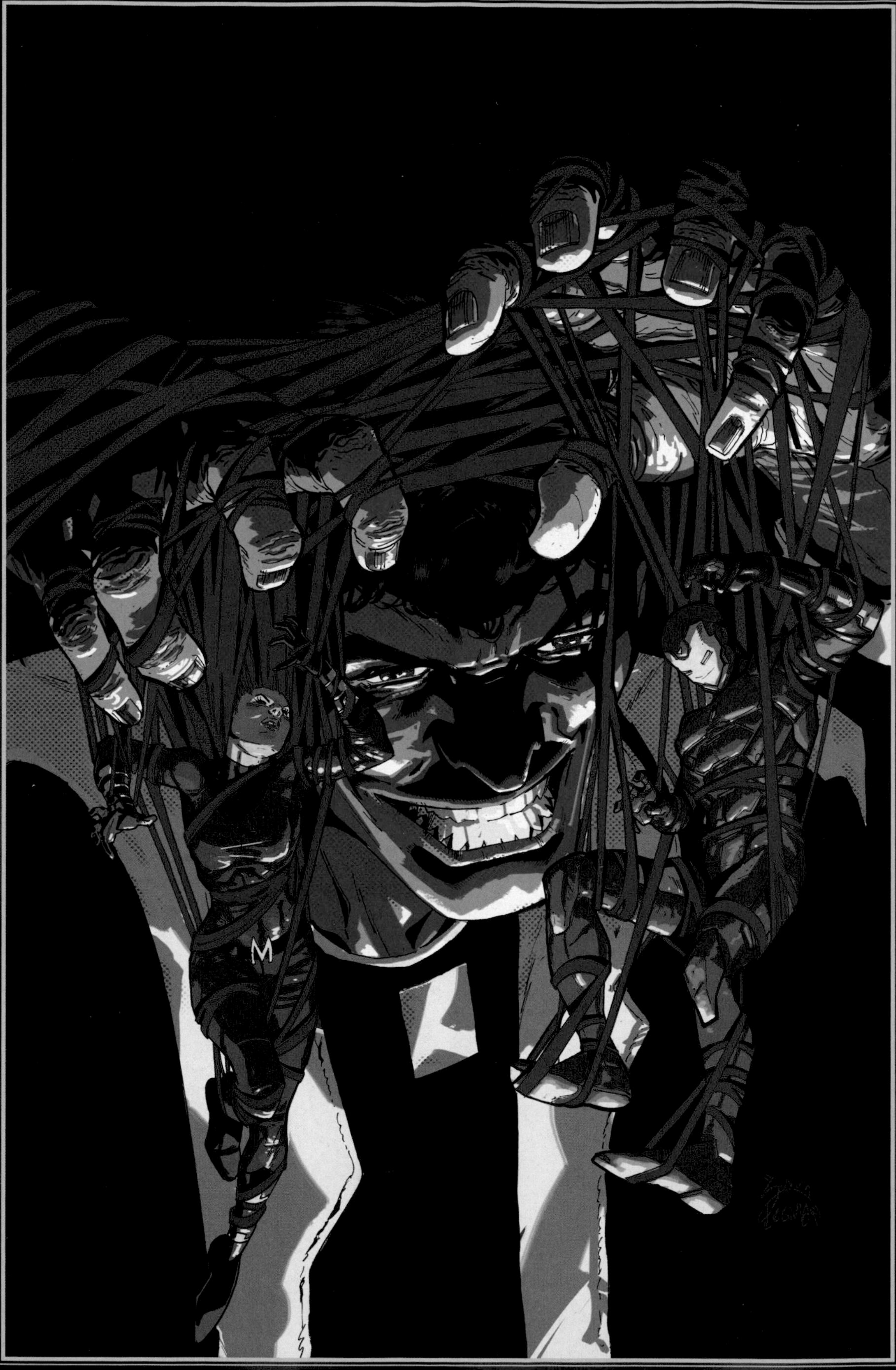

12

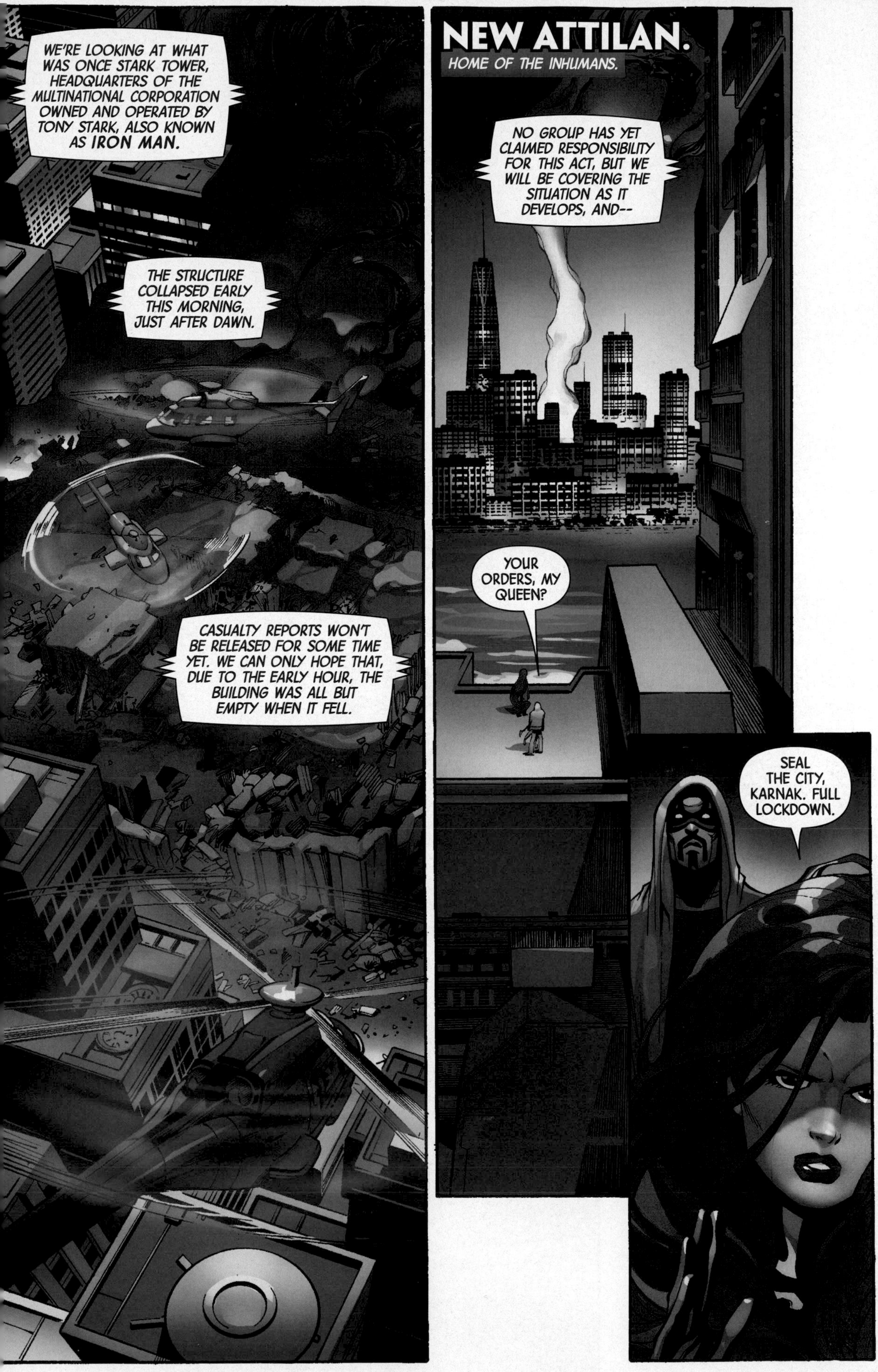
WE'RE LOOKING AT WHAT WAS ONCE STARK TOWER, HEADQUARTERS OF THE MULTINATIONAL CORPORATION OWNED AND OPERATED BY TONY STARK, ALSO KNOWN AS IRON MAN.
THE STRUCTURE COLLAPSED EARLY THIS MORNING, JUST AFTER DAWN.
CASUALTY REPORTS WON'T BE RELEASED FOR SOME TIME YET. WE CAN ONLY HOPE THAT, DUE TO THE EARLY HOUR, THE BUILDING WAS ALL BUT EMPTY WHEN IT FELL.
NEW ATTILAN.
HOME OF THE INHUMANS.
NO GROUP HAS YET CLAIMED RESPONSIBILITY FOR THIS ACT, BUT WE WILL BE COVERING THE SITUATION AS IT DEVELOPS, AND--
YOUR ORDERS, MY QUEEN?
SEAL THE CITY, KARNAK. FULL LOCKDOWN.

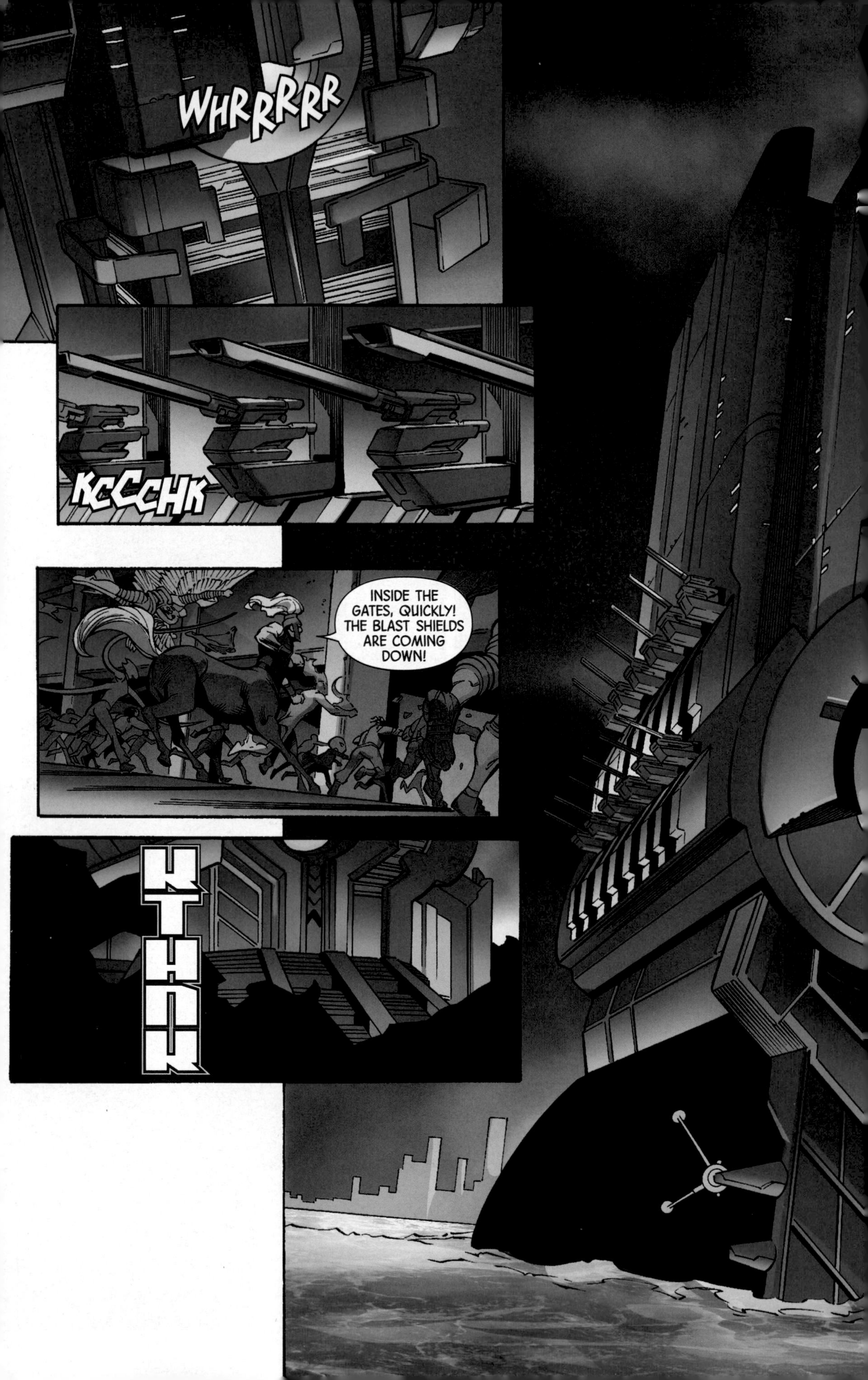
WHRRRRR
KCCCHK
INSIDE THE GATES, QUICKLY! THE BLAST SHIELDS ARE COMING DOWN!
KTHNK

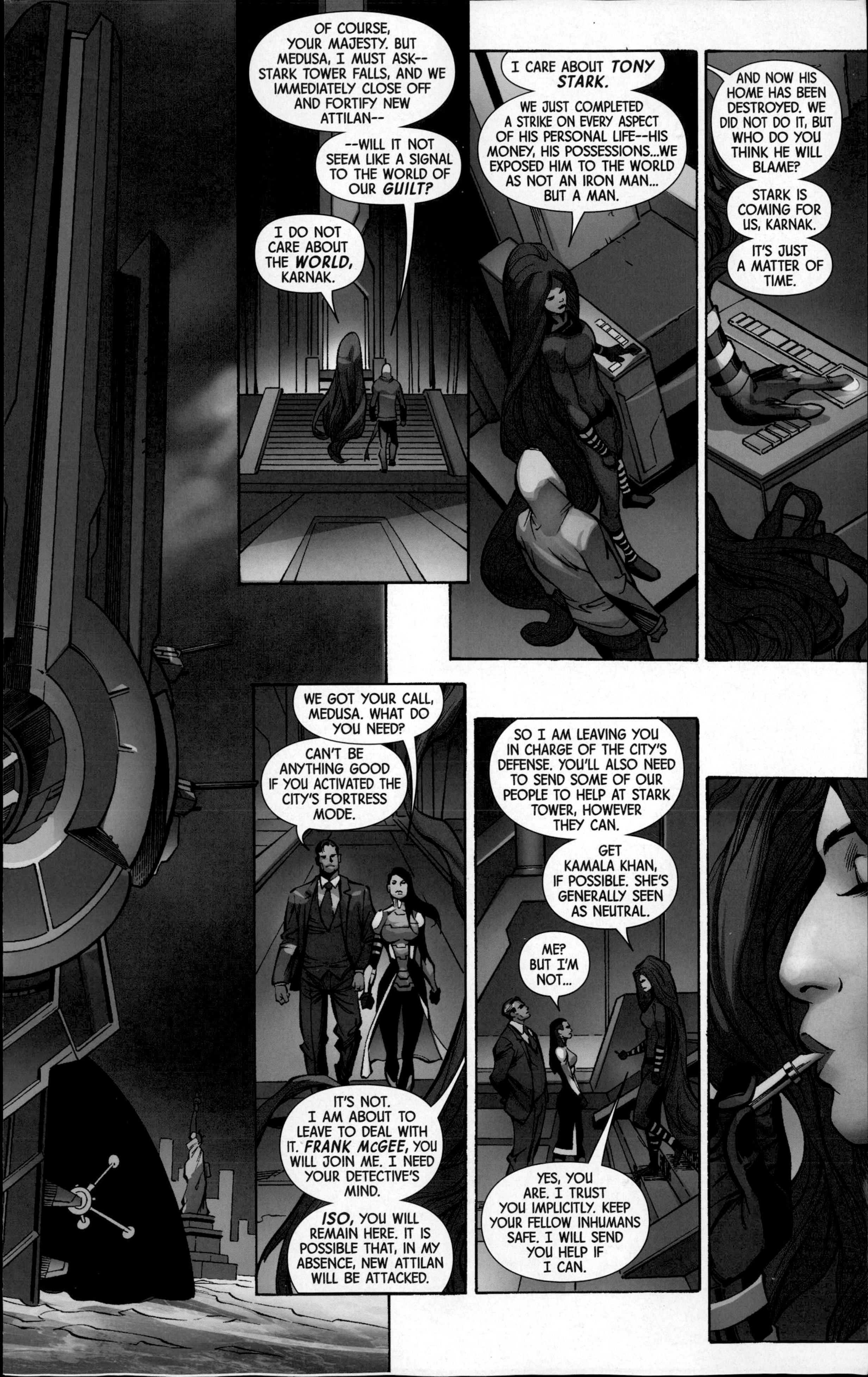
OF COURSE, YOUR MAJESTY. BUT MEDUSA, I MUST ASK-- STARK TOWER FALLS, AND WE IMMEDIATELY CLOSE OFF AND FORTIFY NEW ATTILAN--
--WILL IT NOT SEEM LIKE A SIGNAL TO THE WORLD OF OUR GUILT?
I DO NOT CARE ABOUT THE WORLD, KARNAK.
I CARE ABOUT TONY STARK.
WE JUST COMPLETED A STRIKE ON EVERY ASPECT OF HIS PERSONAL LIFE--HIS MONEY, HIS POSSESSIONS...WE EXPOSED HIM TO THE WORLD AS NOT AN IRON MAN... BUT A MAN.
AND NOW HIS HOME HAS BEEN DESTROYED. WE DID NOT DO IT, BUT WHO DO YOU THINK HE WILL BLAME?
STARK IS COMING FOR US, KARNAK.
IT'S JUST A MATTER OF TIME.
WE GOT YOUR CALL, MEDUSA. WHAT DO YOU NEED?
CAN'T BE ANYTHING GOOD IF YOU ACTIVATED THE CITY'S FORTRESS MODE.
IT'S NOT. I AM ABOUT TO LEAVE TO DEAL WITH IT. FRANK McGEE, YOU WILL JOIN ME. I NEED YOUR DETECTIVE'S MIND.
ISO, YOU WILL REMAIN HERE. IT IS POSSIBLE THAT, IN MY ABSENCE, NEW ATTILAN WILL BE ATTACKED.
SO I AM LEAVING YOU IN CHARGE OF THE CITY'S DEFENSE. YOU'LL ALSO NEED TO SEND SOME OF OUR PEOPLE TO HELP AT STARK TOWER, HOWEVER THEY CAN.
GET KAMALA KHAN, IF POSSIBLE. SHE'S GENERALLY SEEN AS NEUTRAL.
ME? BUT I'M NOT...
YES, YOU ARE. I TRUST YOU IMPLICITLY. KEEP YOUR FELLOW INHUMANS SAFE. I WILL SEND YOU HELP IF I CAN.

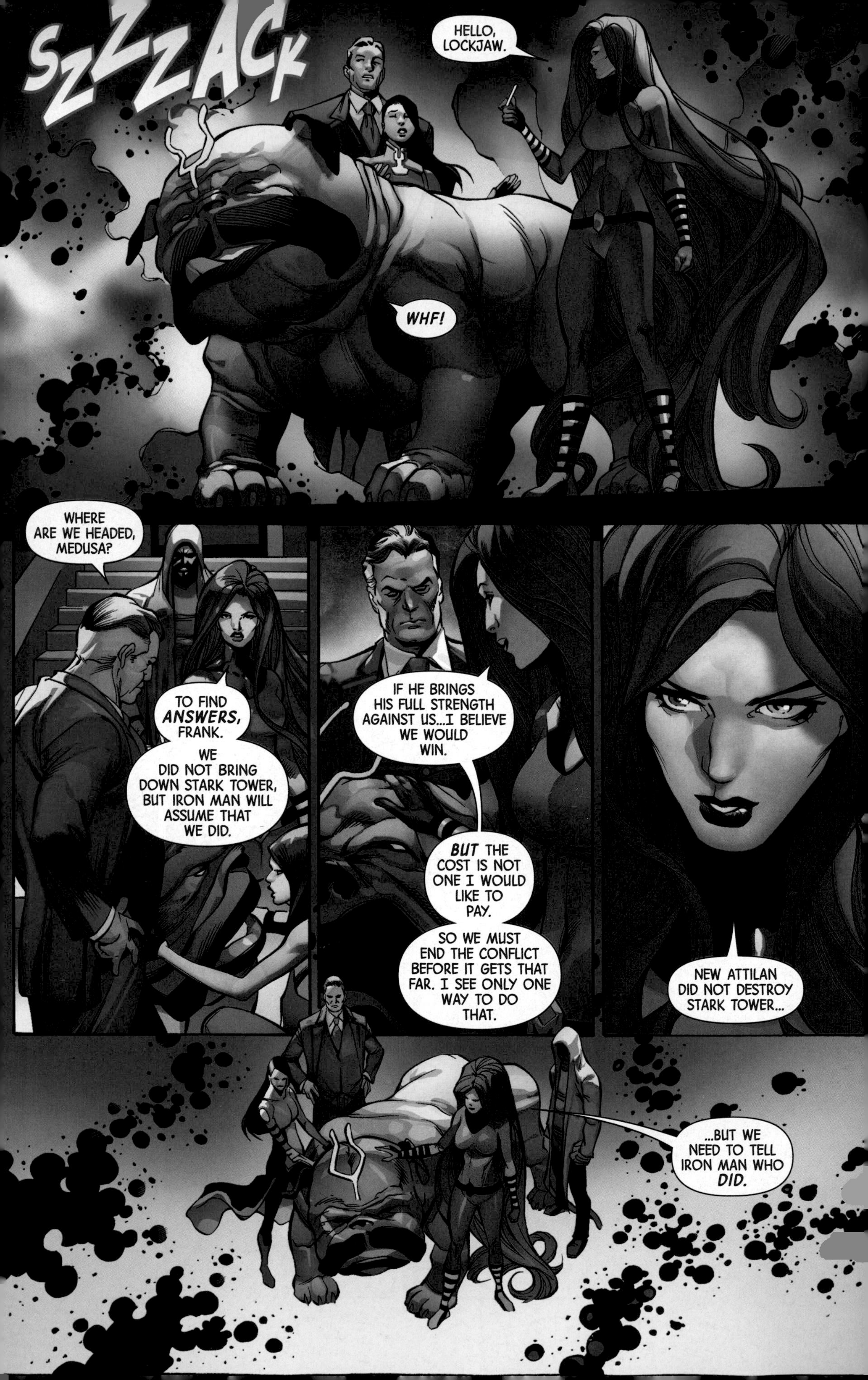
SZZZACK
HELLO, LOCKJAW.
WHF!
WHERE ARE WE HEADED, MEDUSA?
TO FIND ANSWERS, FRANK.
WE DID NOT BRING DOWN STARK TOWER, BUT IRON MAN WILL ASSUME THAT WE DID.
IF HE BRINGS HIS FULL STRENGTH AGAINST US...I BELIEVE WE WOULD WIN.
BUT THE COST IS NOT ONE I WOULD LIKE TO PAY.
SO WE MUST END THE CONFLICT BEFORE IT GETS THAT FAR. I SEE ONLY ONE WAY TO DO THAT.
NEW ATTILAN DID NOT DESTROY STARK TOWER...
...BUT WE NEED TO TELL IRON MAN WHO DID.

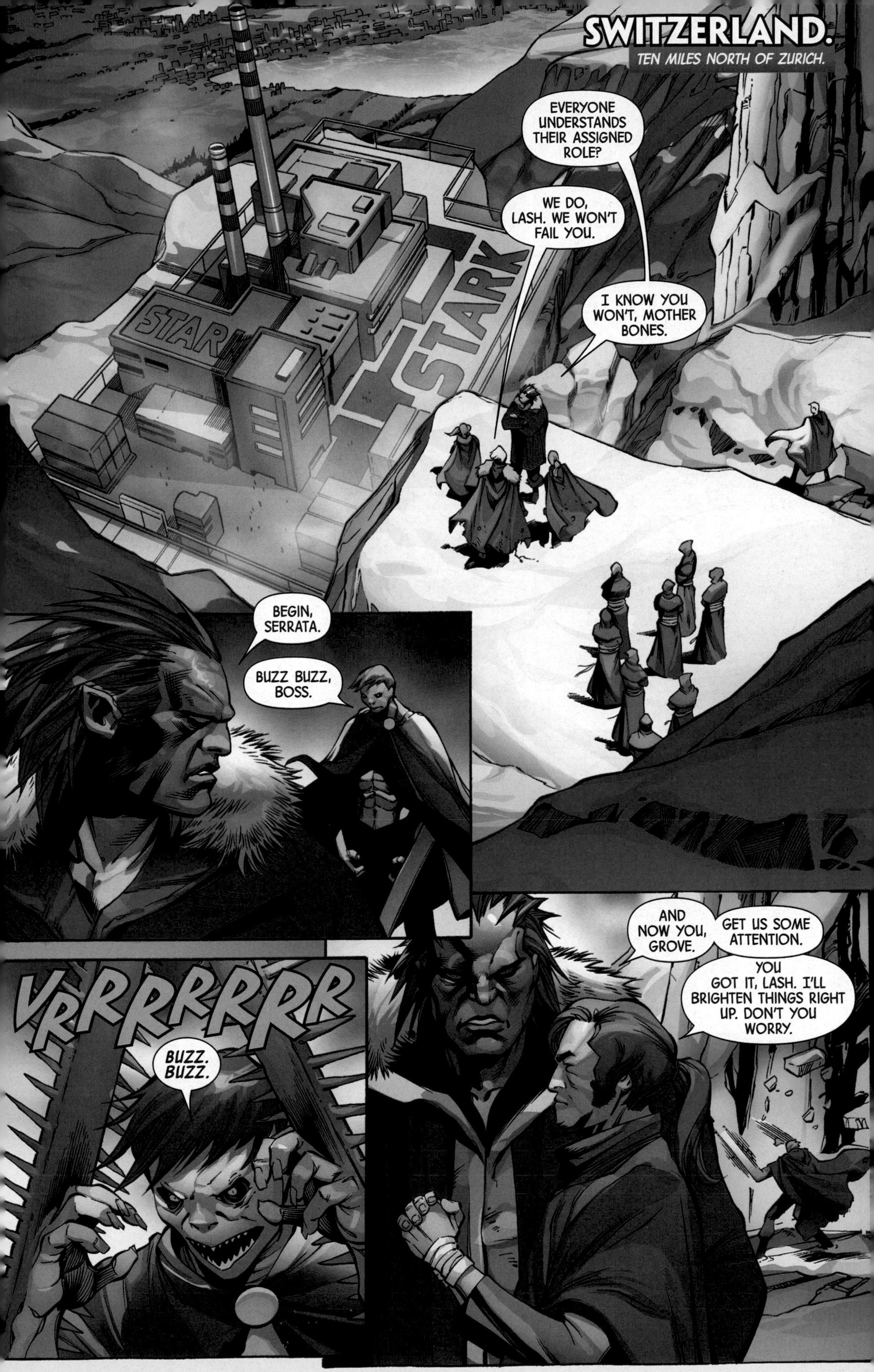
SWITZERLAND.
TEN MILES NORTH OF ZURICH.
EVERYONE UNDERSTANDS THEIR ASSIGNED ROLE?
WE DO, LASH. WE WON'T FAIL YOU.
I KNOW YOU WON'T, MOTHER BONES.
STARK
STARK
BEGIN, SERRATA.
BUZZ BUZZ, BOSS.
VRRRRRRR
BUZZ. BUZZ.
AND NOW YOU, GROVE.
GET US SOME ATTENTION.
YOU GOT IT, LASH. I'LL BRIGHTEN THINGS RIGHT UP. DON'T YOU WORRY.

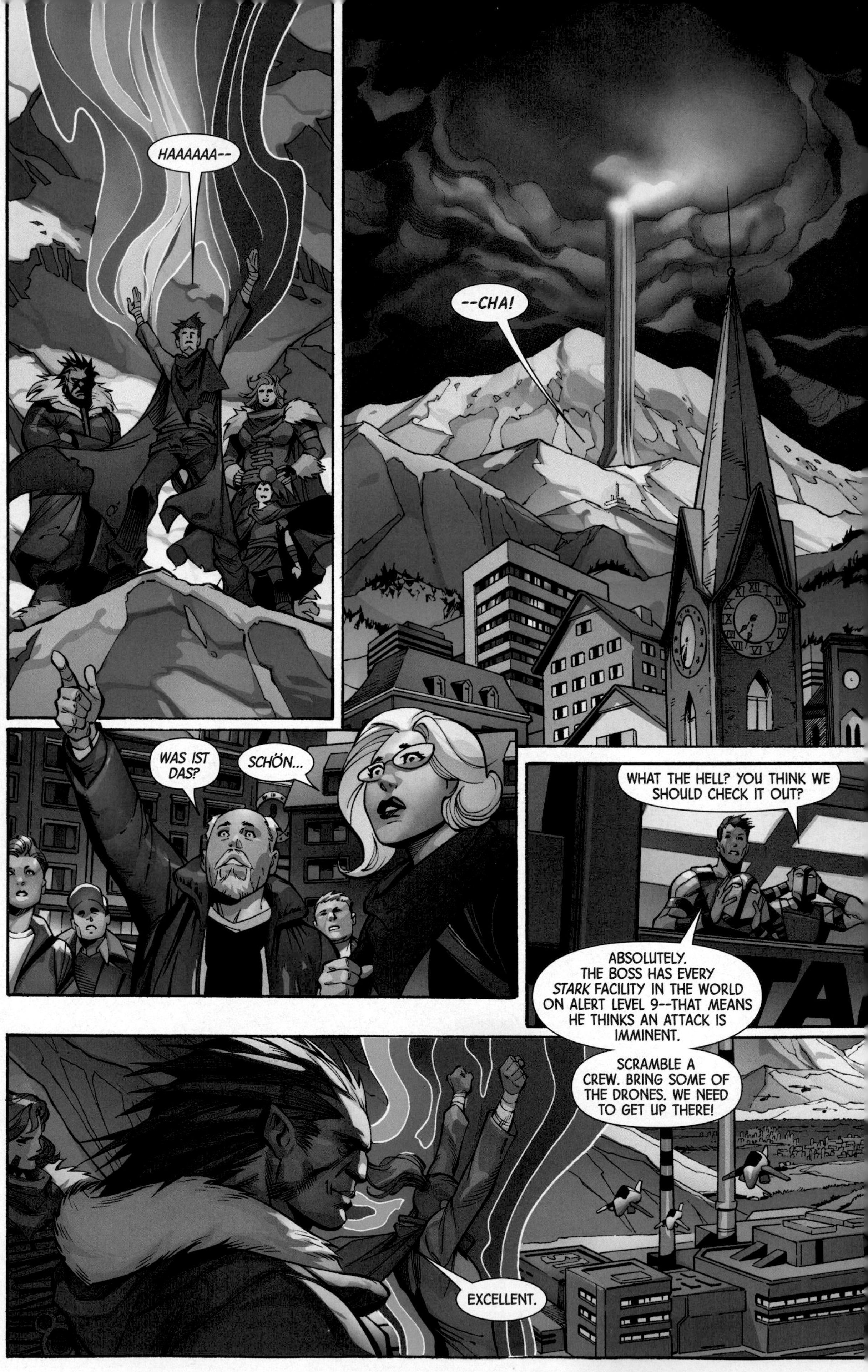
HAAAAAA--
--CHA!
WAS IST DAS?
SCHÖN...
WHAT THE HELL? YOU THINK WE SHOULD CHECK IT OUT?
ABSOLUTELY. THE BOSS HAS EVERY *STARK* FACILITY IN THE WORLD ON ALERT LEVEL 9--THAT MEANS HE THINKS AN ATTACK IS IMMINENT.
SCRAMBLE A CREW. BRING SOME OF THE DRONES. WE NEED TO GET UP THERE!
EXCELLENT.

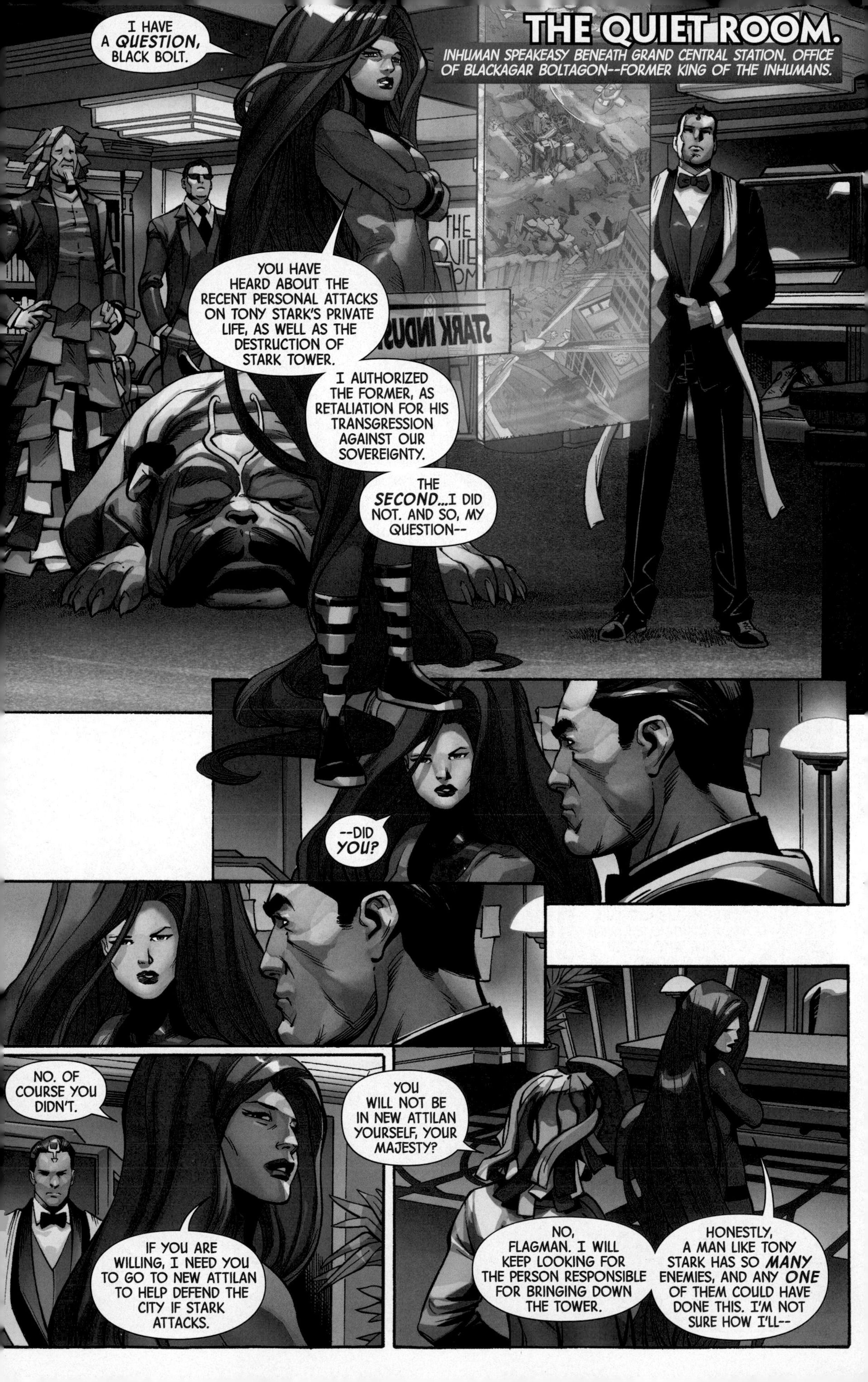
THE QUIET ROOM.
INHUMAN SPEAKEASY BENEATH GRAND CENTRAL STATION. OFFICE OF BLACKAGAR BOLTAGON--FORMER KING OF THE INHUMANS.
I HAVE A QUESTION, BLACK BOLT.
YOU HAVE HEARD ABOUT THE RECENT PERSONAL ATTACKS ON TONY STARK'S PRIVATE LIFE, AS WELL AS THE DESTRUCTION OF STARK TOWER.
I AUTHORIZED THE FORMER, AS RETALIATION FOR HIS TRANSGRESSION AGAINST OUR SOVEREIGNTY.
THE SECOND...I DID NOT. AND SO, MY QUESTION--
--DID YOU?
NO. OF COURSE YOU DIDN'T.
IF YOU ARE WILLING, I NEED YOU TO GO TO NEW ATTILAN TO HELP DEFEND THE CITY IF STARK ATTACKS.
YOU WILL NOT BE IN NEW ATTILAN YOURSELF, YOUR MAJESTY?
NO, FLAGMAN. I WILL KEEP LOOKING FOR THE PERSON RESPONSIBLE FOR BRINGING DOWN THE TOWER.
HONESTLY, A MAN LIKE TONY STARK HAS SO MANY ENEMIES, AND ANY ONE OF THEM COULD HAVE DONE THIS. I'M NOT SURE HOW I'LL--

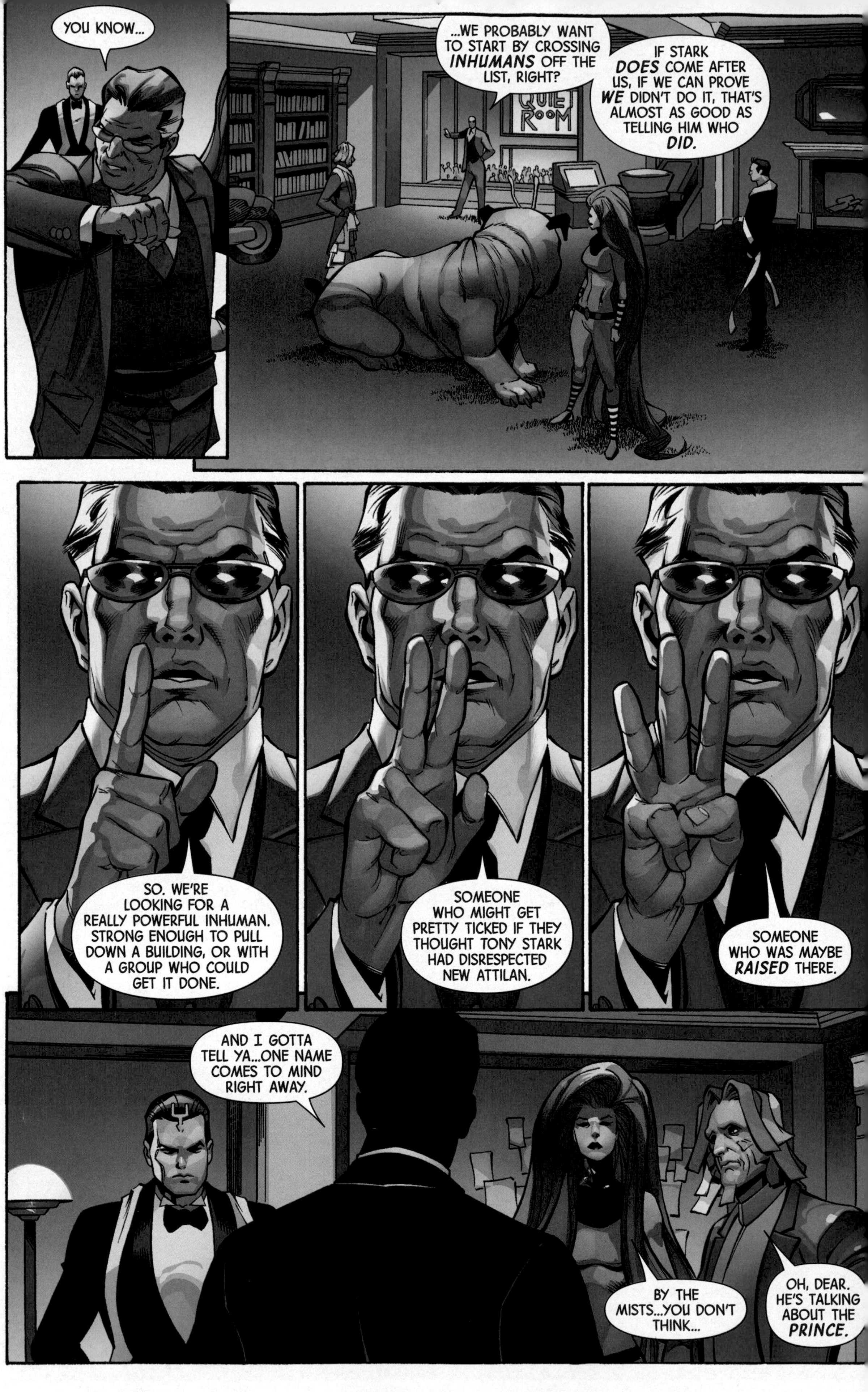
YOU KNOW...
...WE PROBABLY WANT TO START BY CROSSING INHUMANS OFF THE LIST, RIGHT?
QUIET ROOM
IF STARK DOES COME AFTER US, IF WE CAN PROVE WE DIDN'T DO IT, THAT'S ALMOST AS GOOD AS TELLING HIM WHO DID.
SO. WE'RE LOOKING FOR A REALLY POWERFUL INHUMAN. STRONG ENOUGH TO PULL DOWN A BUILDING, OR WITH A GROUP WHO COULD GET IT DONE.
SOMEONE WHO MIGHT GET PRETTY TICKED IF THEY THOUGHT TONY STARK HAD DISRESPECTED NEW ATTILAN.
SOMEONE WHO WAS MAYBE RAISED THERE.
AND I GOTTA TELL YA...ONE NAME COMES TO MIND RIGHT AWAY.
BY THE MISTS...YOU DON'T THINK...
OH, DEAR. HE'S TALKING ABOUT THE PRINCE.

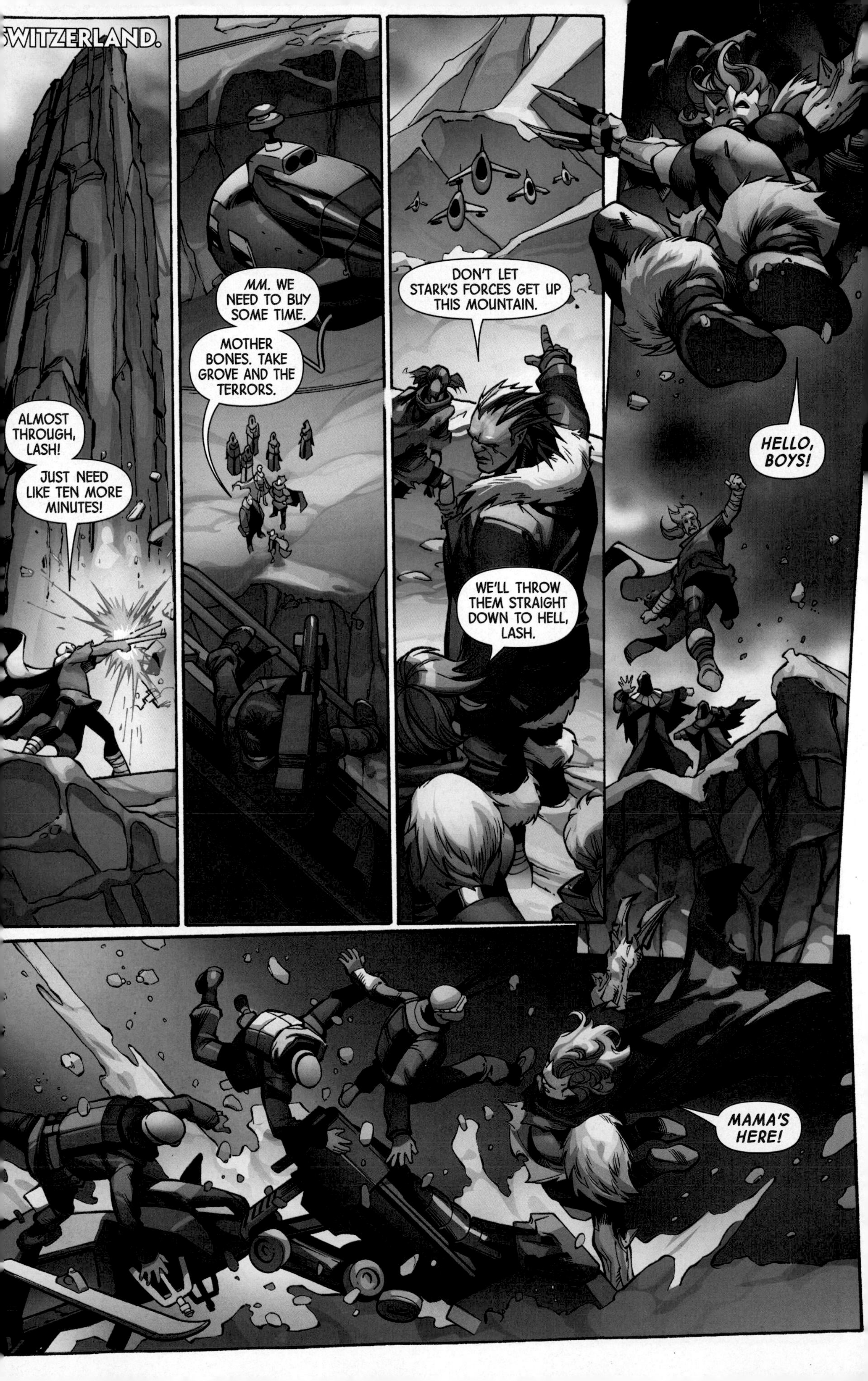
SWITZERLAND.
ALMOST THROUGH, LASH!
JUST NEED LIKE TEN MORE MINUTES!
MM. WE NEED TO BUY SOME TIME.
MOTHER BONES. TAKE GROVE AND THE TERRORS.
DON'T LET STARK'S FORCES GET UP THIS MOUNTAIN.
WE'LL THROW THEM STRAIGHT DOWN TO HELL, LASH.
HELLO, BOYS!
MAMA'S HERE!

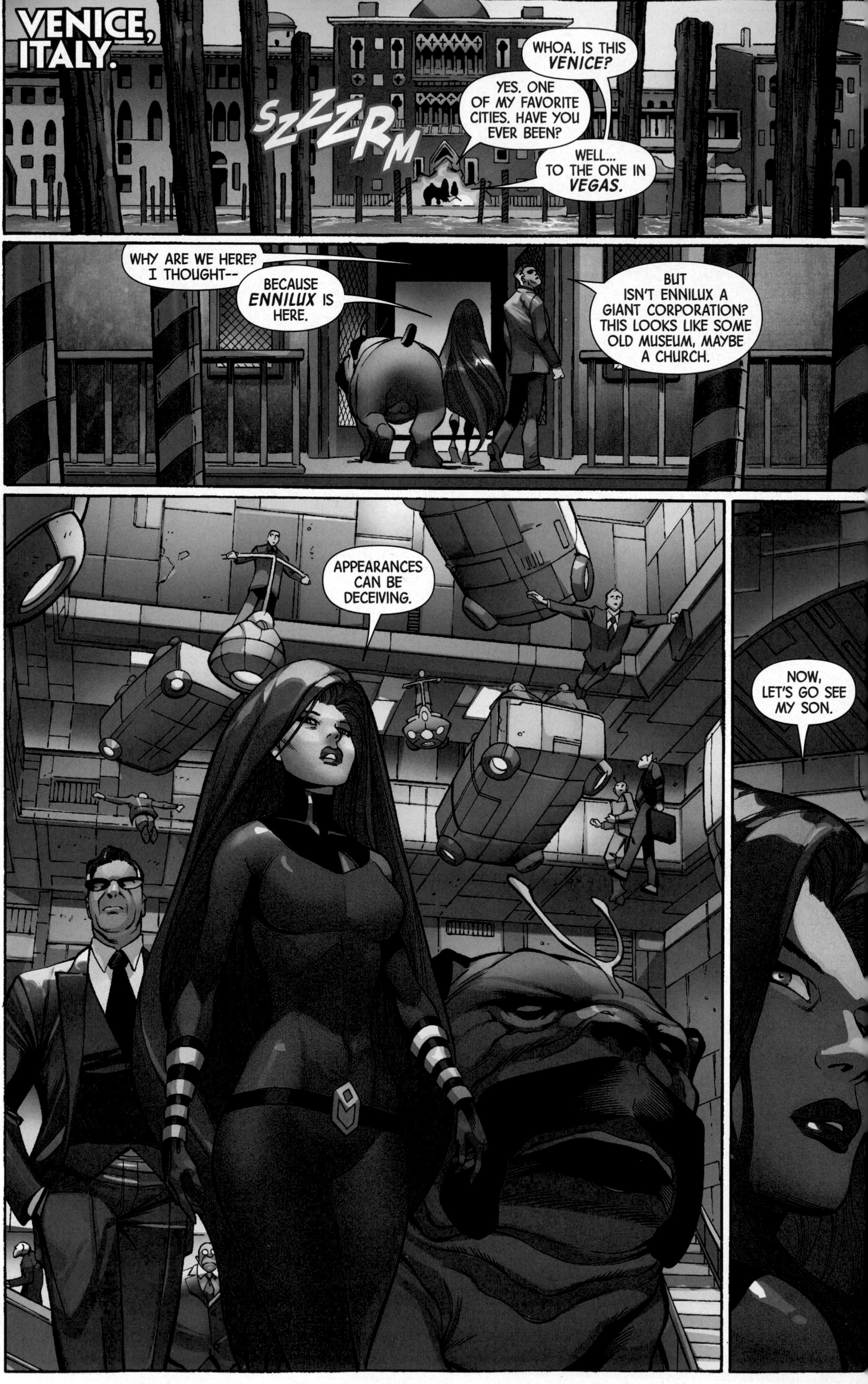
VENICE, ITALY.
SZZZRM
WHOA. IS THIS VENICE?
YES. ONE OF MY FAVORITE CITIES. HAVE YOU EVER BEEN?
WELL... TO THE ONE IN VEGAS.
WHY ARE WE HERE? I THOUGHT--
BECAUSE ENNILUX IS HERE.
BUT ISN'T ENNILUX A GIANT CORPORATION? THIS LOOKS LIKE SOME OLD MUSEUM, MAYBE A CHURCH.
APPEARANCES CAN BE DECEIVING.
NOW, LET'S GO SEE MY SON.

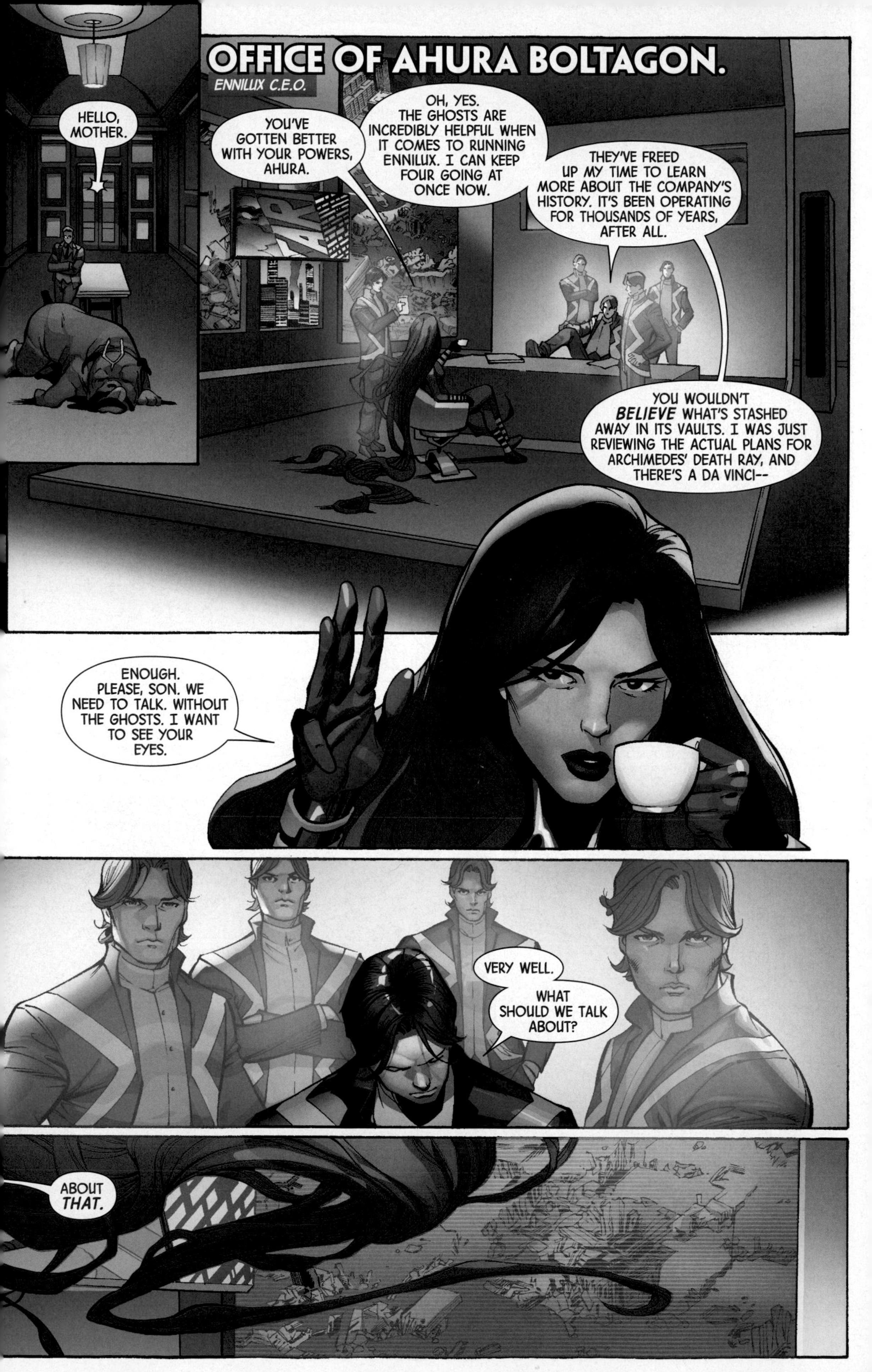
HELLO, MOTHER.
OFFICE OF AHURA BOLTAGON.
ENNILUX C.E.O.
YOU'VE GOTTEN BETTER WITH YOUR POWERS, AHURA.
OH, YES. THE GHOSTS ARE INCREDIBLY HELPFUL WHEN IT COMES TO RUNNING ENNILUX. I CAN KEEP FOUR GOING AT ONCE NOW.
THEY'VE FREED UP MY TIME TO LEARN MORE ABOUT THE COMPANY'S HISTORY. IT'S BEEN OPERATING FOR THOUSANDS OF YEARS, AFTER ALL.
YOU WOULDN'T BELIEVE WHAT'S STASHED AWAY IN ITS VAULTS. I WAS JUST REVIEWING THE ACTUAL PLANS FOR ARCHIMEDES' DEATH RAY, AND THERE'S A DA VINCI--
ENOUGH. PLEASE, SON. WE NEED TO TALK. WITHOUT THE GHOSTS. I WANT TO SEE YOUR EYES.
VERY WELL.
WHAT SHOULD WE TALK ABOUT?
ABOUT THAT.

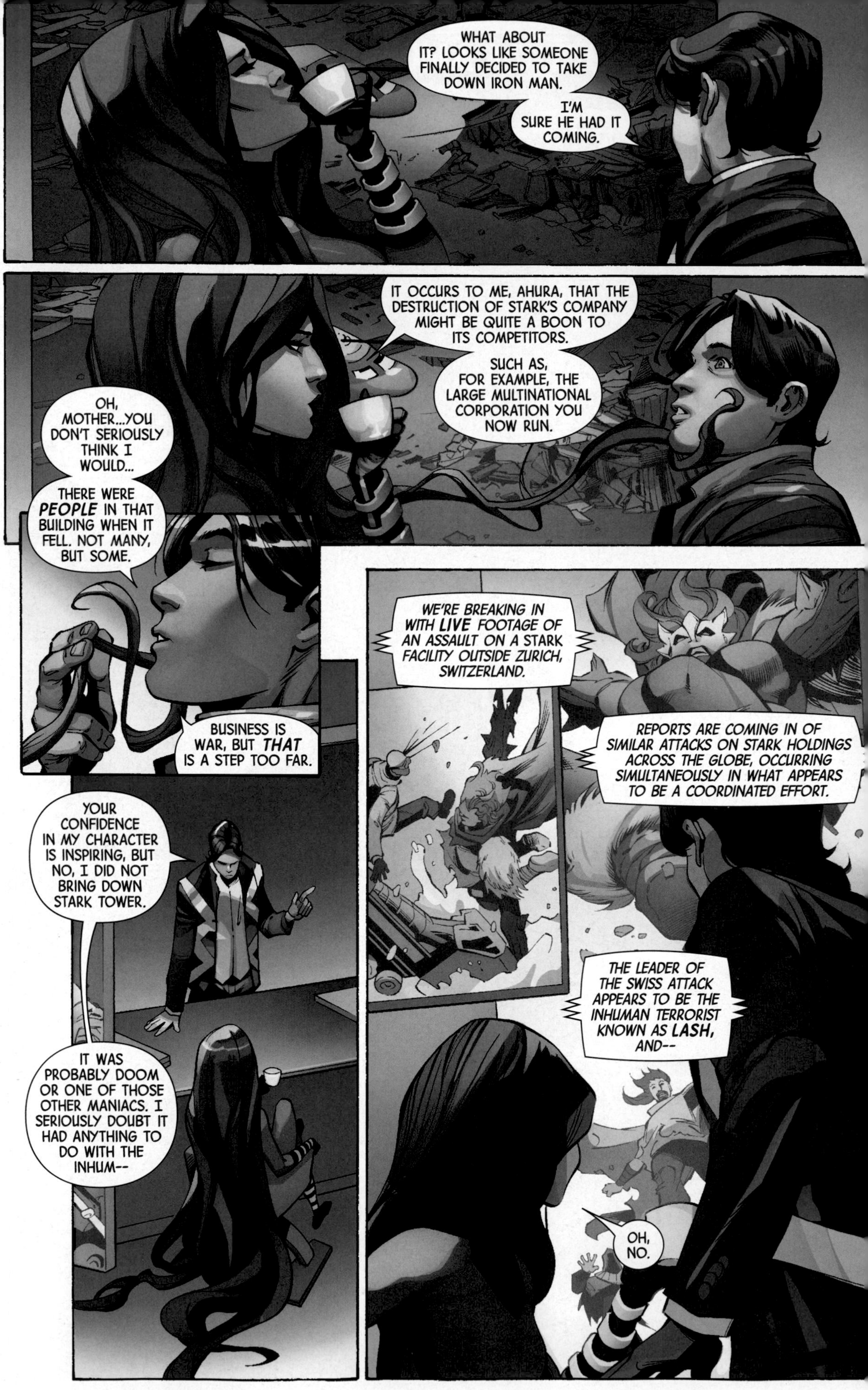
WHAT ABOUT IT? LOOKS LIKE SOMEONE FINALLY DECIDED TO TAKE DOWN IRON MAN.
I'M SURE HE HAD IT COMING.
IT OCCURS TO ME, AHURA, THAT THE DESTRUCTION OF STARK'S COMPANY MIGHT BE QUITE A BOON TO ITS COMPETITORS.
SUCH AS, FOR EXAMPLE, THE LARGE MULTINATIONAL CORPORATION YOU NOW RUN.
OH, MOTHER...YOU DON'T SERIOUSLY THINK I WOULD...
THERE WERE **PEOPLE** IN THAT BUILDING WHEN IT FELL. NOT MANY, BUT SOME.
BUSINESS IS WAR, BUT **THAT** IS A STEP TOO FAR.
YOUR CONFIDENCE IN MY CHARACTER IS INSPIRING, BUT NO, I DID NOT BRING DOWN STARK TOWER.
IT WAS PROBABLY DOOM OR ONE OF THOSE OTHER MANIACS. I SERIOUSLY DOUBT IT HAD ANYTHING TO DO WITH THE INHUM--
*WE'RE BREAKING IN WITH **LIVE** FOOTAGE OF AN ASSAULT ON A STARK FACILITY OUTSIDE ZURICH, SWITZERLAND.*
REPORTS ARE COMING IN OF SIMILAR ATTACKS ON STARK HOLDINGS ACROSS THE GLOBE, OCCURRING SIMULTANEOUSLY IN WHAT APPEARS TO BE A COORDINATED EFFORT.
*THE LEADER OF THE SWISS ATTACK APPEARS TO BE THE INHUMAN TERRORIST KNOWN AS **LASH**, AND--*
OH, NO.

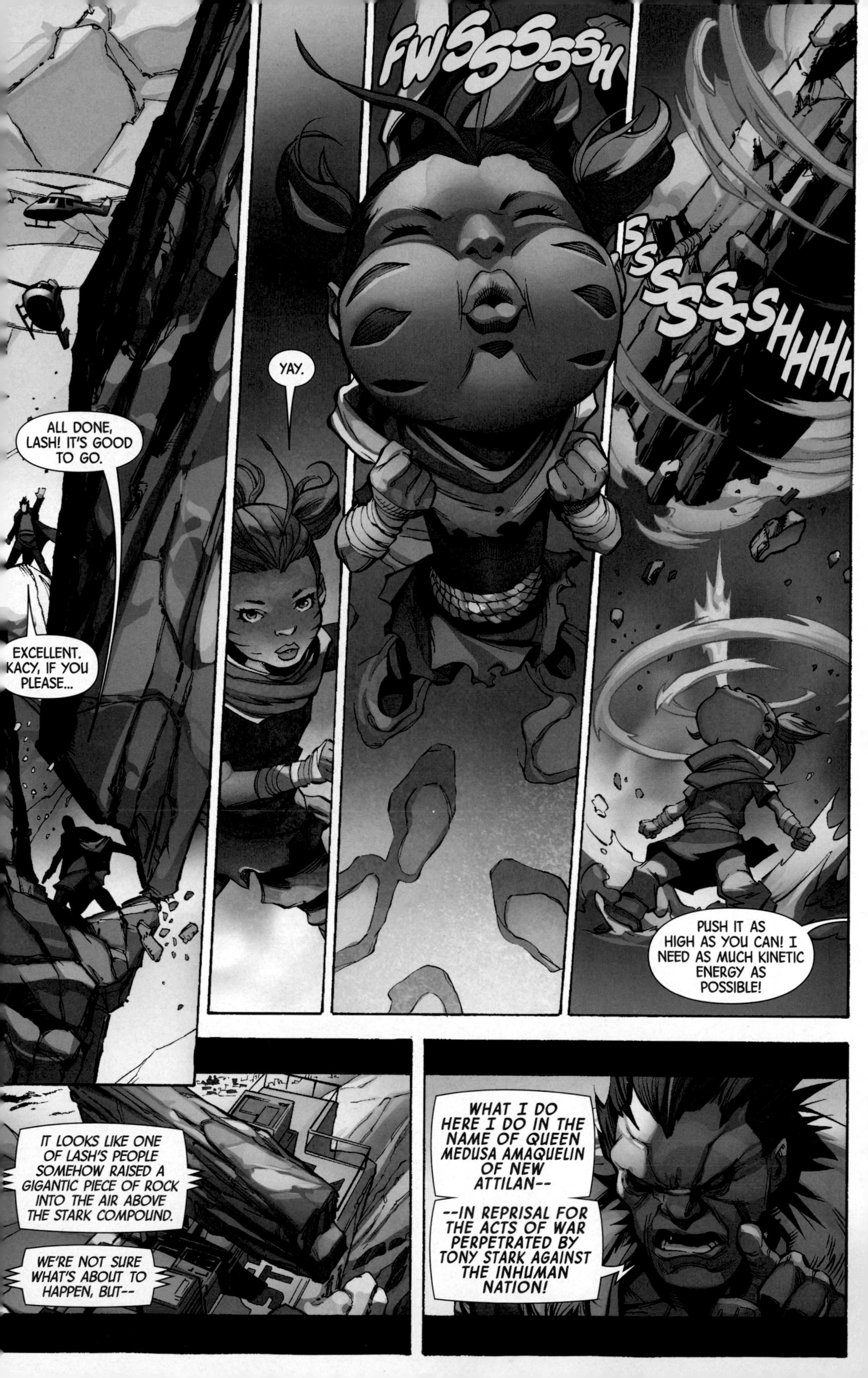
ALL DONE, LASH! IT'S GOOD TO GO.
EXCELLENT. KACY, IF YOU PLEASE...
YAY.
FWSSSSSSH
SSSSSSSHHHH
PUSH IT AS HIGH AS YOU CAN! I NEED AS MUCH KINETIC ENERGY AS POSSIBLE!
IT LOOKS LIKE ONE OF LASH'S PEOPLE SOMEHOW RAISED A GIGANTIC PIECE OF ROCK INTO THE AIR ABOVE THE STARK COMPOUND.
WE'RE NOT SURE WHAT'S ABOUT TO HAPPEN, BUT--
WHAT I DO HERE I DO IN THE NAME OF QUEEN MEDUSA AMAQUELIN OF NEW ATTILAN--
--IN REPRISAL FOR THE ACTS OF WAR PERPETRATED BY TONY STARK AGAINST THE INHUMAN NATION!

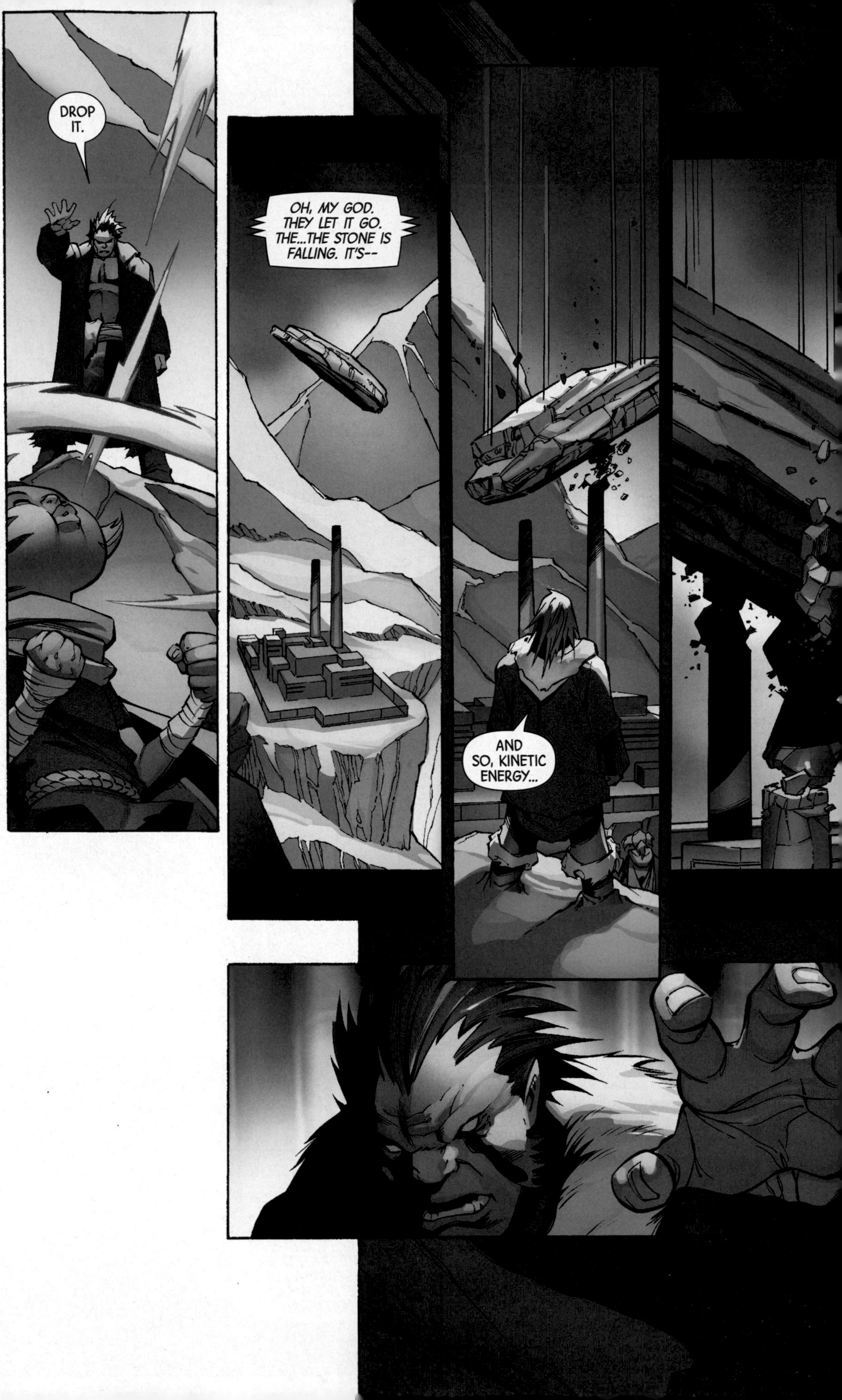
DROP IT.
OH, MY GOD. THEY LET IT GO. THE...THE STONE IS FALLING. IT'S--
AND SO, KINETIC ENERGY...

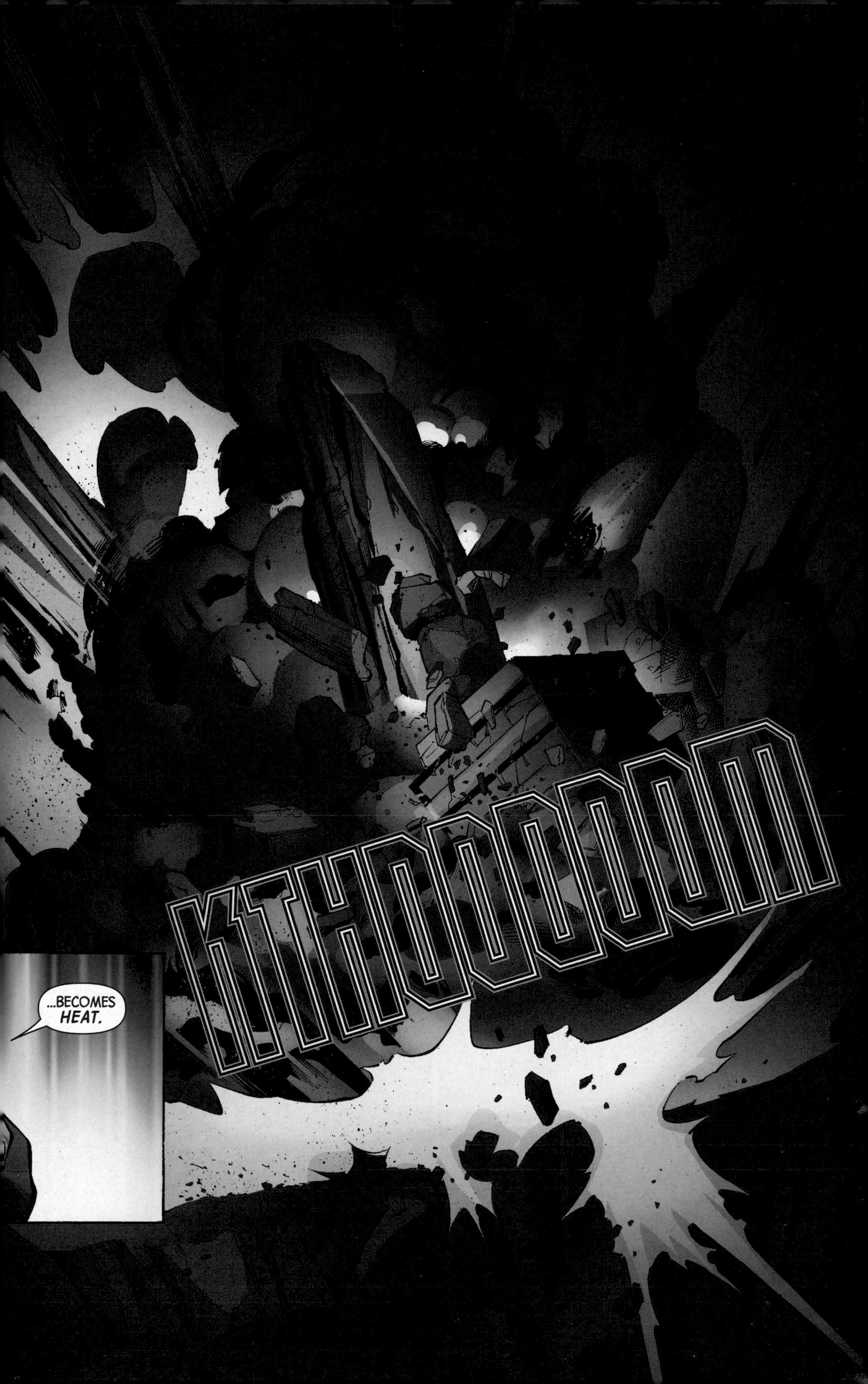
KTHOOOOOM
...BECOMES HEAT.

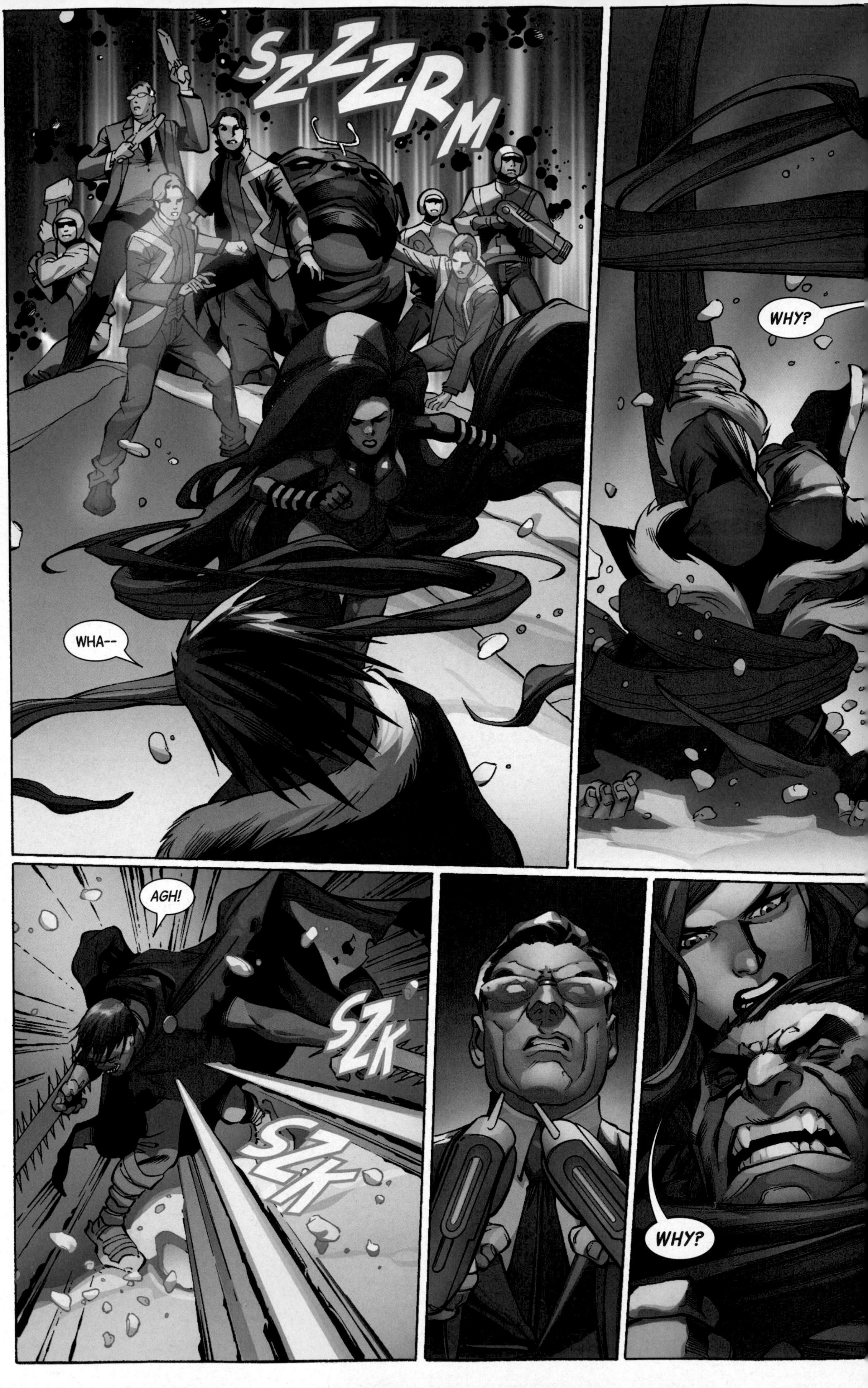
SZZZRM
WHA--
WHY?
AGH!
SZK
SZK
WHY?

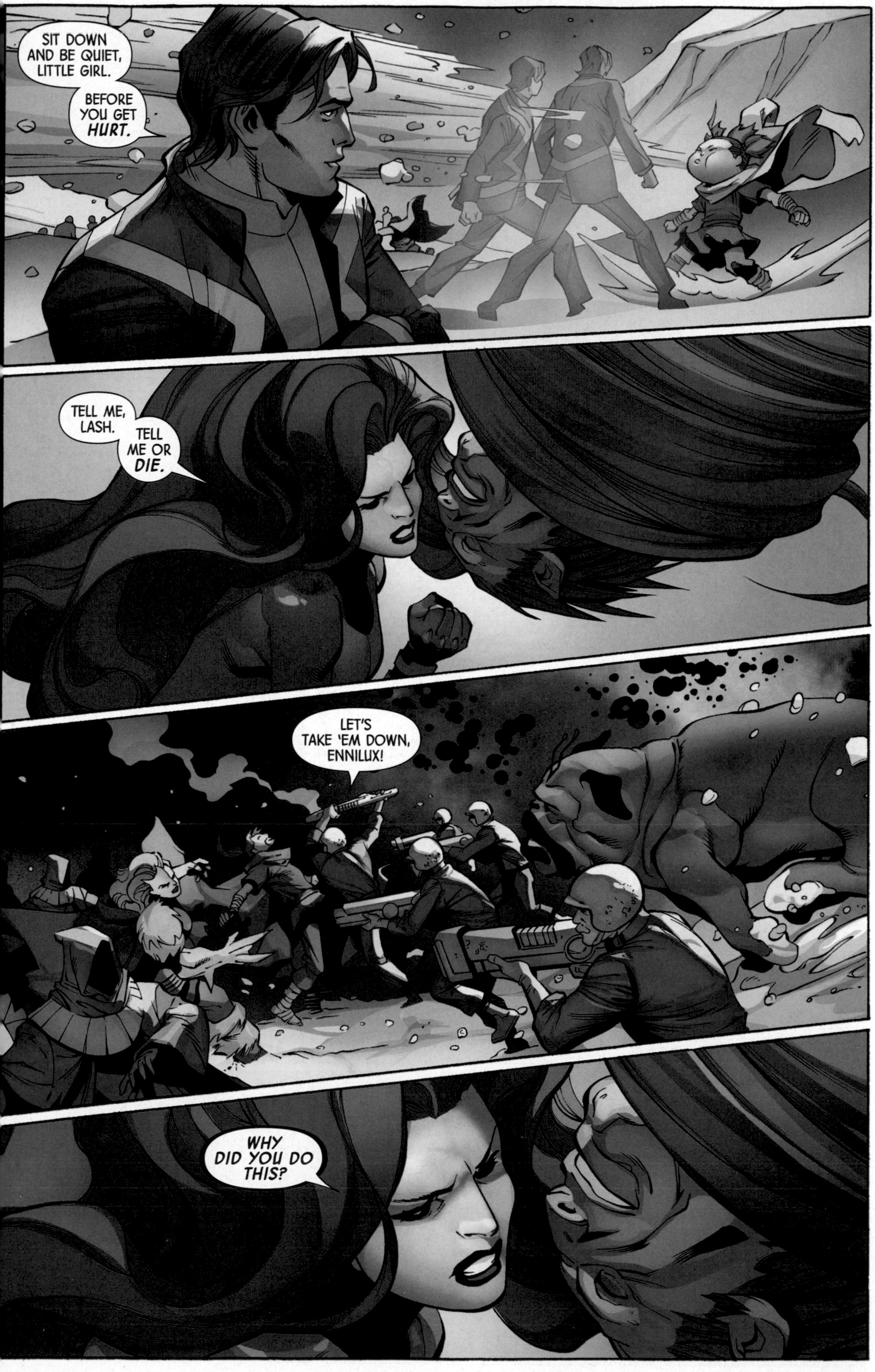
SIT DOWN AND BE QUIET, LITTLE GIRL.
BEFORE YOU GET HURT.
TELL ME, LASH.
TELL ME OR DIE.
LET'S TAKE 'EM DOWN, ENNILUX!
WHY DID YOU DO THIS?

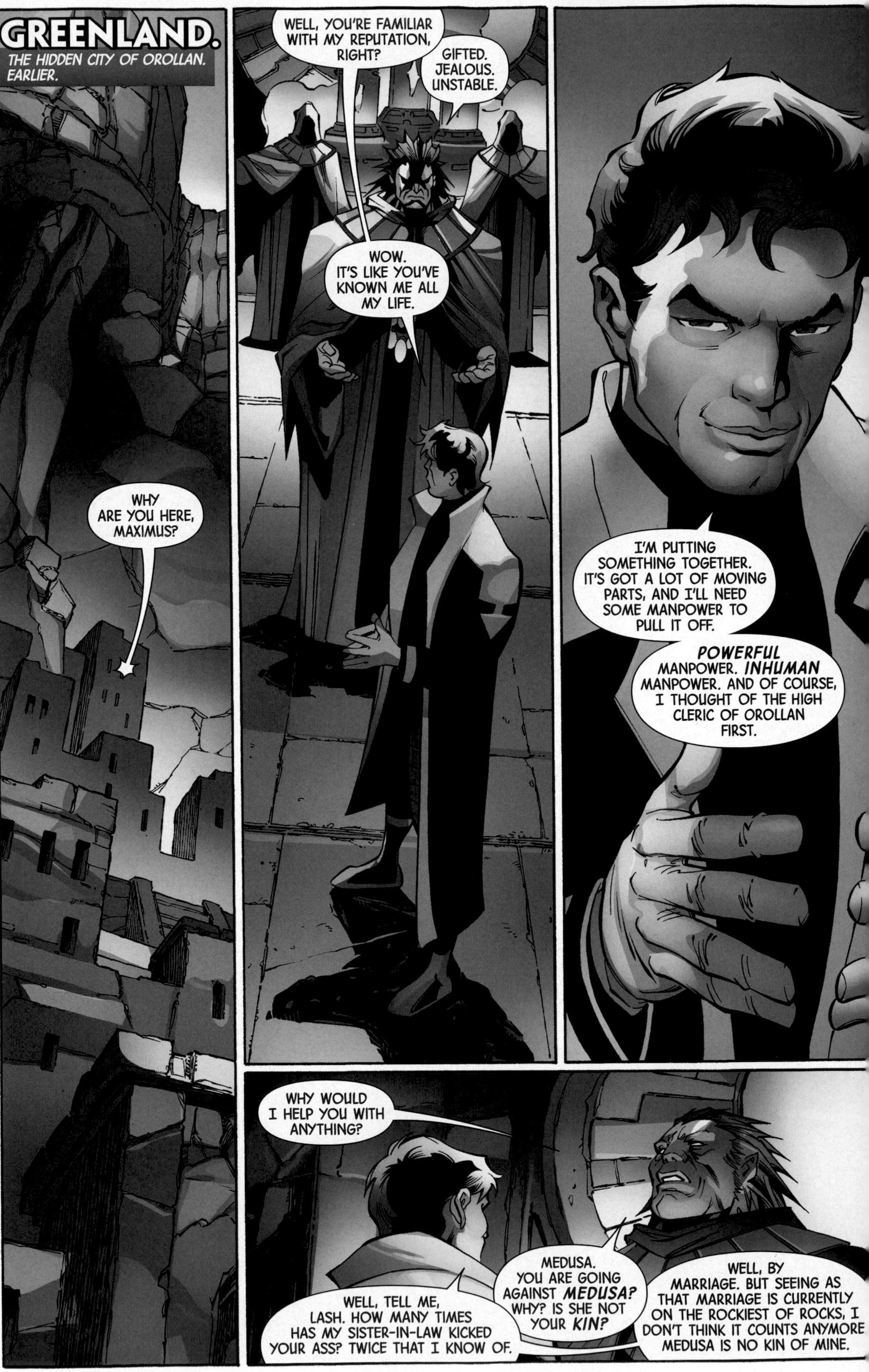
GREENLAND.
THE HIDDEN CITY OF OROLLAN. EARLIER.
WHY ARE YOU HERE, MAXIMUS?
WELL, YOU'RE FAMILIAR WITH MY REPUTATION, RIGHT?
GIFTED. JEALOUS. UNSTABLE.
WOW. IT'S LIKE YOU'VE KNOWN ME ALL MY LIFE.
I'M PUTTING SOMETHING TOGETHER. IT'S GOT A LOT OF MOVING PARTS, AND I'LL NEED SOME MANPOWER TO PULL IT OFF.
POWERFUL MANPOWER. INHUMAN MANPOWER. AND OF COURSE, I THOUGHT OF THE HIGH CLERIC OF OROLLAN FIRST.
WHY WOULD I HELP YOU WITH ANYTHING?
WELL, TELL ME, LASH. HOW MANY TIMES HAS MY SISTER-IN-LAW KICKED YOUR ASS? TWICE THAT I KNOW OF.
MEDUSA. YOU ARE GOING AGAINST MEDUSA? WHY? IS SHE NOT YOUR KIN?
WELL, BY MARRIAGE. BUT SEEING AS THAT MARRIAGE IS CURRENTLY ON THE ROCKIEST OF ROCKS, I DON'T THINK IT COUNTS ANYMORE. MEDUSA IS NO KIN OF MINE.

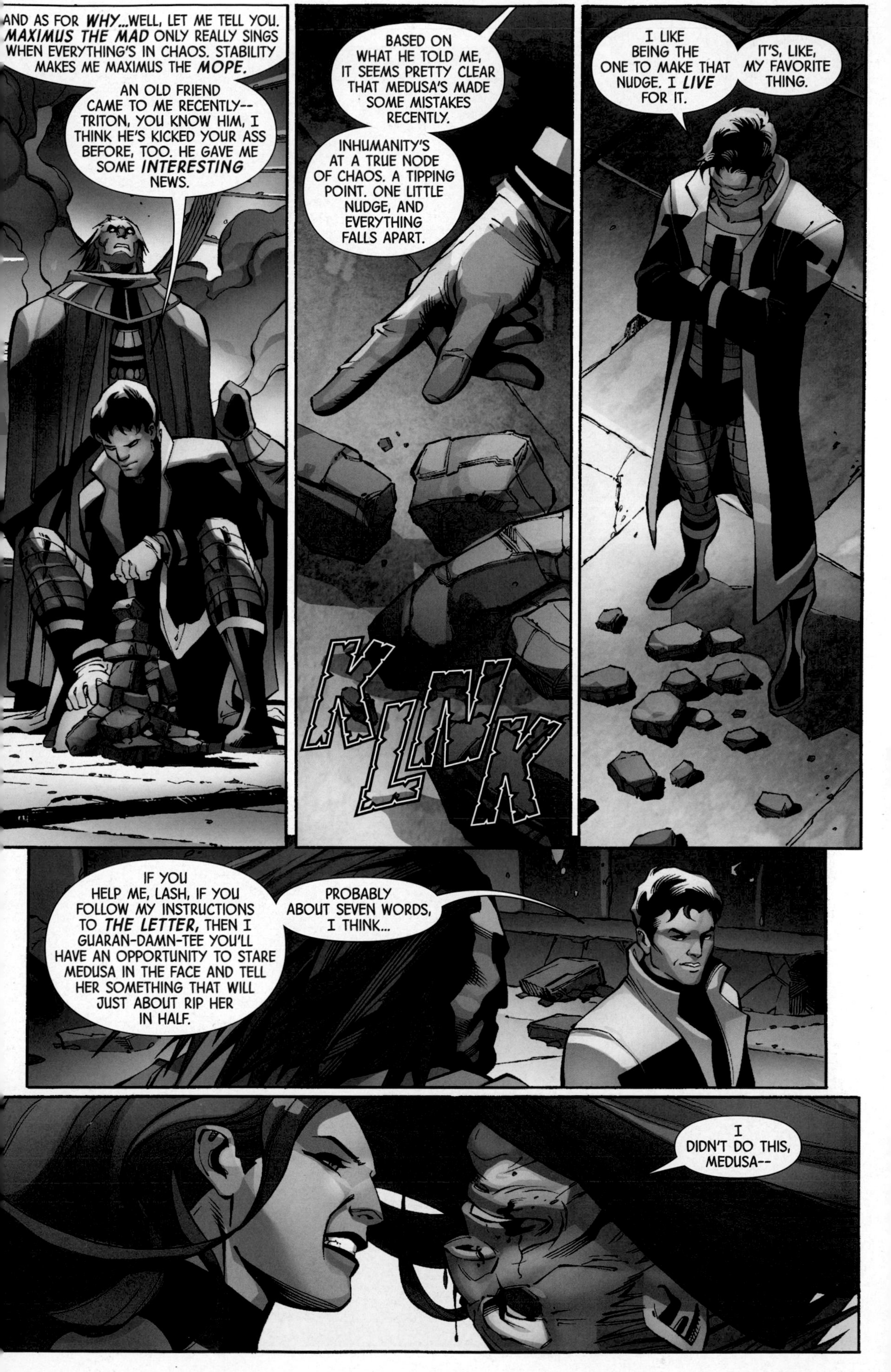
AND AS FOR WHY...WELL, LET ME TELL YOU. MAXIMUS THE MAD ONLY REALLY SINGS WHEN EVERYTHING'S IN CHAOS. STABILITY MAKES ME MAXIMUS THE MOPE.
AN OLD FRIEND CAME TO ME RECENTLY-- TRITON, YOU KNOW HIM, I THINK HE'S KICKED YOUR ASS BEFORE, TOO. HE GAVE ME SOME INTERESTING NEWS.
BASED ON WHAT HE TOLD ME, IT SEEMS PRETTY CLEAR THAT MEDUSA'S MADE SOME MISTAKES RECENTLY.
INHUMANITY'S AT A TRUE NODE OF CHAOS. A TIPPING POINT. ONE LITTLE NUDGE, AND EVERYTHING FALLS APART.
KLINK
I LIKE BEING THE ONE TO MAKE THAT NUDGE. I LIVE FOR IT.
IT'S, LIKE, MY FAVORITE THING.
IF YOU HELP ME, LASH, IF YOU FOLLOW MY INSTRUCTIONS TO THE LETTER, THEN I GUARAN-DAMN-TEE YOU'LL HAVE AN OPPORTUNITY TO STARE MEDUSA IN THE FACE AND TELL HER SOMETHING THAT WILL JUST ABOUT RIP HER IN HALF.
PROBABLY ABOUT SEVEN WORDS, I THINK...
I DIDN'T DO THIS, MEDUSA--

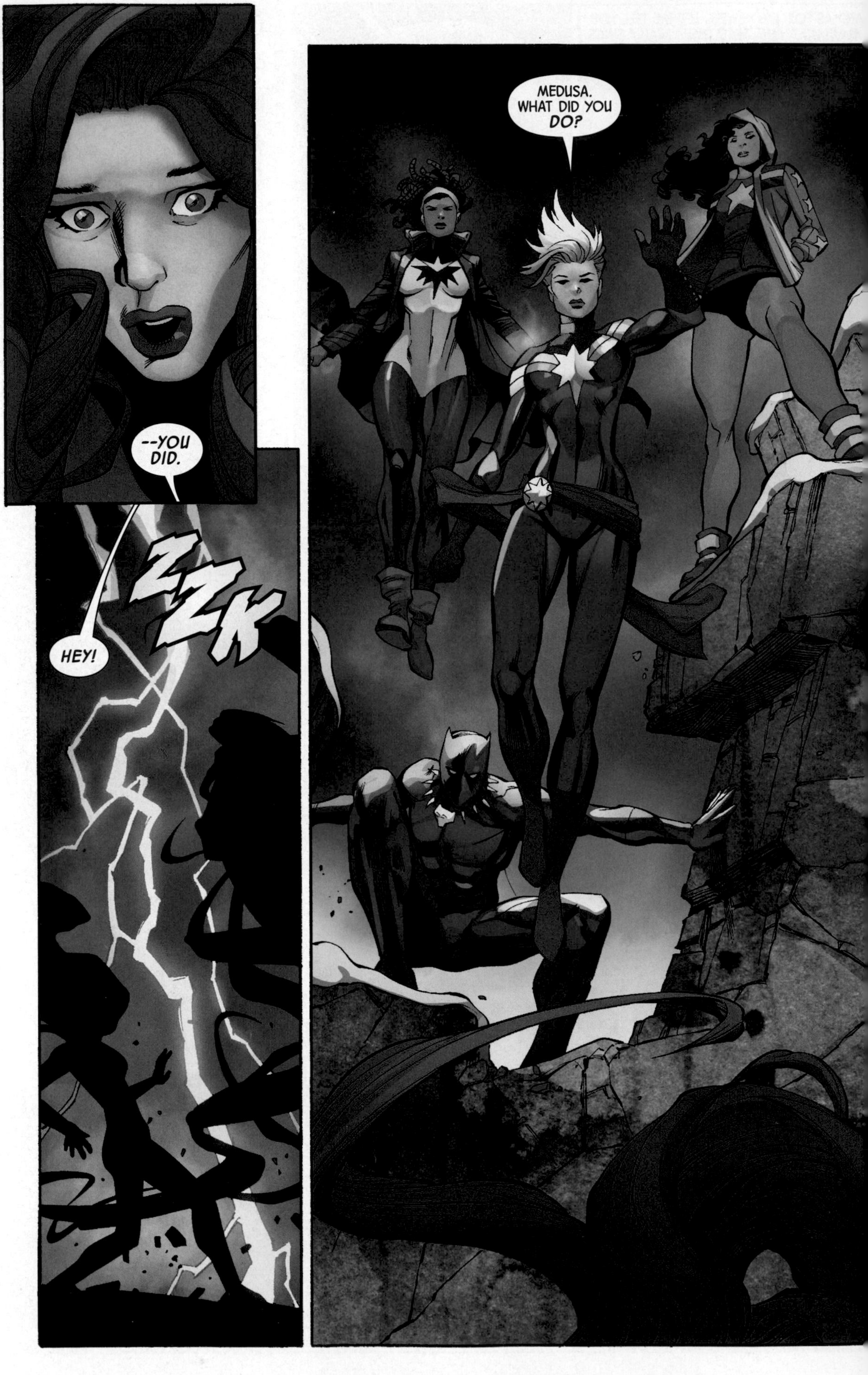
--YOU DID.
HEY!
ZZZK
MEDUSA. WHAT DID YOU DO?

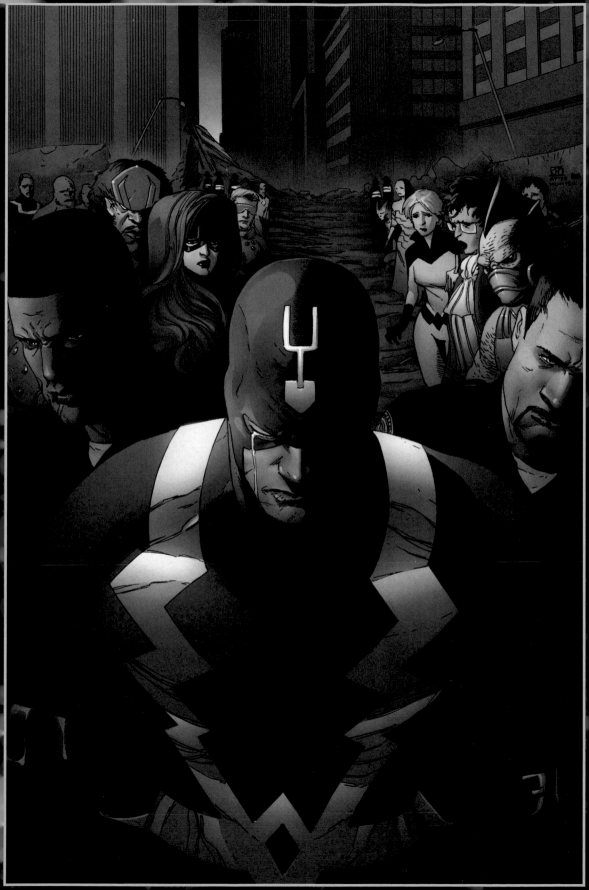

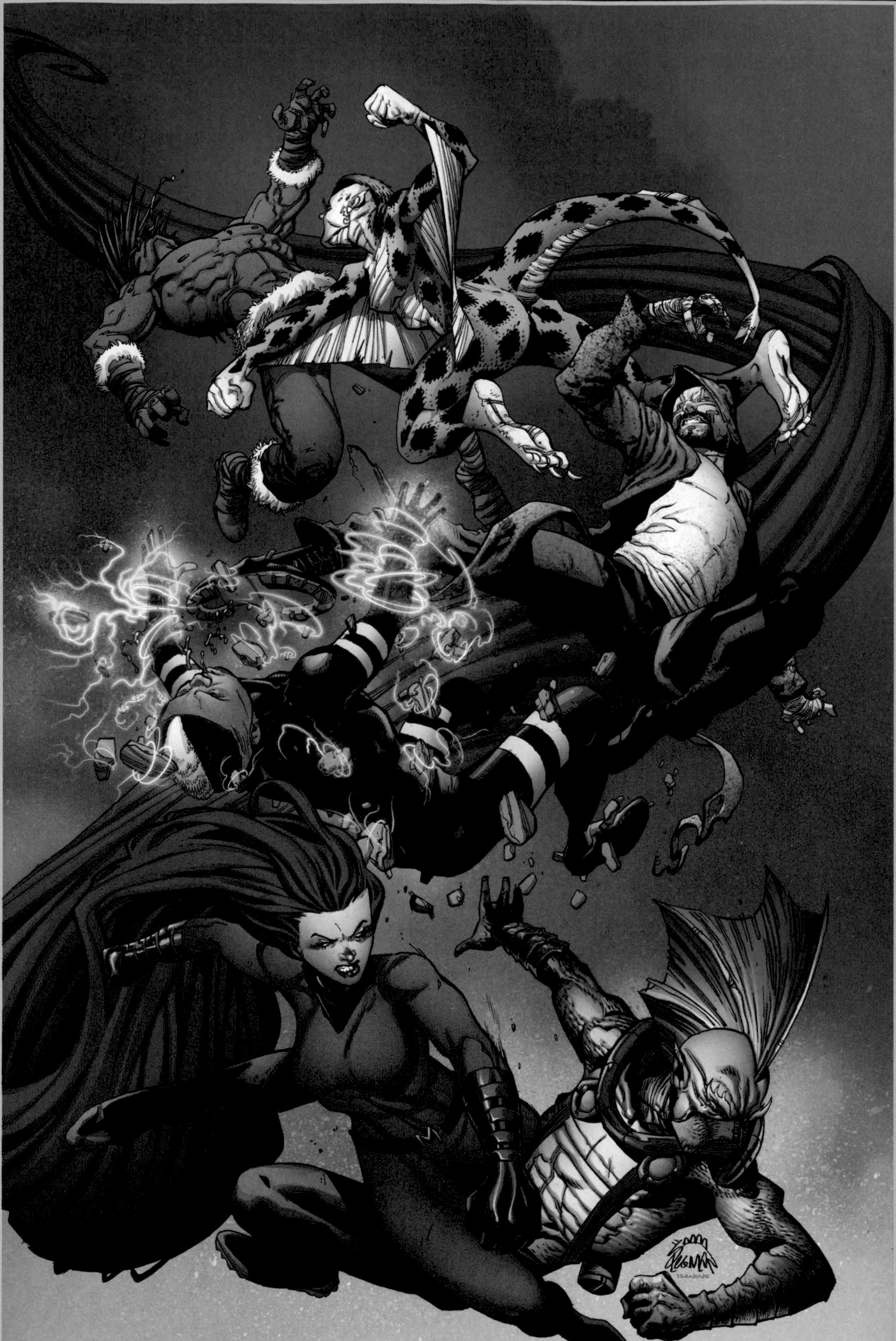

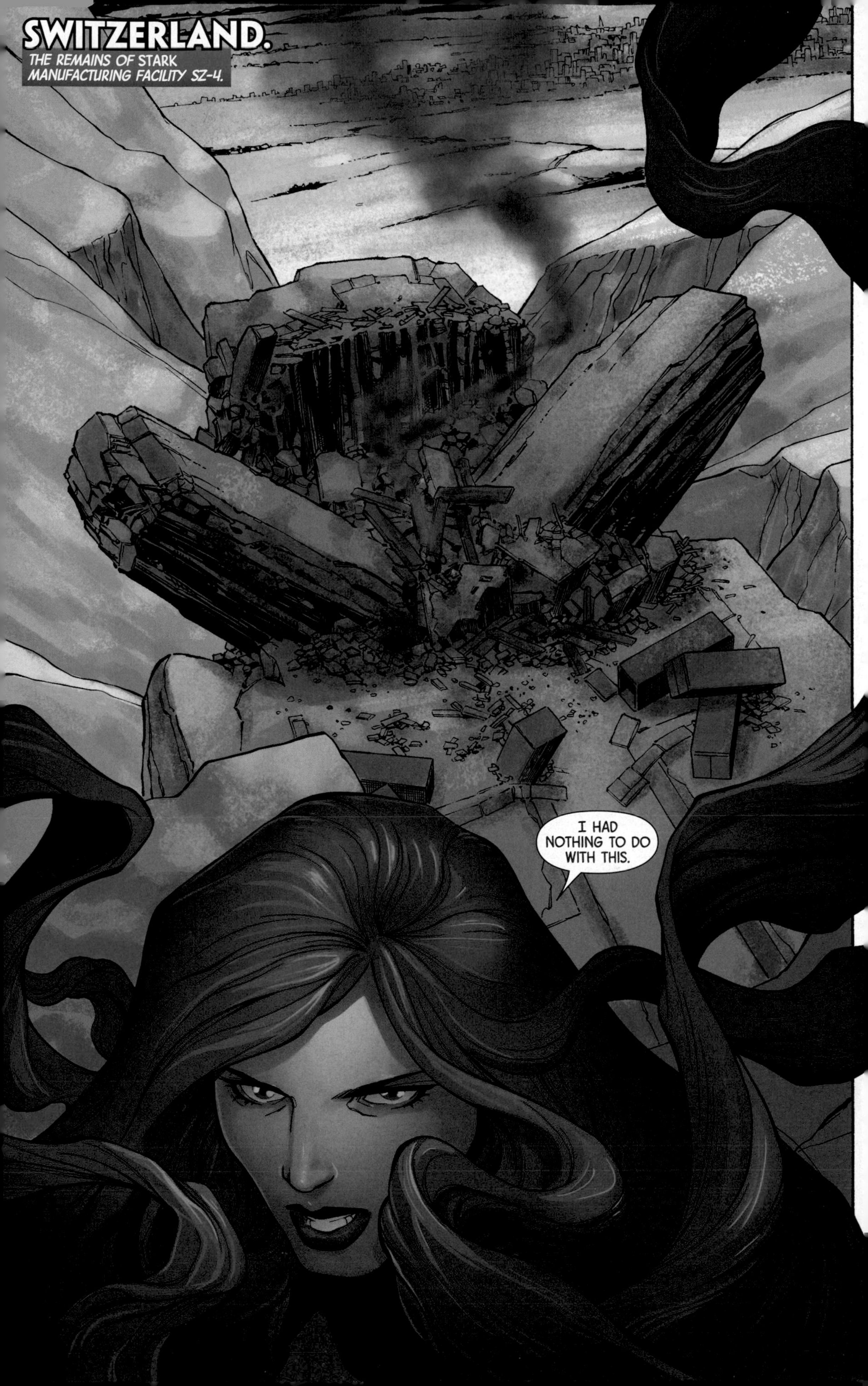
SWITZERLAND.
THE REMAINS OF STARK MANUFACTURING FACILITY SZ-4.
I HAD NOTHING TO DO WITH THIS.

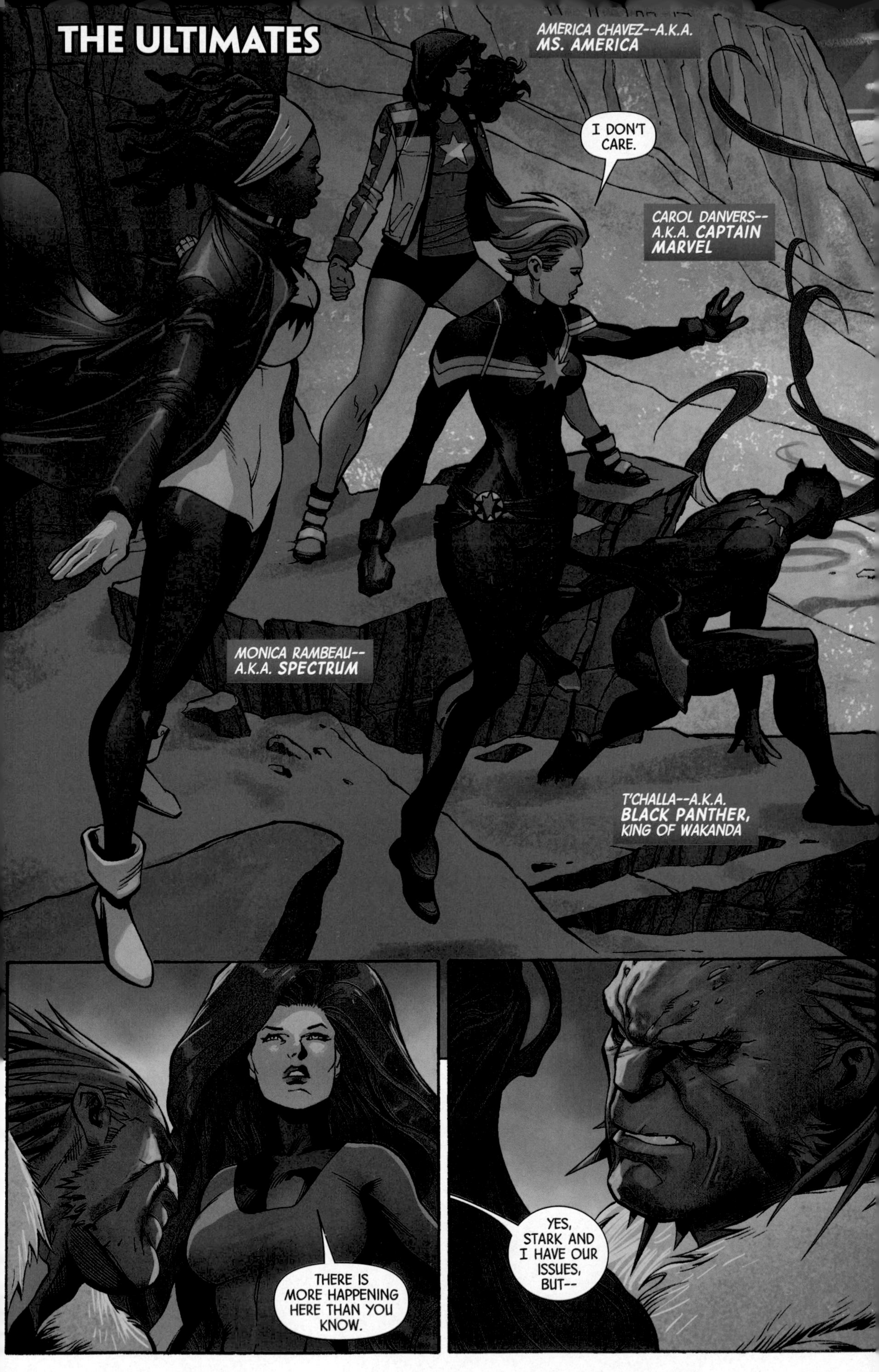
THE ULTIMATES
AMERICA CHAVEZ--A.K.A. MS. AMERICA
I DON'T CARE.
CAROL DANVERS--A.K.A. CAPTAIN MARVEL
MONICA RAMBEAU--A.K.A. SPECTRUM
T'CHALLA--A.K.A. BLACK PANTHER, KING OF WAKANDA
THERE IS MORE HAPPENING HERE THAN YOU KNOW.
YES, STARK AND I HAVE OUR ISSUES, BUT--

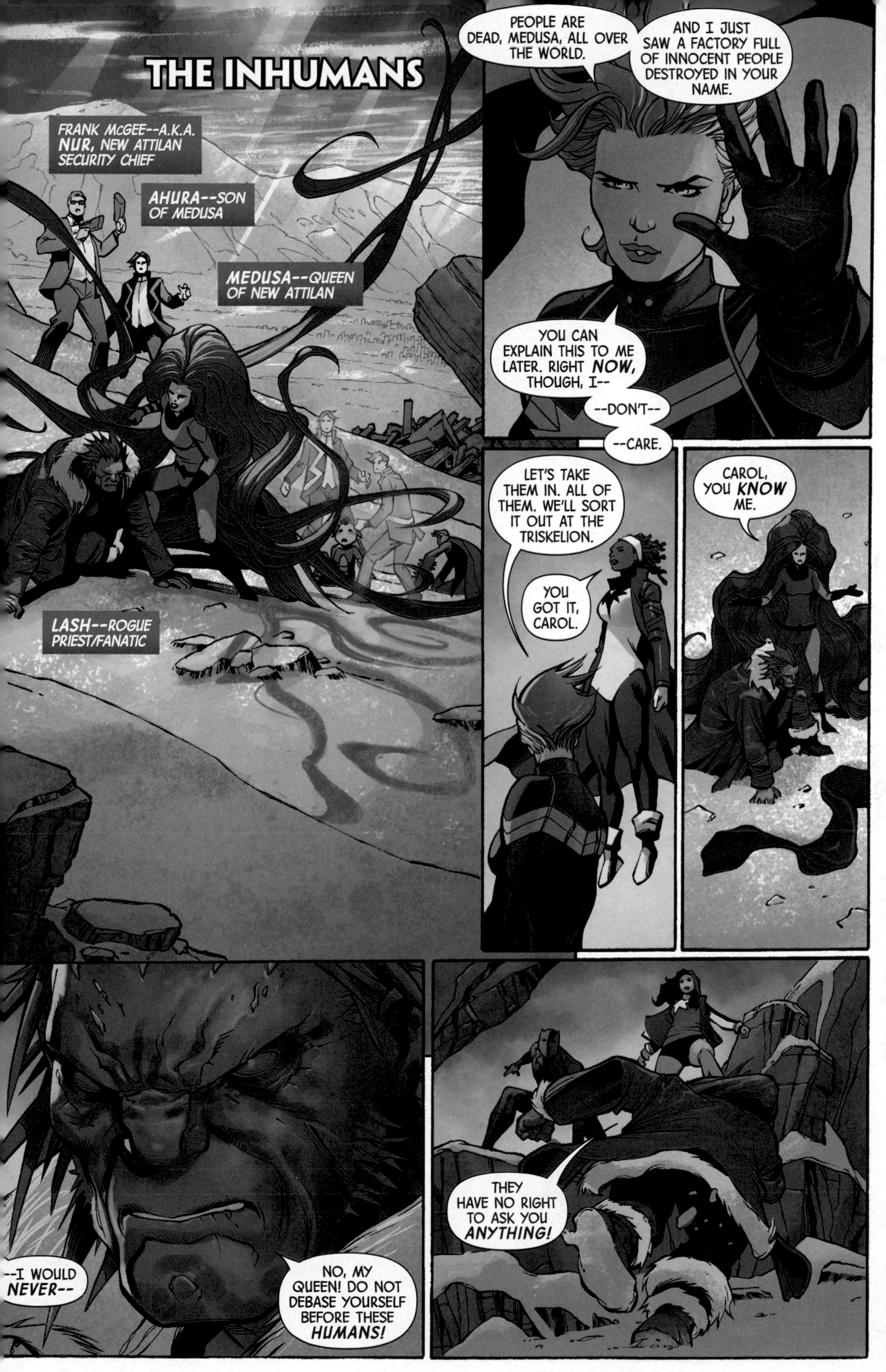
THE INHUMANS
FRANK McGEE--A.K.A. NUR, NEW ATTILAN SECURITY CHIEF
AHURA--SON OF MEDUSA
MEDUSA--QUEEN OF NEW ATTILAN
LASH--ROGUE PRIEST/FANATIC
PEOPLE ARE DEAD, MEDUSA, ALL OVER THE WORLD.
AND I JUST SAW A FACTORY FULL OF INNOCENT PEOPLE DESTROYED IN YOUR NAME.
YOU CAN EXPLAIN THIS TO ME LATER. RIGHT NOW, THOUGH, I--
--DON'T--
--CARE.
LET'S TAKE THEM IN. ALL OF THEM. WE'LL SORT IT OUT AT THE TRISKELION.
YOU GOT IT, CAROL.
CAROL, YOU KNOW ME.
--I WOULD NEVER--
NO, MY QUEEN! DO NOT DEBASE YOURSELF BEFORE THESE HUMANS!
THEY HAVE NO RIGHT TO ASK YOU ANYTHING!

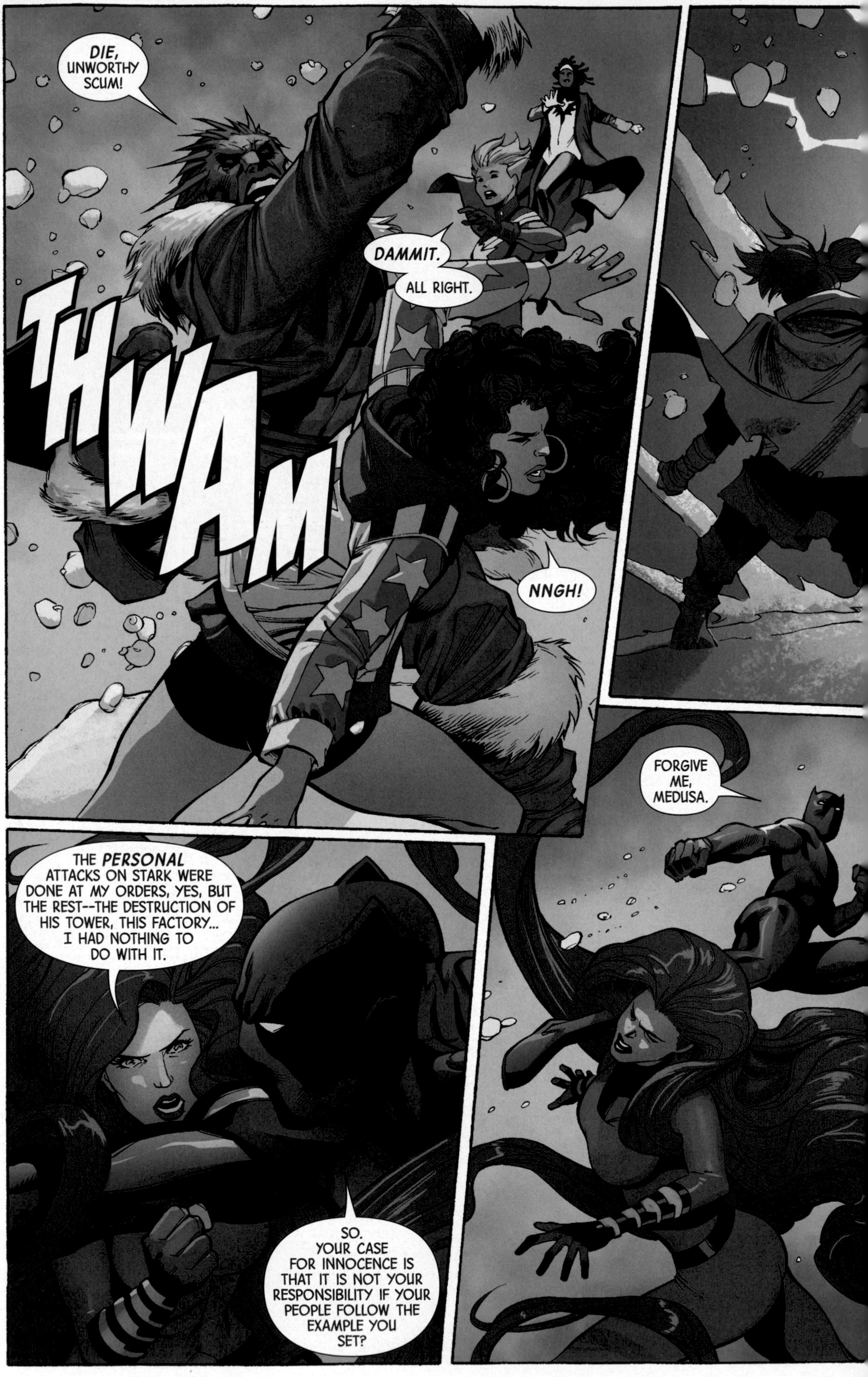
DIE, UNWORTHY SCUM!
DAMMIT.
ALL RIGHT.
THWAM
NNGH!
FORGIVE ME, MEDUSA.
THE PERSONAL ATTACKS ON STARK WERE DONE AT MY ORDERS, YES, BUT THE REST--THE DESTRUCTION OF HIS TOWER, THIS FACTORY... I HAD NOTHING TO DO WITH IT.
SO. YOUR CASE FOR INNOCENCE IS THAT IT IS NOT YOUR RESPONSIBILITY IF YOUR PEOPLE FOLLOW THE EXAMPLE YOU SET?

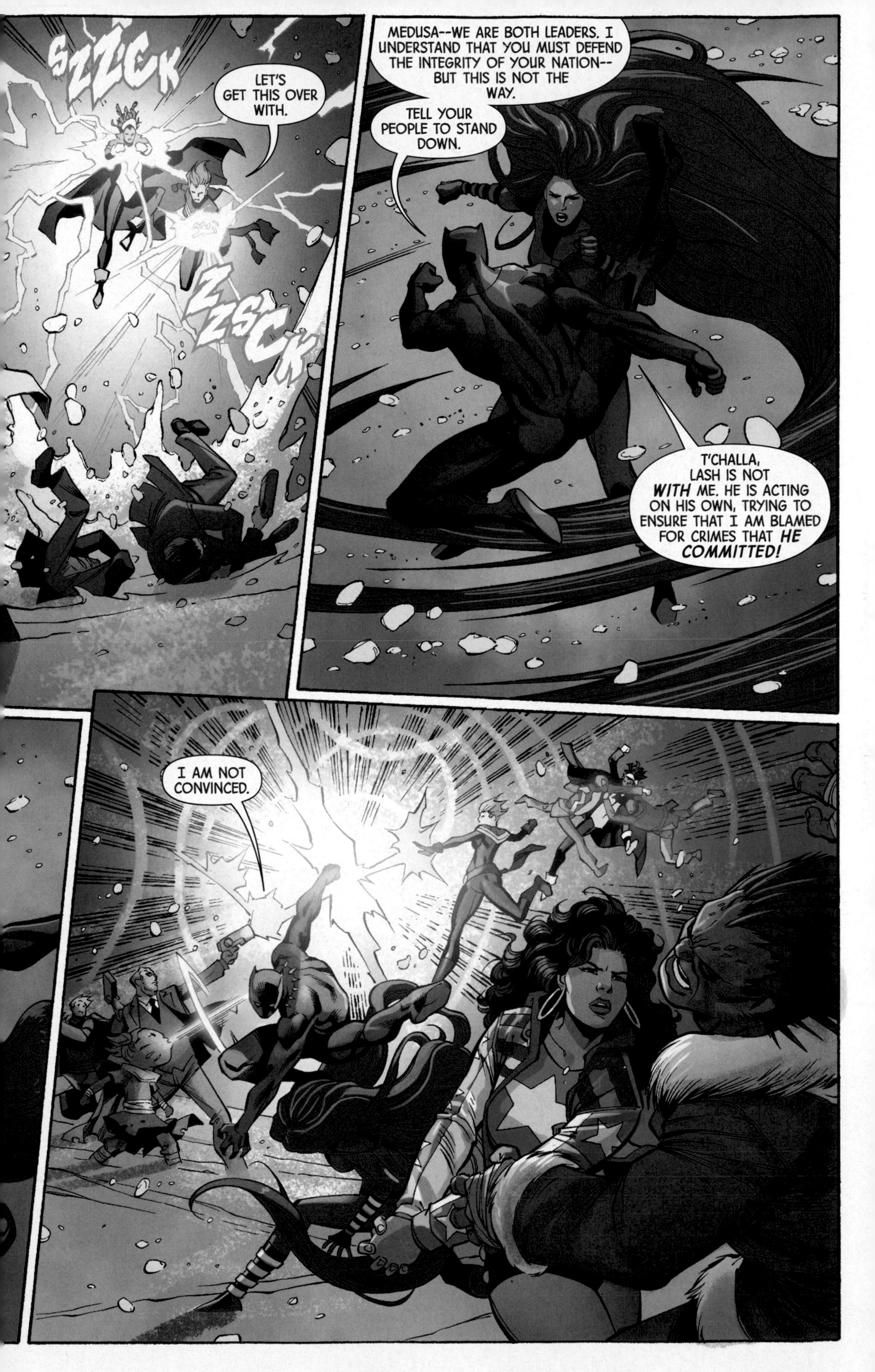
SZZCK
LET'S GET THIS OVER WITH.
ZZSCK
MEDUSA--WE ARE BOTH LEADERS. I UNDERSTAND THAT YOU MUST DEFEND THE INTEGRITY OF YOUR NATION-- BUT THIS IS NOT THE WAY.
TELL YOUR PEOPLE TO STAND DOWN.
T'CHALLA, LASH IS NOT *WITH* ME. HE IS ACTING ON HIS OWN, TRYING TO ENSURE THAT I AM BLAMED FOR CRIMES THAT *HE COMMITTED!*
I AM NOT CONVINCED.

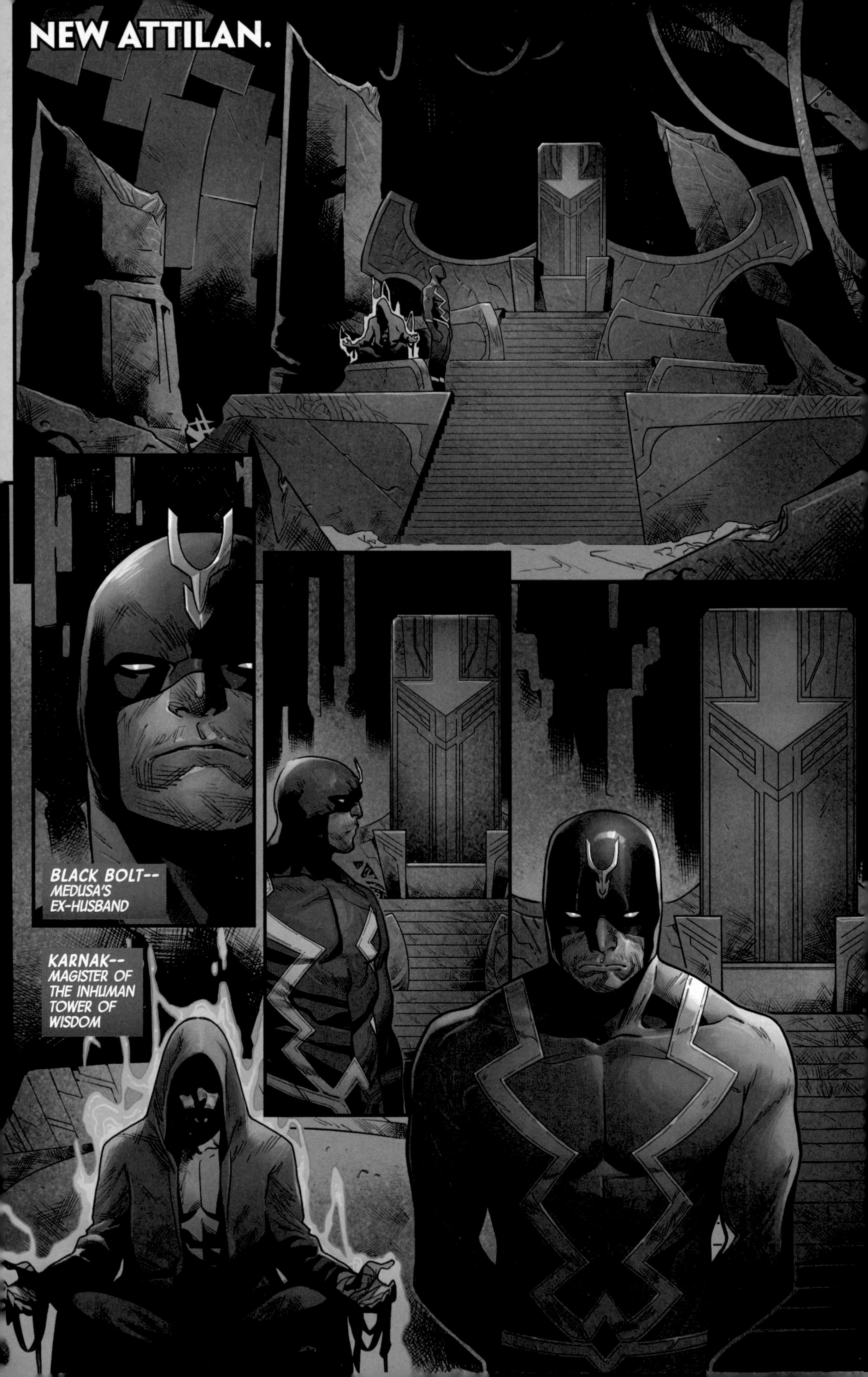
NEW ATTILAN.
BLACK BOLT-- MEDUSA'S EX-HUSBAND
KARNAK-- MAGISTER OF THE INHUMAN TOWER OF WISDOM

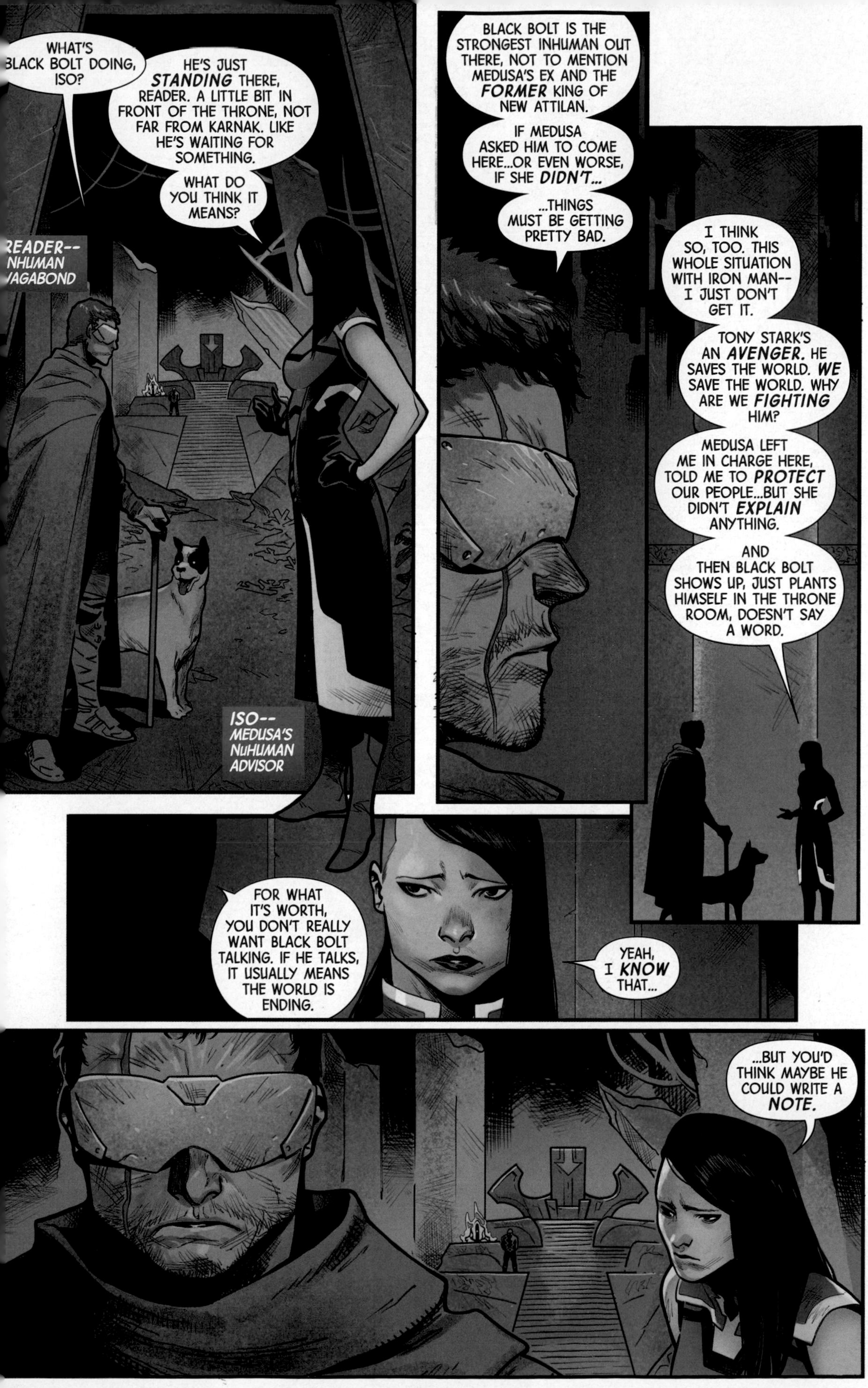
WHAT'S BLACK BOLT DOING, ISO?
HE'S JUST STANDING THERE, READER. A LITTLE BIT IN FRONT OF THE THRONE, NOT FAR FROM KARNAK. LIKE HE'S WAITING FOR SOMETHING.
WHAT DO YOU THINK IT MEANS?
READER-- NHUMAN VAGABOND
ISO-- MEDUSA'S NUHUMAN ADVISOR
BLACK BOLT IS THE STRONGEST INHUMAN OUT THERE, NOT TO MENTION MEDUSA'S EX AND THE FORMER KING OF NEW ATTILAN.
IF MEDUSA ASKED HIM TO COME HERE...OR EVEN WORSE, IF SHE DIDN'T...
...THINGS MUST BE GETTING PRETTY BAD.
I THINK SO, TOO. THIS WHOLE SITUATION WITH IRON MAN-- I JUST DON'T GET IT.
TONY STARK'S AN AVENGER. HE SAVES THE WORLD. WE SAVE THE WORLD. WHY ARE WE FIGHTING HIM?
MEDUSA LEFT ME IN CHARGE HERE, TOLD ME TO PROTECT OUR PEOPLE...BUT SHE DIDN'T EXPLAIN ANYTHING.
AND THEN BLACK BOLT SHOWS UP, JUST PLANTS HIMSELF IN THE THRONE ROOM, DOESN'T SAY A WORD.
FOR WHAT IT'S WORTH, YOU DON'T REALLY WANT BLACK BOLT TALKING. IF HE TALKS, IT USUALLY MEANS THE WORLD IS ENDING.
YEAH, I KNOW THAT...
...BUT YOU'D THINK MAYBE HE COULD WRITE A NOTE.

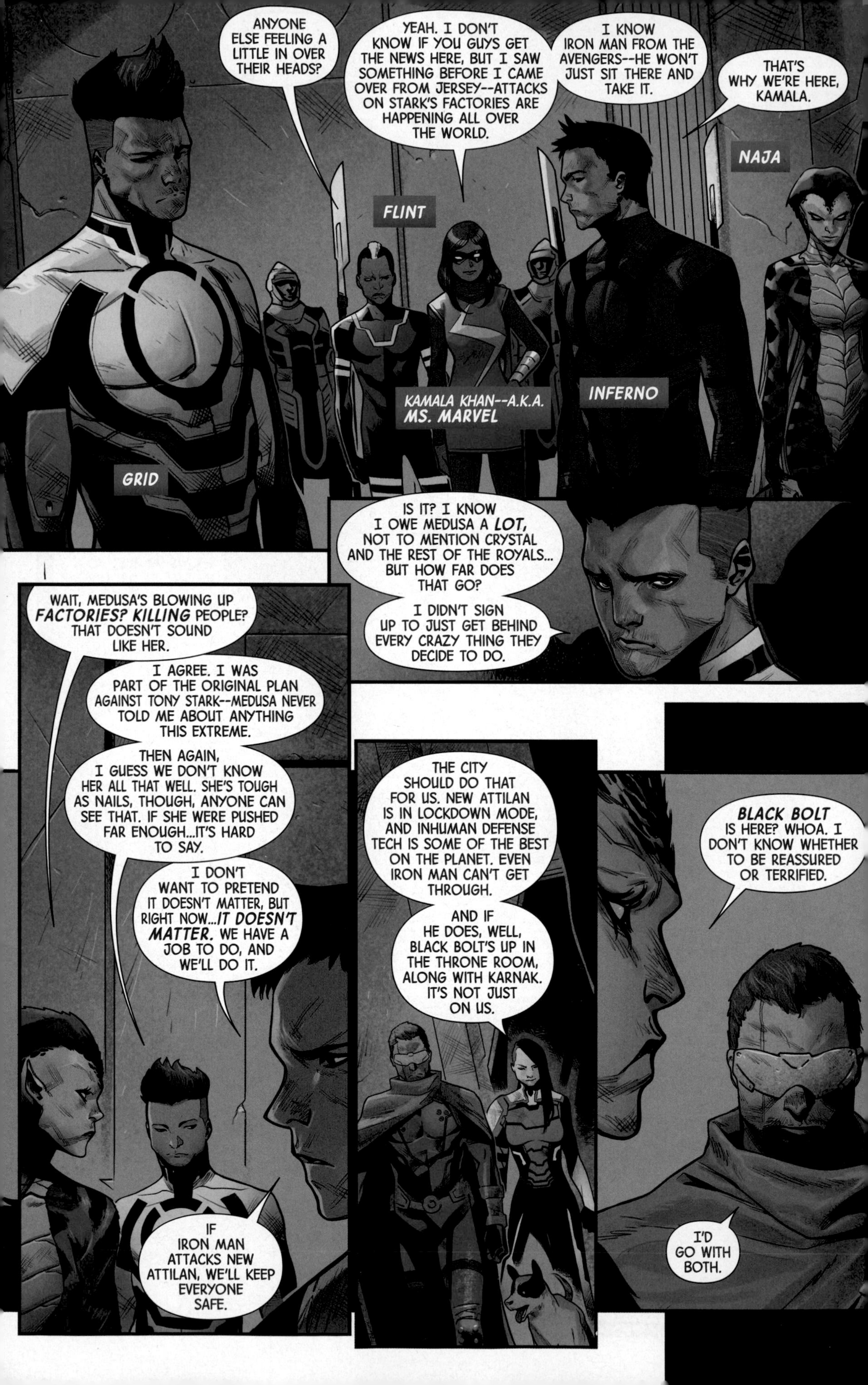
ANYONE ELSE FEELING A LITTLE IN OVER THEIR HEADS?
YEAH. I DON'T KNOW IF YOU GUYS GET THE NEWS HERE, BUT I SAW SOMETHING BEFORE I CAME OVER FROM JERSEY--ATTACKS ON STARK'S FACTORIES ARE HAPPENING ALL OVER THE WORLD.
I KNOW IRON MAN FROM THE AVENGERS--HE WON'T JUST SIT THERE AND TAKE IT.
THAT'S WHY WE'RE HERE, KAMALA.
NAJA
FLINT
KAMALA KHAN--A.K.A. MS. MARVEL
INFERNO
GRID
IS IT? I KNOW I OWE MEDUSA A LOT, NOT TO MENTION CRYSTAL AND THE REST OF THE ROYALS... BUT HOW FAR DOES THAT GO?
I DIDN'T SIGN UP TO JUST GET BEHIND EVERY CRAZY THING THEY DECIDE TO DO.
WAIT, MEDUSA'S BLOWING UP FACTORIES? KILLING PEOPLE? THAT DOESN'T SOUND LIKE HER.
I AGREE. I WAS PART OF THE ORIGINAL PLAN AGAINST TONY STARK--MEDUSA NEVER TOLD ME ABOUT ANYTHING THIS EXTREME.
THEN AGAIN, I GUESS WE DON'T KNOW HER ALL THAT WELL. SHE'S TOUGH AS NAILS, THOUGH, ANYONE CAN SEE THAT. IF SHE WERE PUSHED FAR ENOUGH...IT'S HARD TO SAY.
I DON'T WANT TO PRETEND IT DOESN'T MATTER, BUT RIGHT NOW...IT DOESN'T MATTER. WE HAVE A JOB TO DO, AND WE'LL DO IT.
IF IRON MAN ATTACKS NEW ATTILAN, WE'LL KEEP EVERYONE SAFE.
THE CITY SHOULD DO THAT FOR US. NEW ATTILAN IS IN LOCKDOWN MODE, AND INHUMAN DEFENSE TECH IS SOME OF THE BEST ON THE PLANET. EVEN IRON MAN CAN'T GET THROUGH.
AND IF HE DOES, WELL, BLACK BOLT'S UP IN THE THRONE ROOM, ALONG WITH KARNAK. IT'S NOT JUST ON US.
BLACK BOLT IS HERE? WHOA. I DON'T KNOW WHETHER TO BE REASSURED OR TERRIFIED.
I'D GO WITH BOTH.

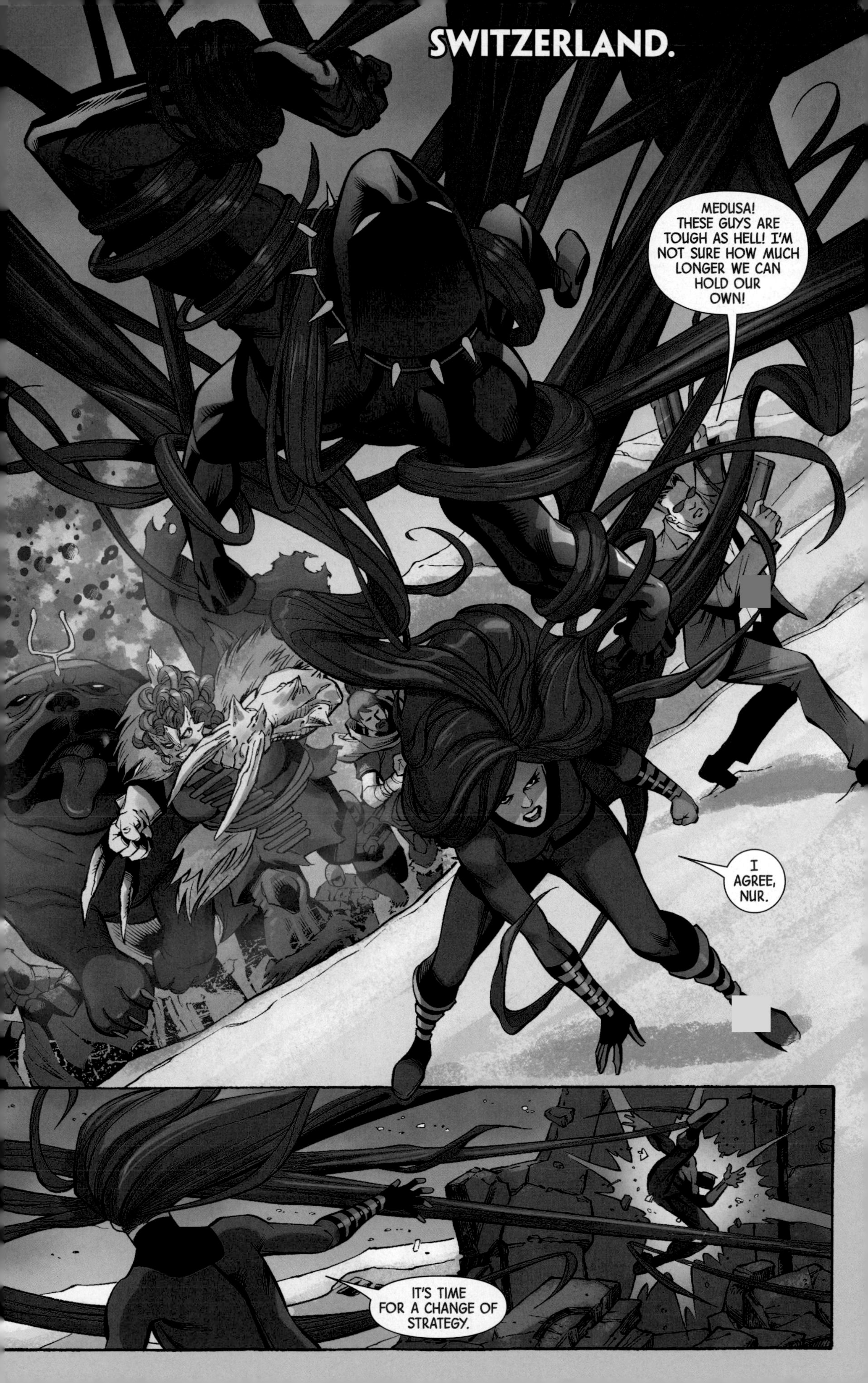
SWITZERLAND.
MEDUSA! THESE GUYS ARE TOUGH AS HELL! I'M NOT SURE HOW MUCH LONGER WE CAN HOLD OUR OWN!
I AGREE, NUR.
IT'S TIME FOR A CHANGE OF STRATEGY.

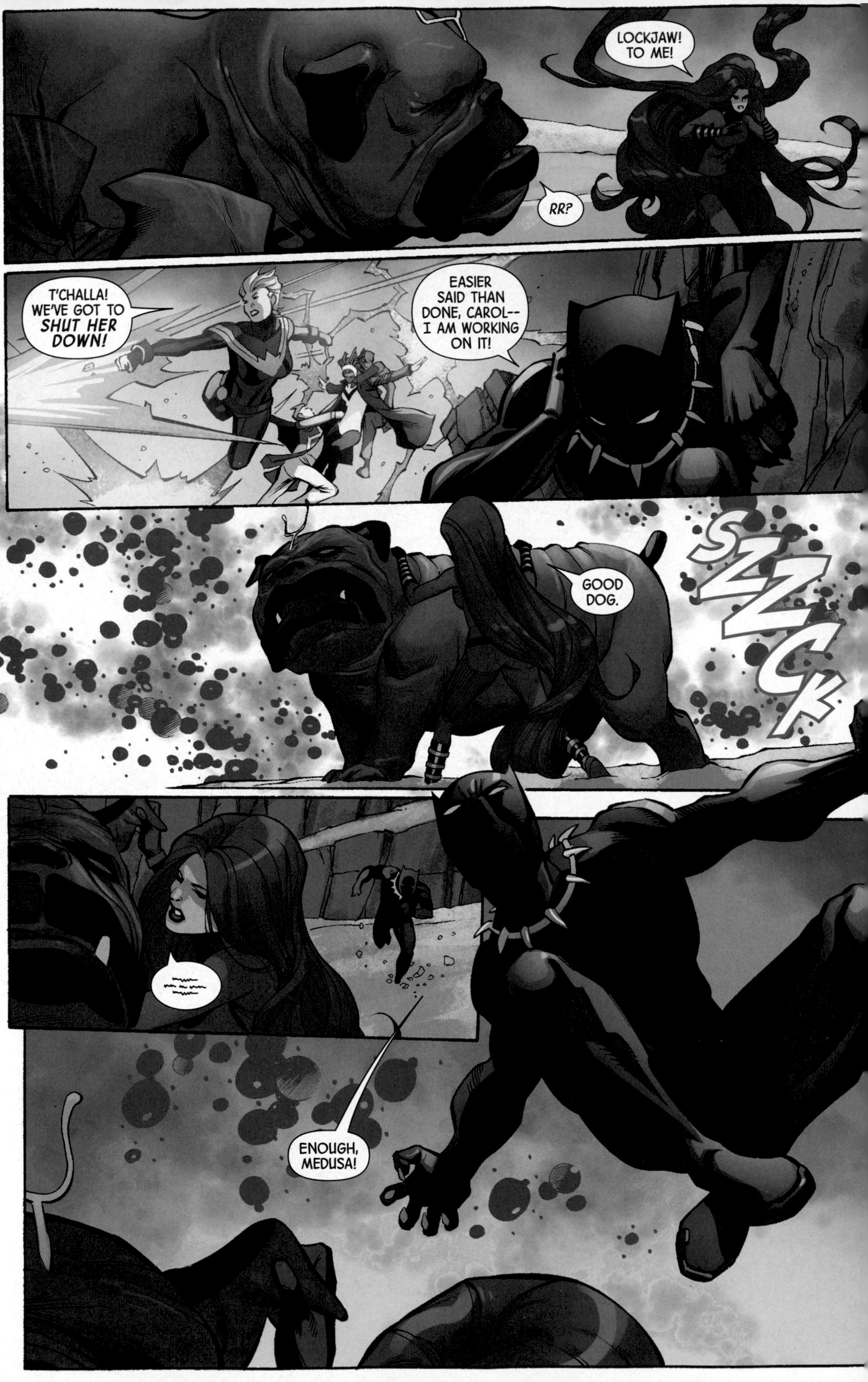
LOCKJAW! TO ME!
RR?
T'CHALLA! WE'VE GOT TO SHUT HER DOWN!
EASIER SAID THAN DONE, CAROL-- I AM WORKING ON IT!
SZZCK
GOOD DOG.
ENOUGH, MEDUSA!

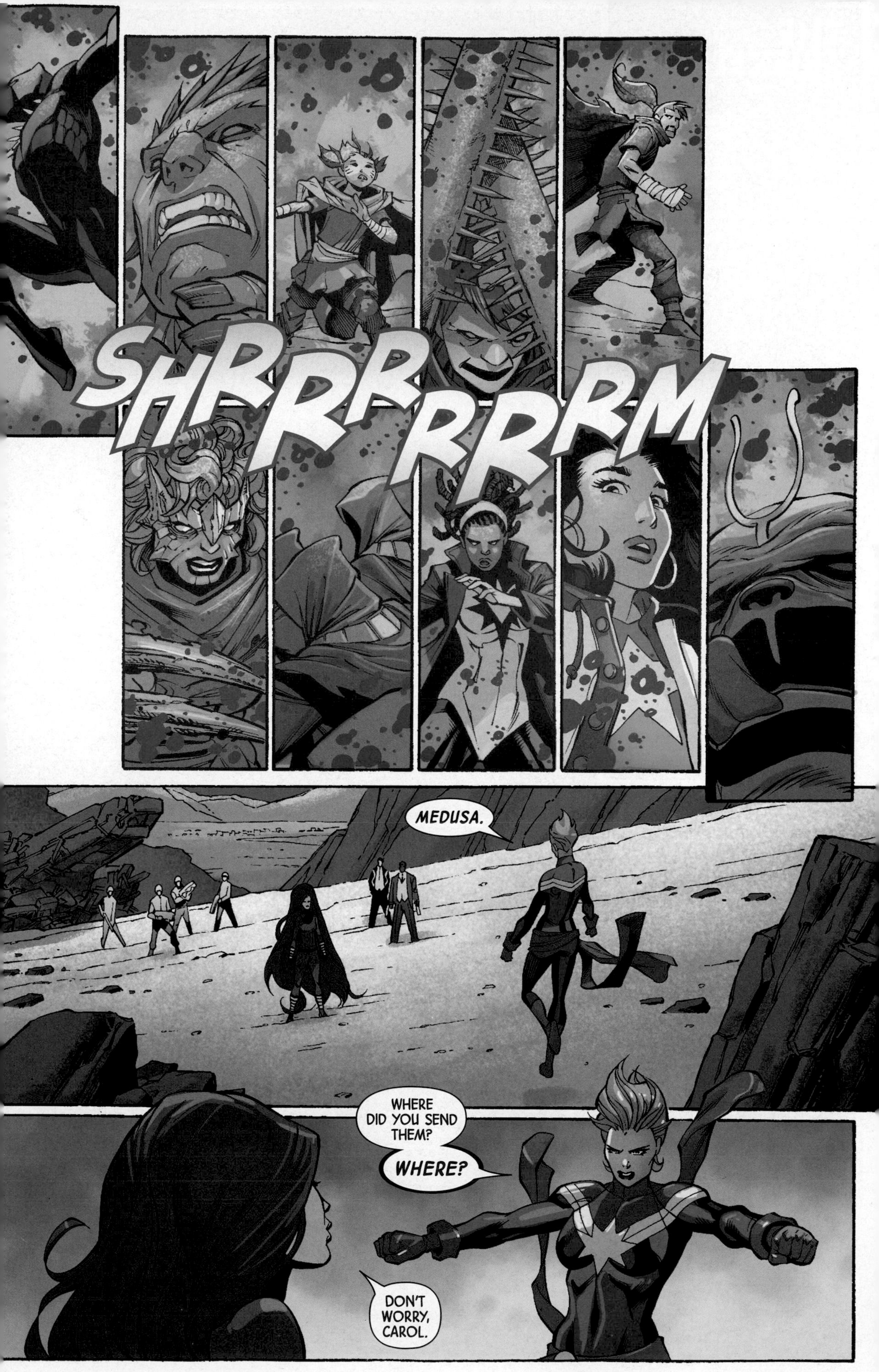
SHRRRRRRRM
MEDUSA.
WHERE DID YOU SEND THEM?
WHERE?
DON'T WORRY, CAROL.

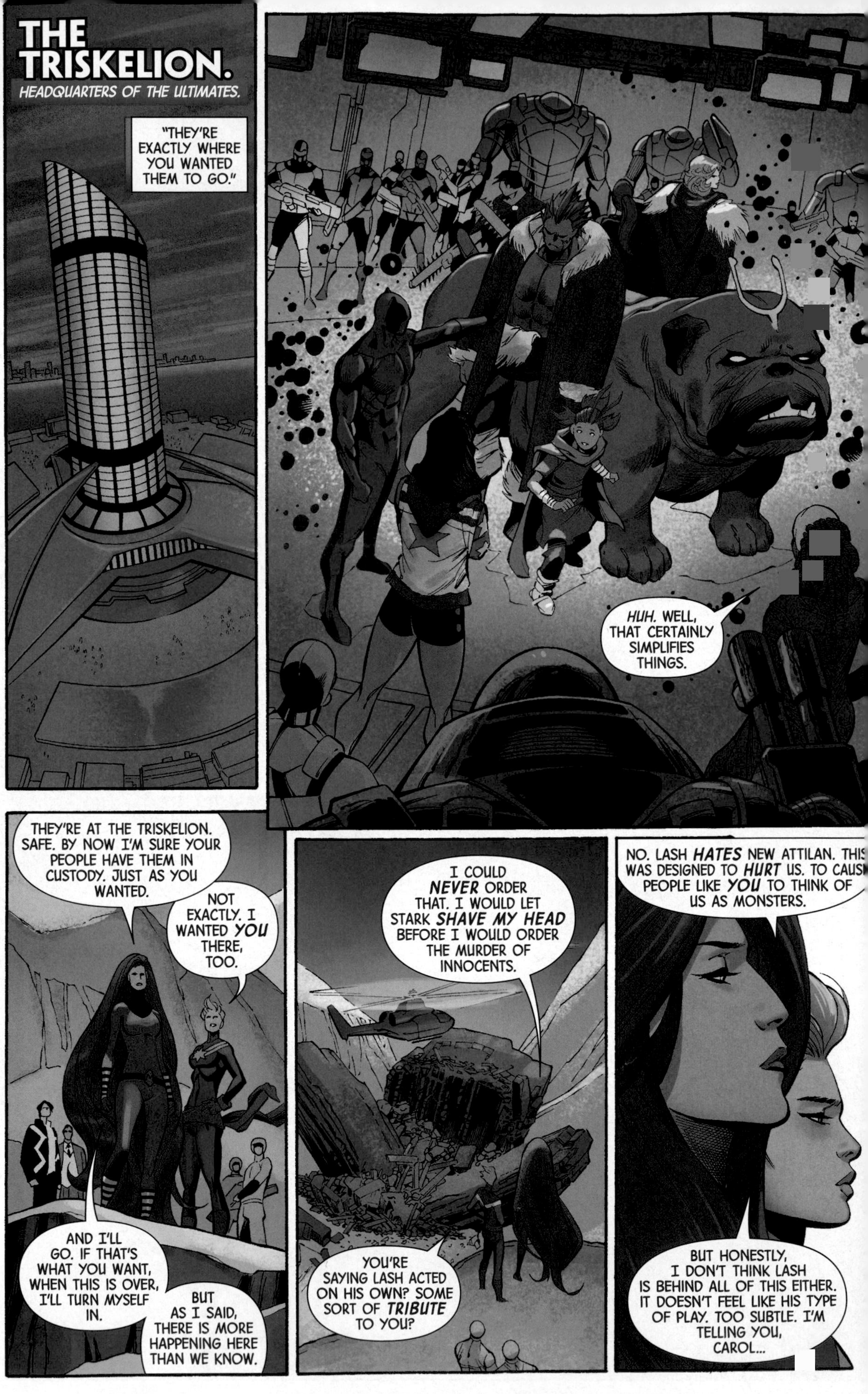
THE TRISKELION.
HEADQUARTERS OF THE ULTIMATES.
"THEY'RE EXACTLY WHERE YOU WANTED THEM TO GO."
HUH. WELL, THAT CERTAINLY SIMPLIFIES THINGS.
THEY'RE AT THE TRISKELION. SAFE. BY NOW I'M SURE YOUR PEOPLE HAVE THEM IN CUSTODY. JUST AS YOU WANTED.
NOT EXACTLY. I WANTED YOU THERE, TOO.
AND I'LL GO. IF THAT'S WHAT YOU WANT, WHEN THIS IS OVER, I'LL TURN MYSELF IN.
BUT AS I SAID, THERE IS MORE HAPPENING HERE THAN WE KNOW.
I COULD NEVER ORDER THAT. I WOULD LET STARK SHAVE MY HEAD BEFORE I WOULD ORDER THE MURDER OF INNOCENTS.
YOU'RE SAYING LASH ACTED ON HIS OWN? SOME SORT OF TRIBUTE TO YOU?
NO. LASH HATES NEW ATTILAN. THIS WAS DESIGNED TO HURT US. TO CAUSE PEOPLE LIKE YOU TO THINK OF US AS MONSTERS.
BUT HONESTLY, I DON'T THINK LASH IS BEHIND ALL OF THIS EITHER. IT DOESN'T FEEL LIKE HIS TYPE OF PLAY. TOO SUBTLE. I'M TELLING YOU, CAROL...

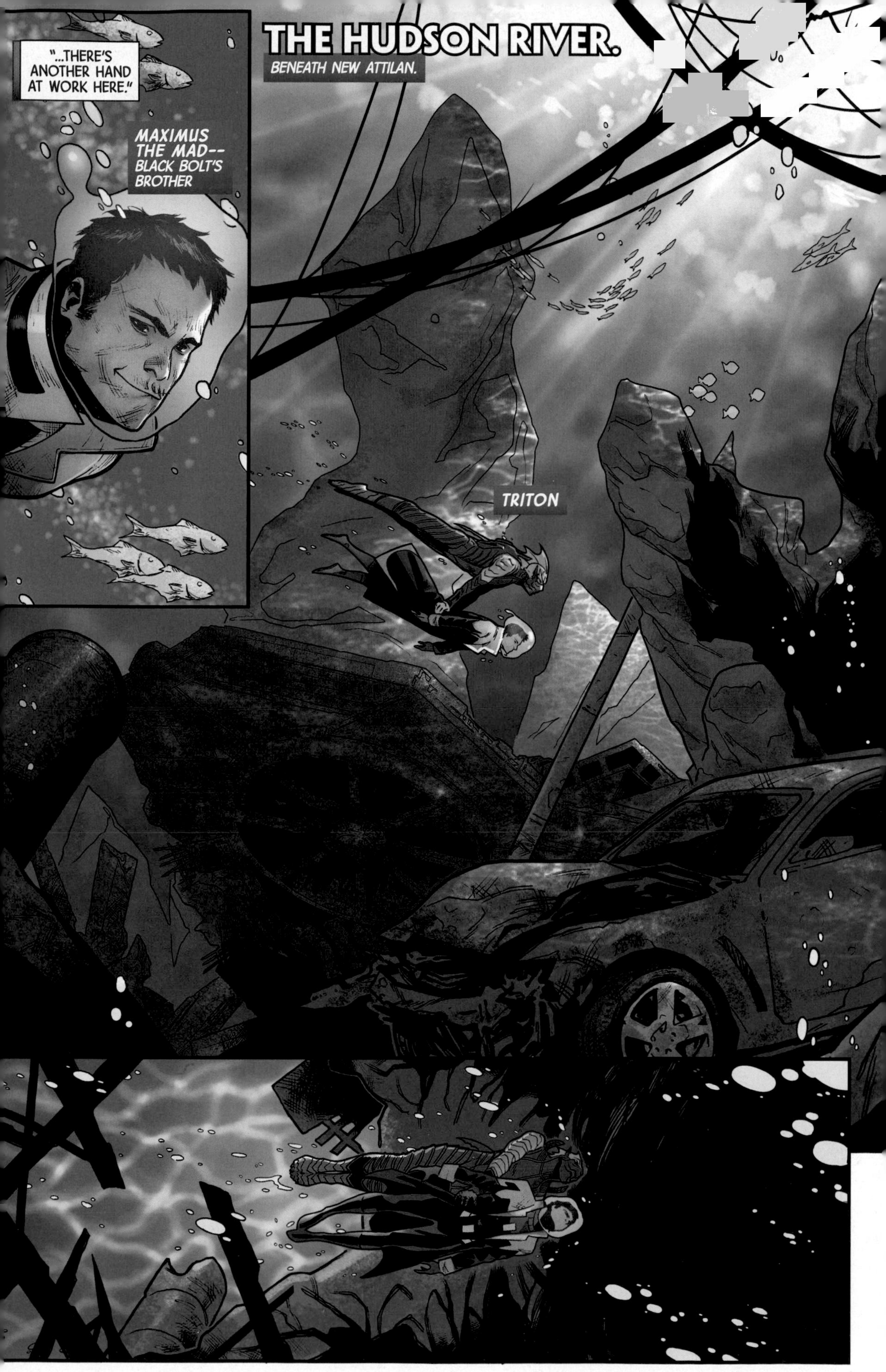

THE HUDSON RIVER.
BENEATH NEW ATTILAN.
"...THERE'S ANOTHER HAND AT WORK HERE."
MAXIMUS THE MAD-- BLACK BOLT'S BROTHER
TRITON

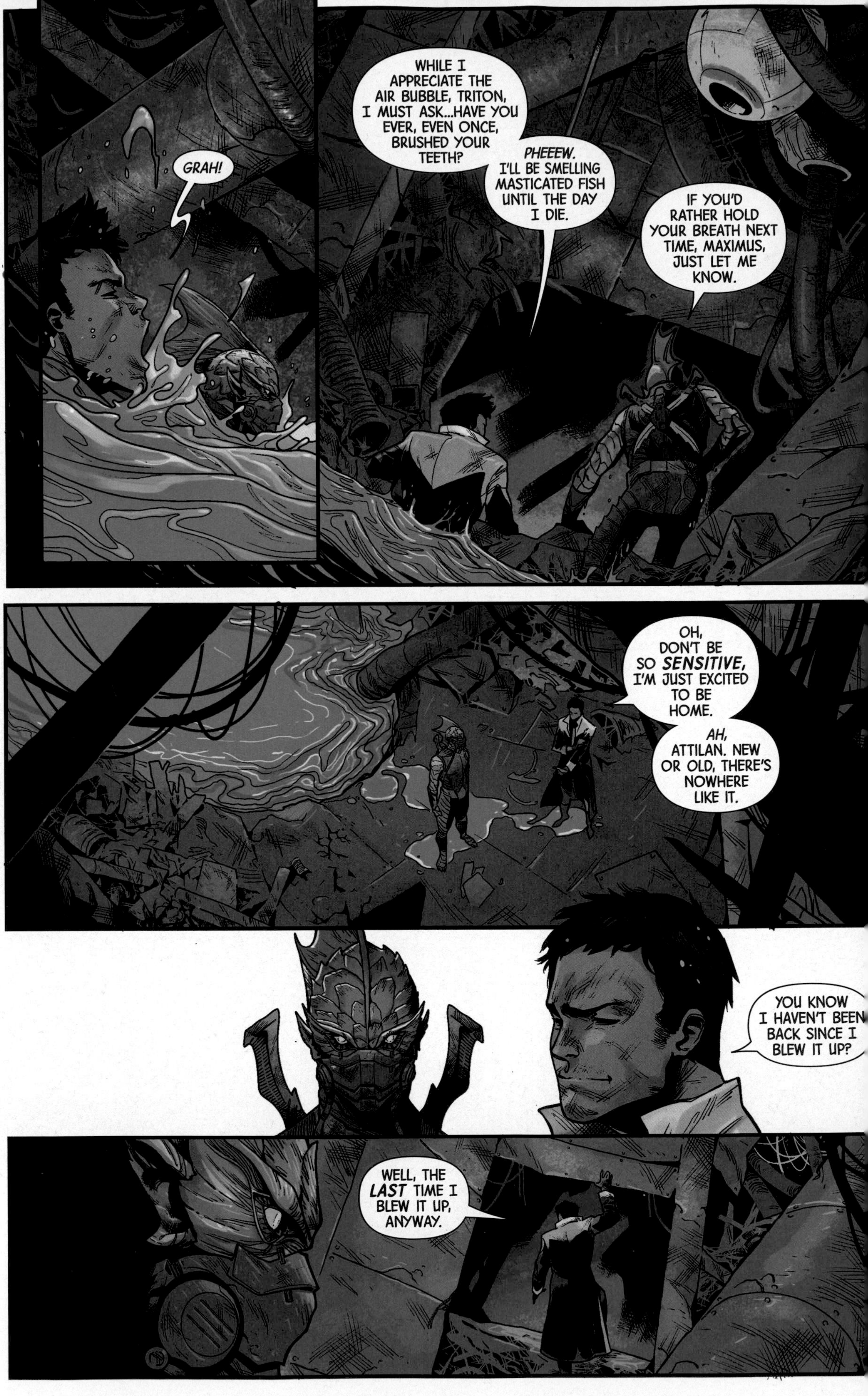
GRAH!
WHILE I APPRECIATE THE AIR BUBBLE, TRITON, I MUST ASK...HAVE YOU EVER, EVEN ONCE, BRUSHED YOUR TEETH?
PHEEEW. I'LL BE SMELLING MASTICATED FISH UNTIL THE DAY I DIE.
IF YOU'D RATHER HOLD YOUR BREATH NEXT TIME, MAXIMUS, JUST LET ME KNOW.
OH, DON'T BE SO SENSITIVE, I'M JUST EXCITED TO BE HOME.
AH, ATTILAN. NEW OR OLD, THERE'S NOWHERE LIKE IT.
YOU KNOW I HAVEN'T BEEN BACK SINCE I BLEW IT UP?
WELL, THE LAST TIME I BLEW IT UP, ANYWAY.

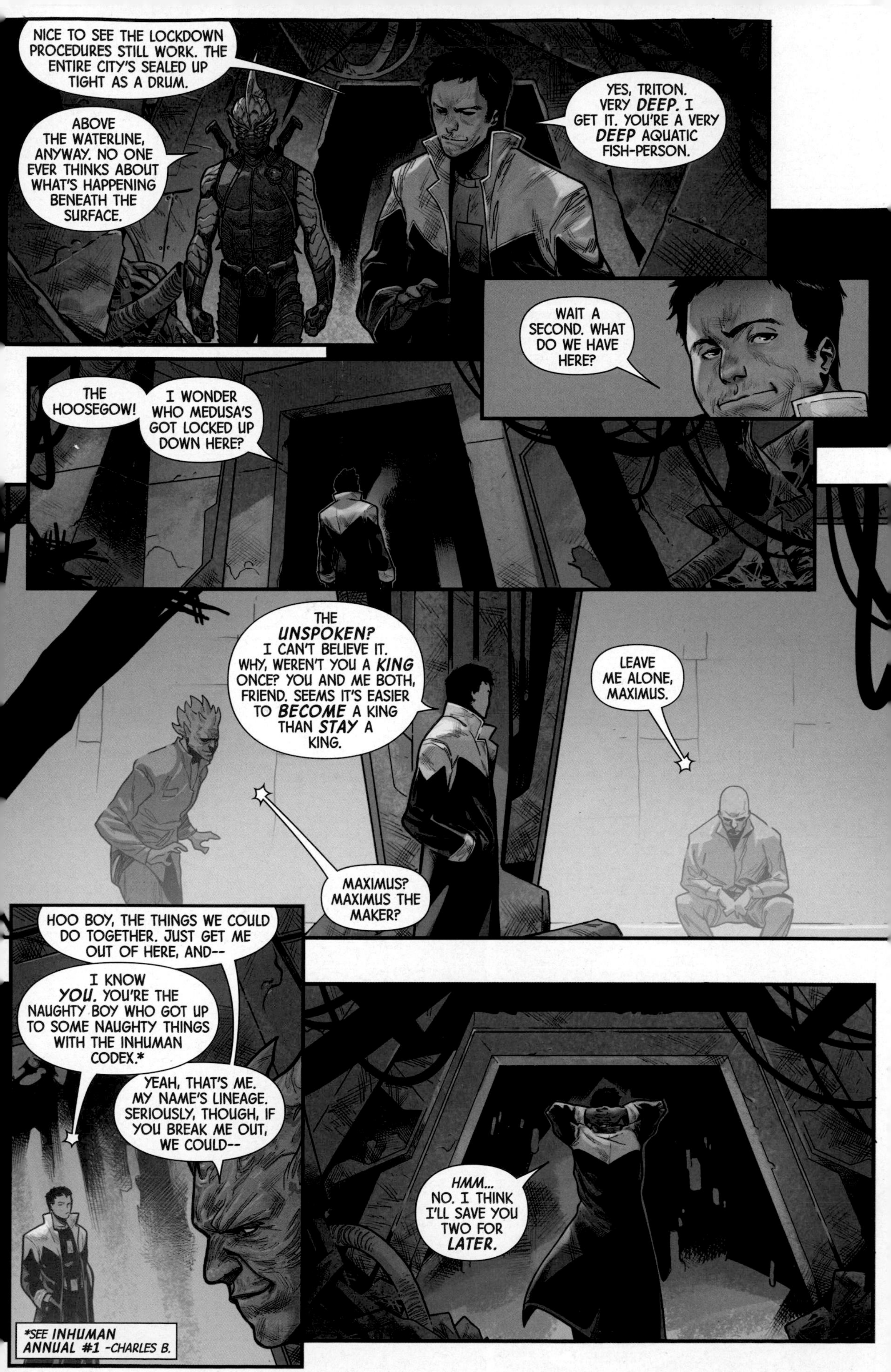
NICE TO SEE THE LOCKDOWN PROCEDURES STILL WORK. THE ENTIRE CITY'S SEALED UP TIGHT AS A DRUM.
ABOVE THE WATERLINE, ANYWAY. NO ONE EVER THINKS ABOUT WHAT'S HAPPENING BENEATH THE SURFACE.
YES, TRITON. VERY DEEP. I GET IT. YOU'RE A VERY DEEP AQUATIC FISH-PERSON.
WAIT A SECOND. WHAT DO WE HAVE HERE?
THE HOOSEGOW!
I WONDER WHO MEDUSA'S GOT LOCKED UP DOWN HERE?
THE UNSPOKEN? I CAN'T BELIEVE IT. WHY, WEREN'T YOU A KING ONCE? YOU AND ME BOTH, FRIEND. SEEMS IT'S EASIER TO BECOME A KING THAN STAY A KING.
LEAVE ME ALONE, MAXIMUS.
MAXIMUS? MAXIMUS THE MAKER?
HOO BOY, THE THINGS WE COULD DO TOGETHER. JUST GET ME OUT OF HERE, AND--
I KNOW YOU. YOU'RE THE NAUGHTY BOY WHO GOT UP TO SOME NAUGHTY THINGS WITH THE INHUMAN CODEX.*
YEAH, THAT'S ME. MY NAME'S LINEAGE. SERIOUSLY, THOUGH, IF YOU BREAK ME OUT, WE COULD--
*SEE INHUMAN ANNUAL #1 -CHARLES B.
HMM... NO. I THINK I'LL SAVE YOU TWO FOR LATER.

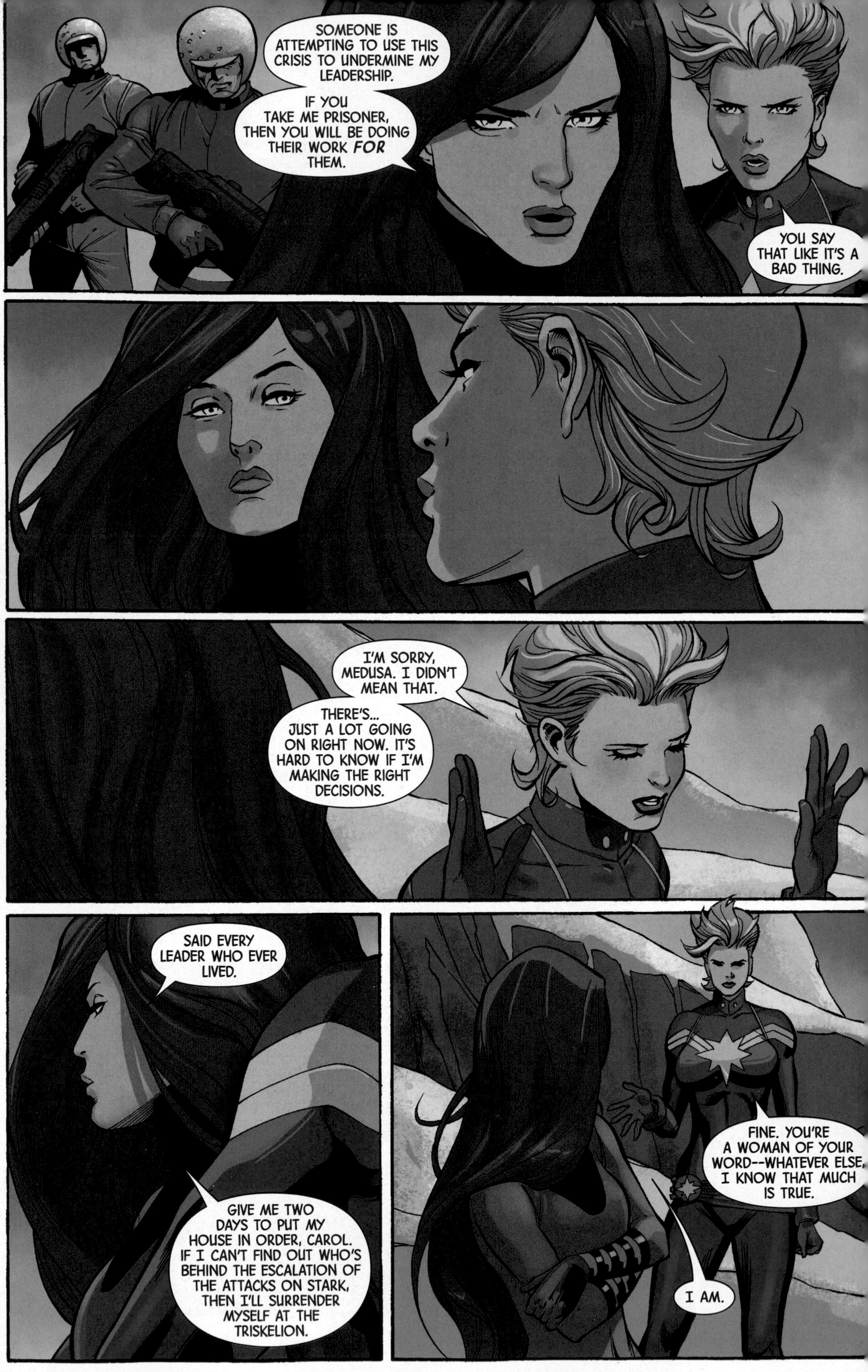
SOMEONE IS ATTEMPTING TO USE THIS CRISIS TO UNDERMINE MY LEADERSHIP.
IF YOU TAKE ME PRISONER, THEN YOU WILL BE DOING THEIR WORK FOR THEM.
YOU SAY THAT LIKE IT'S A BAD THING.
I'M SORRY, MEDUSA. I DIDN'T MEAN THAT.
THERE'S... JUST A LOT GOING ON RIGHT NOW. IT'S HARD TO KNOW IF I'M MAKING THE RIGHT DECISIONS.
SAID EVERY LEADER WHO EVER LIVED.
GIVE ME TWO DAYS TO PUT MY HOUSE IN ORDER, CAROL. IF I CAN'T FIND OUT WHO'S BEHIND THE ESCALATION OF THE ATTACKS ON STARK, THEN I'LL SURRENDER MYSELF AT THE TRISKELION.
FINE. YOU'RE A WOMAN OF YOUR WORD--WHATEVER ELSE, I KNOW THAT MUCH IS TRUE.
I AM.

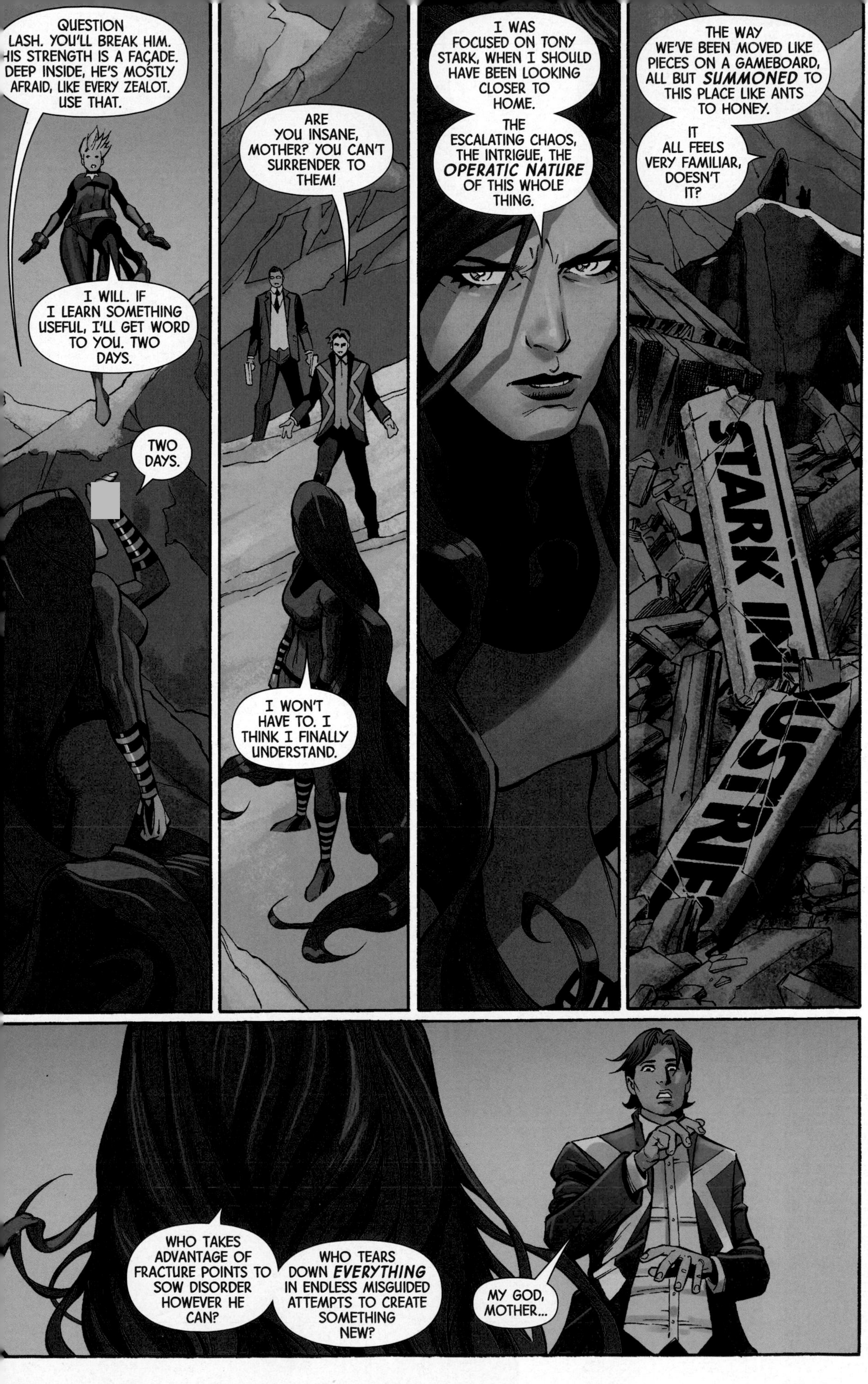

QUESTION LASH. YOU'LL BREAK HIM. HIS STRENGTH IS A FAÇADE. DEEP INSIDE, HE'S MOSTLY AFRAID, LIKE EVERY ZEALOT. USE THAT.
I WILL. IF I LEARN SOMETHING USEFUL, I'LL GET WORD TO YOU. TWO DAYS.
TWO DAYS.
ARE YOU INSANE, MOTHER? YOU CAN'T SURRENDER TO THEM!
I WON'T HAVE TO. I THINK I FINALLY UNDERSTAND.
I WAS FOCUSED ON TONY STARK, WHEN I SHOULD HAVE BEEN LOOKING CLOSER TO HOME.
THE ESCALATING CHAOS, THE INTRIGUE, THE *OPERATIC NATURE* OF THIS WHOLE THING.
THE WAY WE'VE BEEN MOVED LIKE PIECES ON A GAMEBOARD, ALL BUT ***SUMMONED*** TO THIS PLACE LIKE ANTS TO HONEY.
IT ALL FEELS VERY FAMILIAR, DOESN'T IT?
STARK
WHO TAKES ADVANTAGE OF FRACTURE POINTS TO SOW DISORDER HOWEVER HE CAN?
WHO TEARS DOWN *EVERYTHING* IN ENDLESS MISGUIDED ATTEMPTS TO CREATE SOMETHING NEW?
MY GOD, MOTHER...

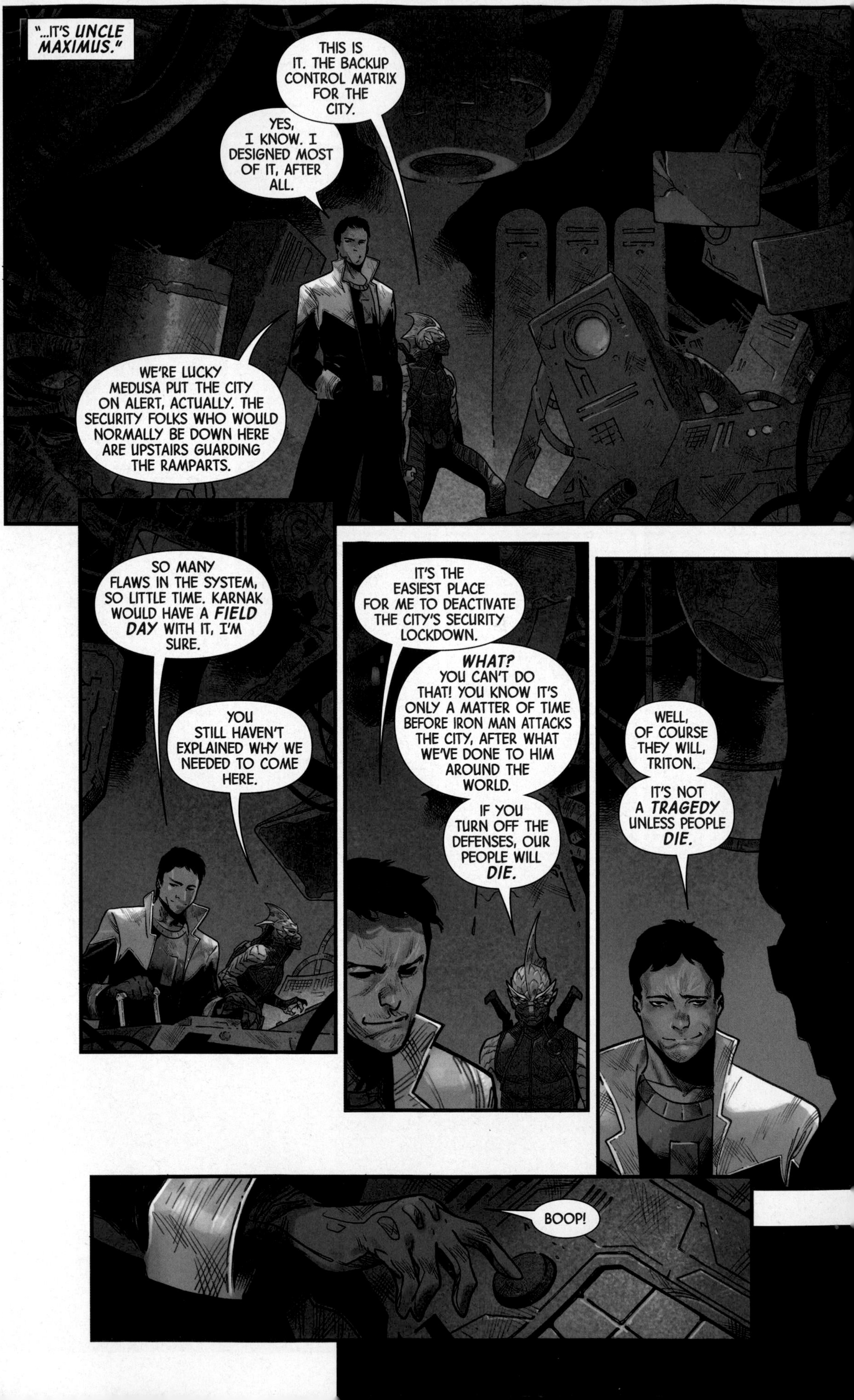
"...IT'S UNCLE MAXIMUS."
THIS IS IT. THE BACKUP CONTROL MATRIX FOR THE CITY.
YES, I KNOW. I DESIGNED MOST OF IT, AFTER ALL.
WE'RE LUCKY MEDUSA PUT THE CITY ON ALERT, ACTUALLY. THE SECURITY FOLKS WHO WOULD NORMALLY BE DOWN HERE ARE UPSTAIRS GUARDING THE RAMPARTS.
SO MANY FLAWS IN THE SYSTEM, SO LITTLE TIME. KARNAK WOULD HAVE A FIELD DAY WITH IT, I'M SURE.
YOU STILL HAVEN'T EXPLAINED WHY WE NEEDED TO COME HERE.
IT'S THE EASIEST PLACE FOR ME TO DEACTIVATE THE CITY'S SECURITY LOCKDOWN.
WHAT? YOU CAN'T DO THAT! YOU KNOW IT'S ONLY A MATTER OF TIME BEFORE IRON MAN ATTACKS THE CITY, AFTER WHAT WE'VE DONE TO HIM AROUND THE WORLD.
IF YOU TURN OFF THE DEFENSES, OUR PEOPLE WILL DIE.
WELL, OF COURSE THEY WILL, TRITON.
IT'S NOT A TRAGEDY UNLESS PEOPLE DIE.
BOOP!

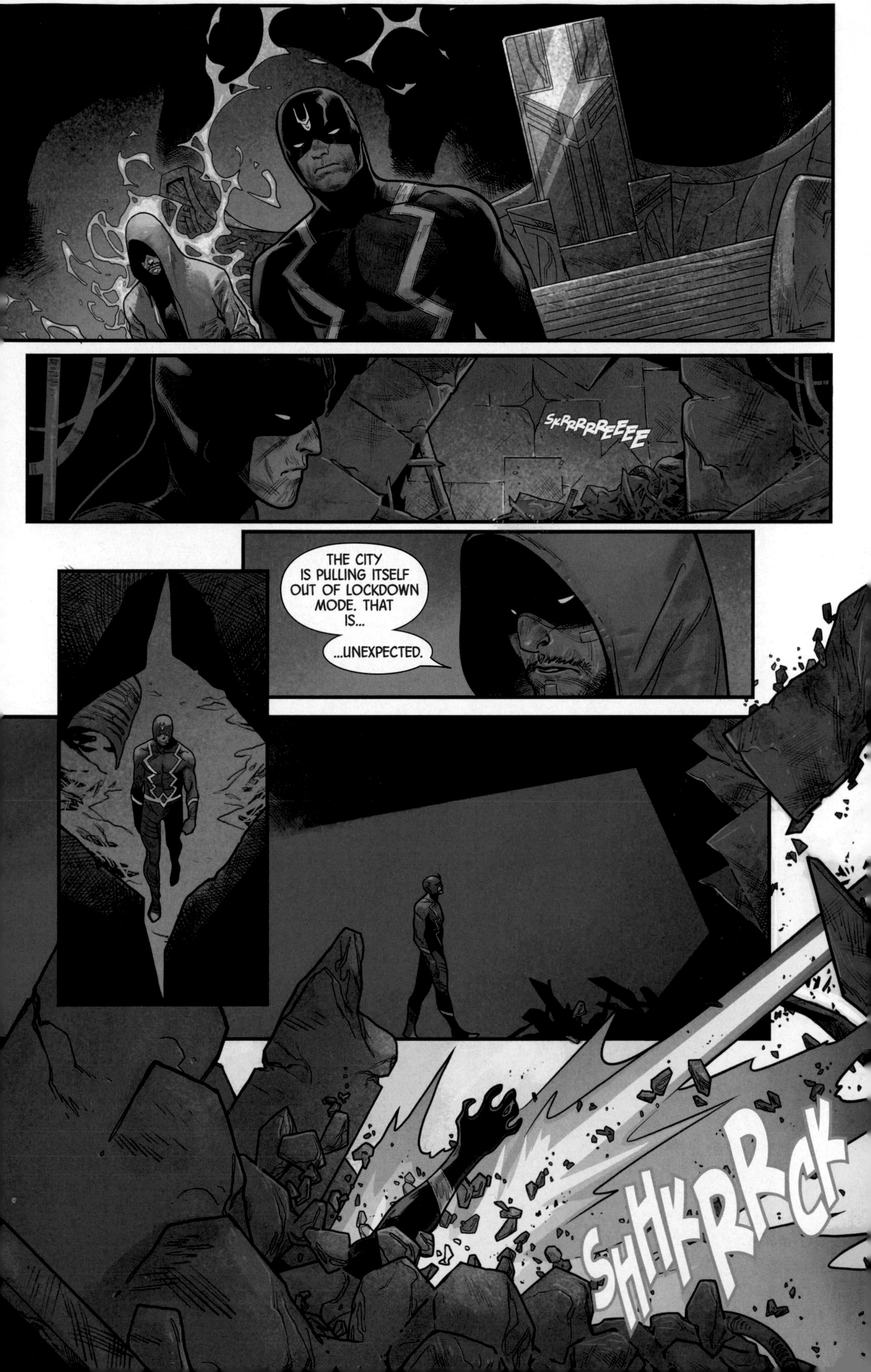
SKRRRRREEEE
THE CITY IS PULLING ITSELF OUT OF LOCKDOWN MODE. THAT IS...
...UNEXPECTED.
SHKRRCK

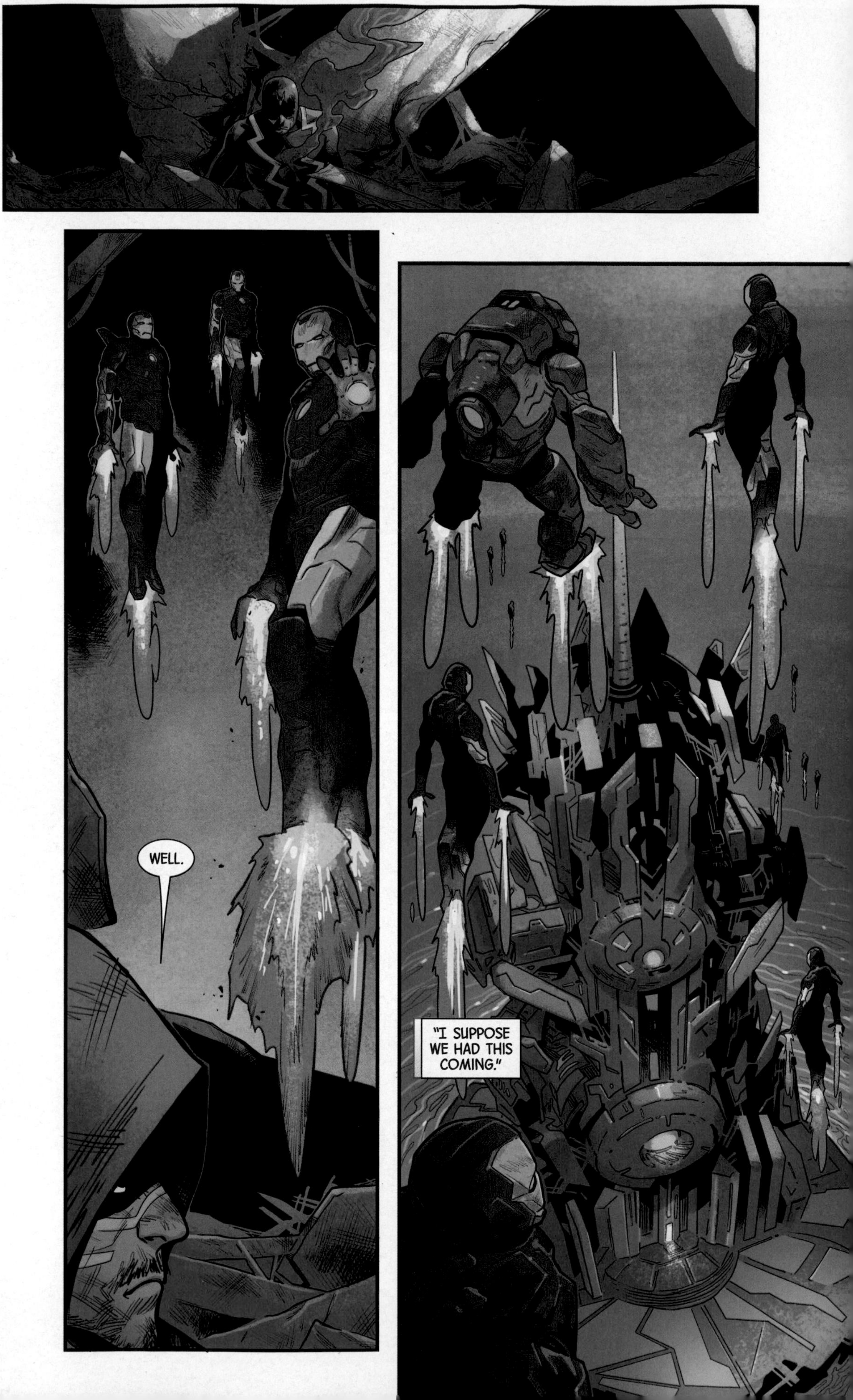
WELL.
"I SUPPOSE WE HAD THIS COMING."

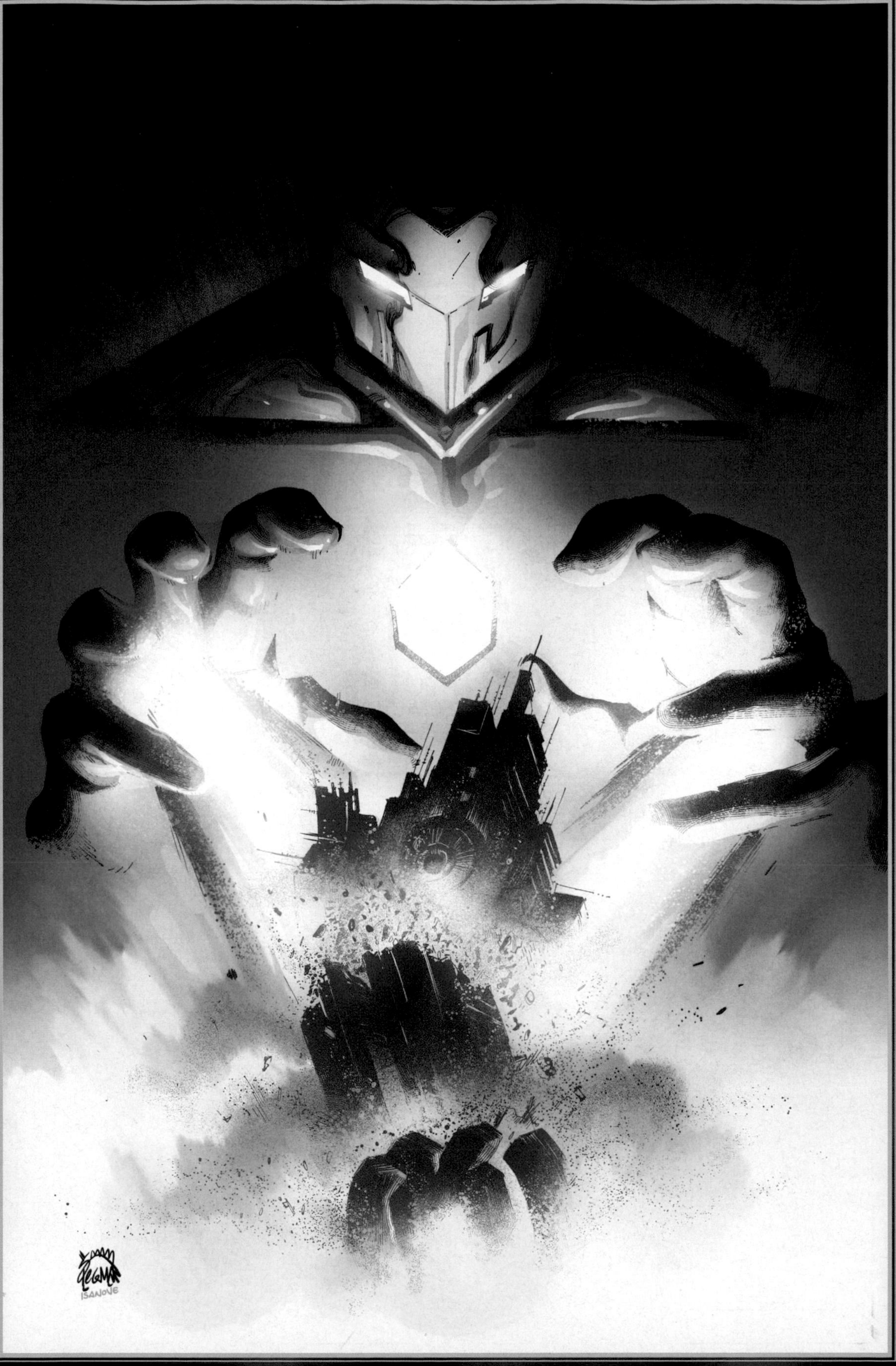

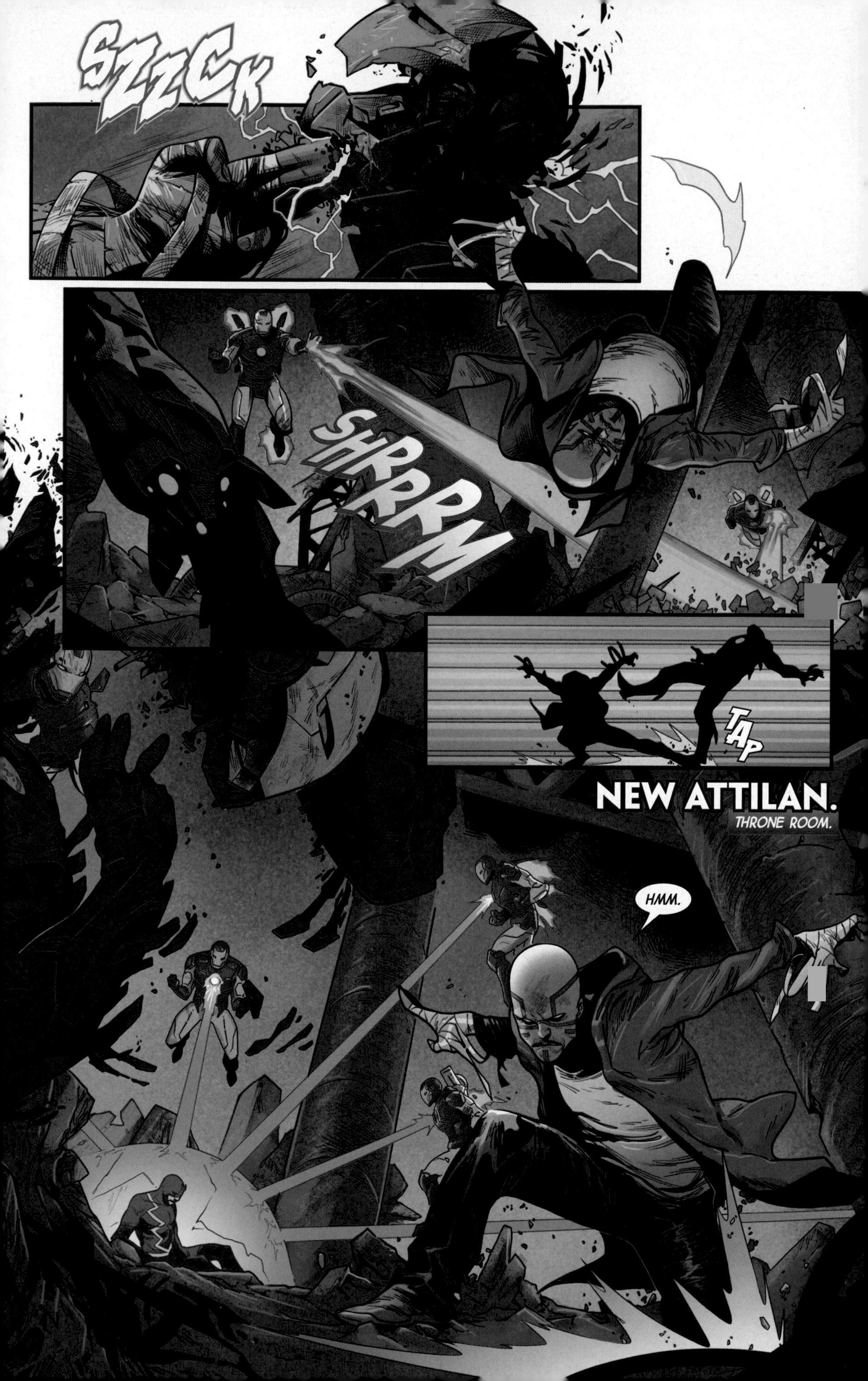
SZZCK
SHRRM
TAP
NEW ATTILAN.
THRONE ROOM.
HMM.

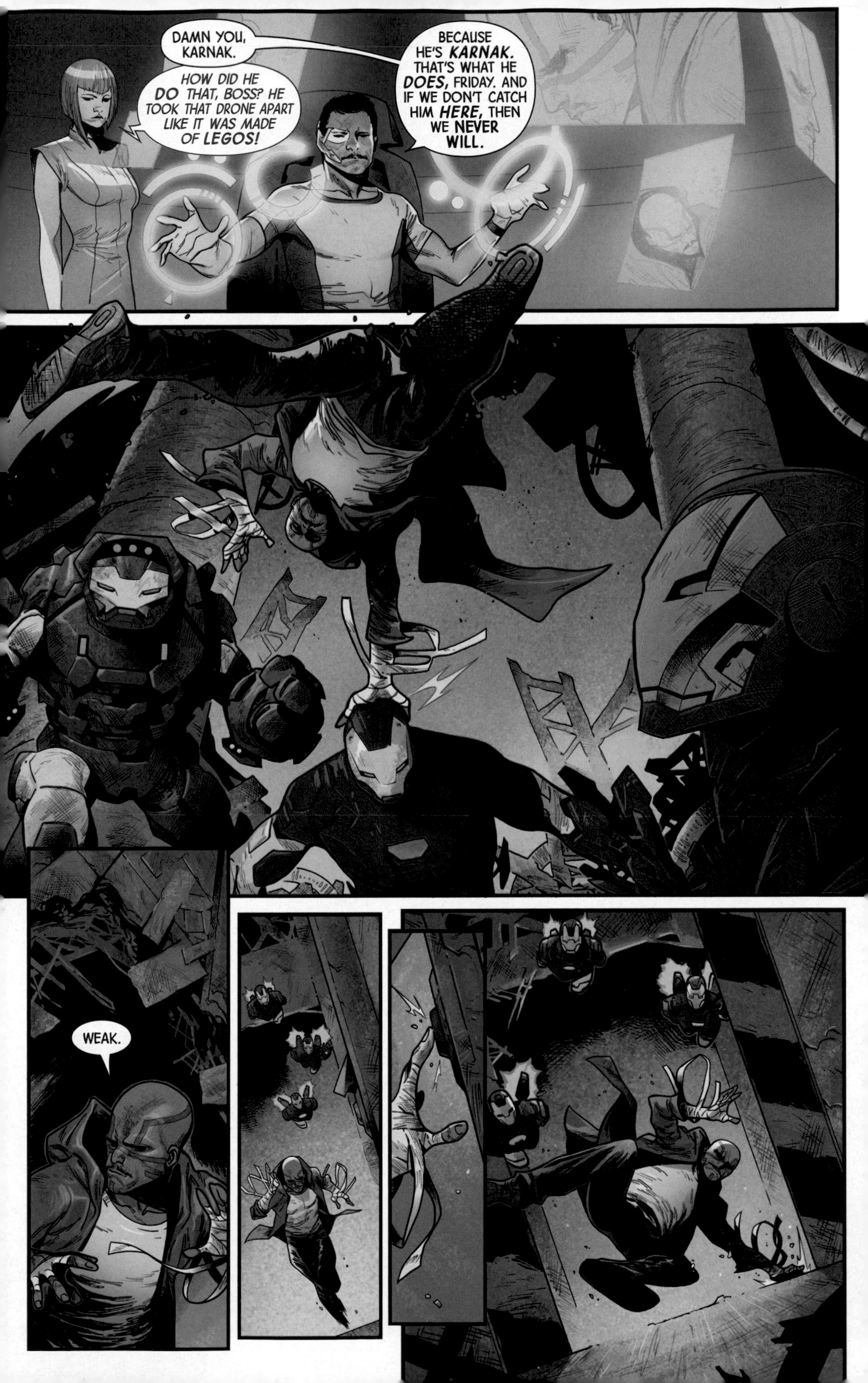
DAMN YOU, KARNAK.
HOW DID HE DO THAT, BOSS? HE TOOK THAT DRONE APART LIKE IT WAS MADE OF LEGOS!
BECAUSE HE'S KARNAK. THAT'S WHAT HE DOES, FRIDAY. AND IF WE DON'T CATCH HIM HERE, THEN WE NEVER WILL.
WEAK.

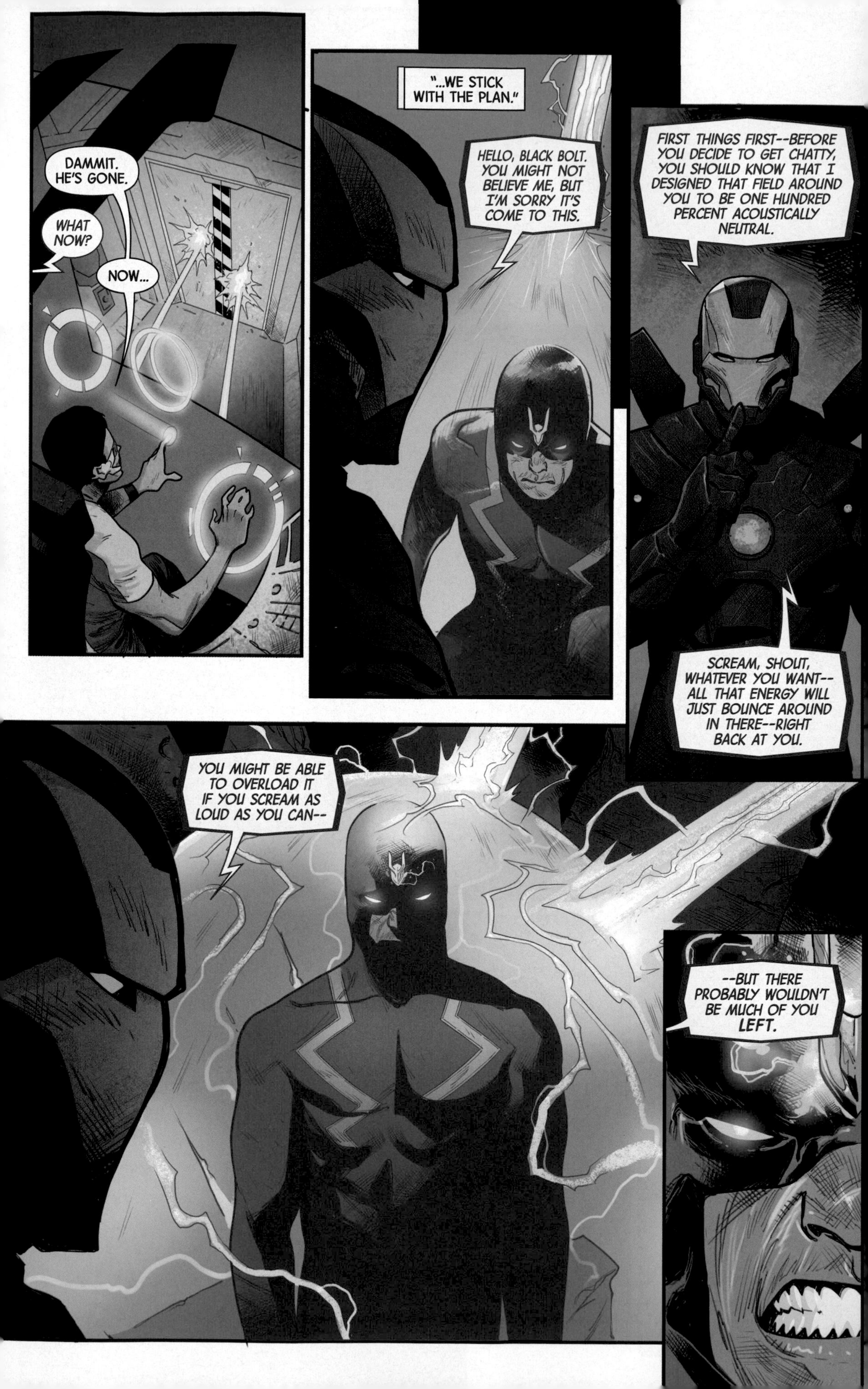
DAMMIT. HE'S GONE.
WHAT NOW?
NOW...
"...WE STICK WITH THE PLAN."
HELLO, BLACK BOLT. YOU MIGHT NOT BELIEVE ME, BUT I'M SORRY IT'S COME TO THIS.
FIRST THINGS FIRST--BEFORE YOU DECIDE TO GET CHATTY, YOU SHOULD KNOW THAT I DESIGNED THAT FIELD AROUND YOU TO BE ONE HUNDRED PERCENT ACOUSTICALLY NEUTRAL.
SCREAM, SHOUT, WHATEVER YOU WANT--ALL THAT ENERGY WILL JUST BOUNCE AROUND IN THERE--RIGHT BACK AT YOU.
YOU MIGHT BE ABLE TO OVERLOAD IT IF YOU SCREAM AS LOUD AS YOU CAN--
--BUT THERE PROBABLY WOULDN'T BE MUCH OF YOU LEFT.

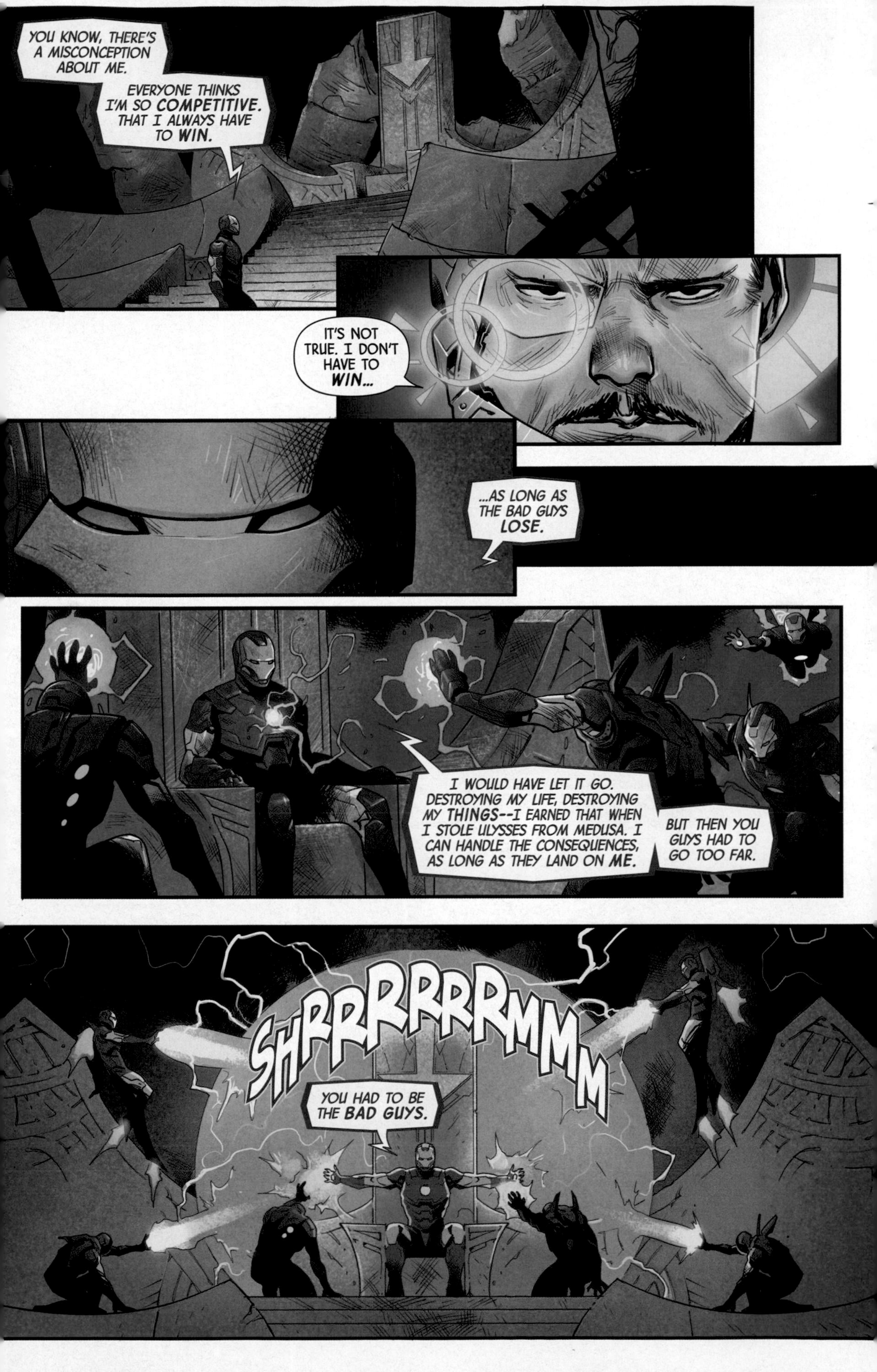
YOU KNOW, THERE'S A MISCONCEPTION ABOUT ME.
EVERYONE THINKS I'M SO COMPETITIVE. THAT I ALWAYS HAVE TO WIN.
IT'S NOT TRUE. I DON'T HAVE TO WIN...
...AS LONG AS THE BAD GUYS LOSE.
I WOULD HAVE LET IT GO. DESTROYING MY LIFE, DESTROYING MY THINGS--I EARNED THAT WHEN I STOLE ULYSSES FROM MEDUSA. I CAN HANDLE THE CONSEQUENCES, AS LONG AS THEY LAND ON ME.
BUT THEN YOU GUYS HAD TO GO TOO FAR.
SHRRRRRRMMMM
YOU HAD TO BE THE BAD GUYS.

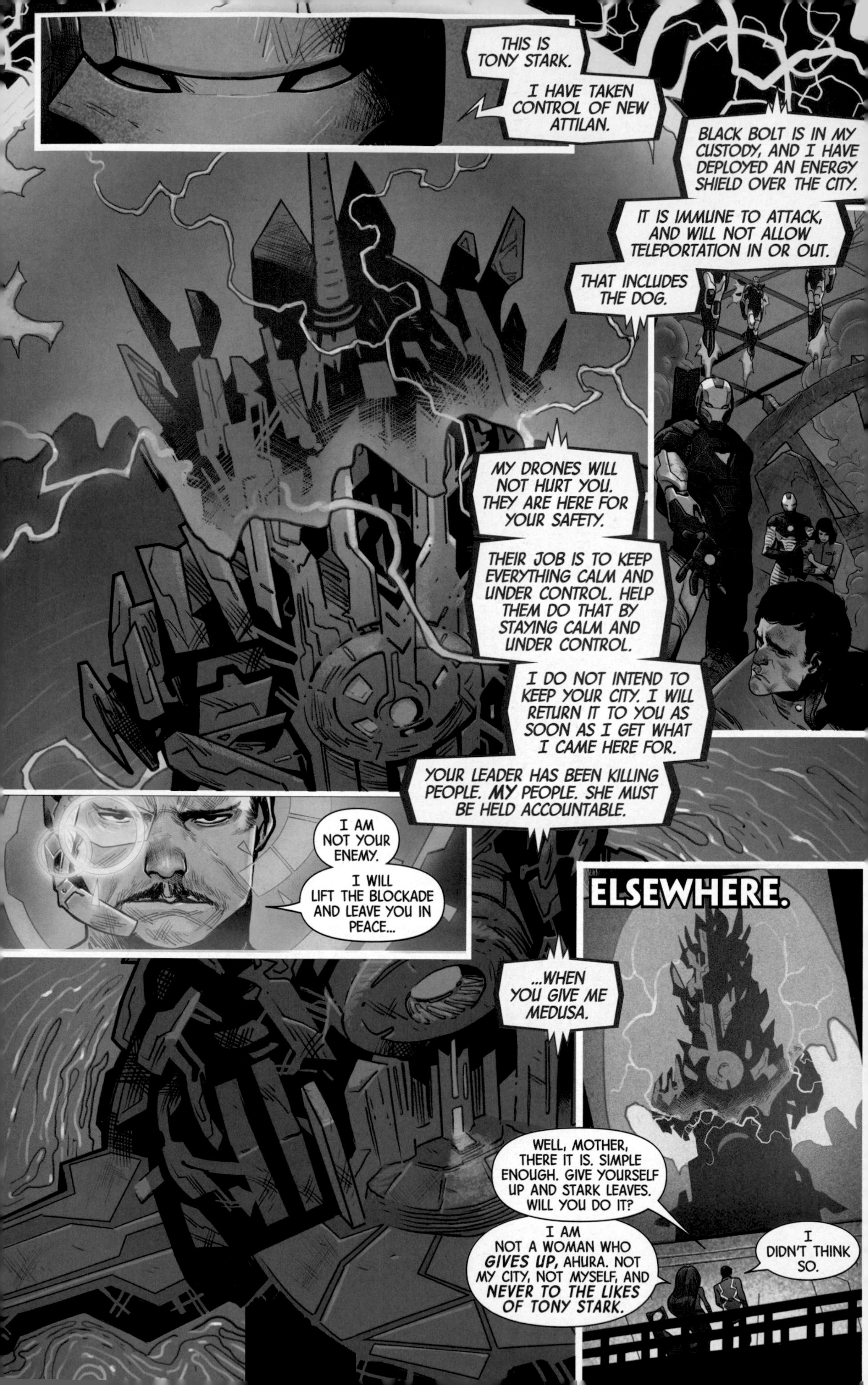
THIS IS TONY STARK.
I HAVE TAKEN CONTROL OF NEW ATTILAN.
BLACK BOLT IS IN MY CUSTODY, AND I HAVE DEPLOYED AN ENERGY SHIELD OVER THE CITY.
IT IS IMMUNE TO ATTACK, AND WILL NOT ALLOW TELEPORTATION IN OR OUT.
THAT INCLUDES THE DOG.
MY DRONES WILL NOT HURT YOU. THEY ARE HERE FOR YOUR SAFETY.
THEIR JOB IS TO KEEP EVERYTHING CALM AND UNDER CONTROL. HELP THEM DO THAT BY STAYING CALM AND UNDER CONTROL.
I DO NOT INTEND TO KEEP YOUR CITY. I WILL RETURN IT TO YOU AS SOON AS I GET WHAT I CAME HERE FOR.
YOUR LEADER HAS BEEN KILLING PEOPLE. *MY* PEOPLE. SHE MUST BE HELD ACCOUNTABLE.
I AM NOT YOUR ENEMY.
I WILL LIFT THE BLOCKADE AND LEAVE YOU IN PEACE...
...WHEN YOU GIVE ME MEDUSA.
ELSEWHERE.
WELL, MOTHER, THERE IT IS. SIMPLE ENOUGH. GIVE YOURSELF UP AND STARK LEAVES. WILL YOU DO IT?
I AM NOT A WOMAN WHO ***GIVES UP,*** AHURA. NOT MY CITY, NOT MYSELF, AND ***NEVER TO THE LIKES OF TONY STARK.***
I DIDN'T THINK SO.

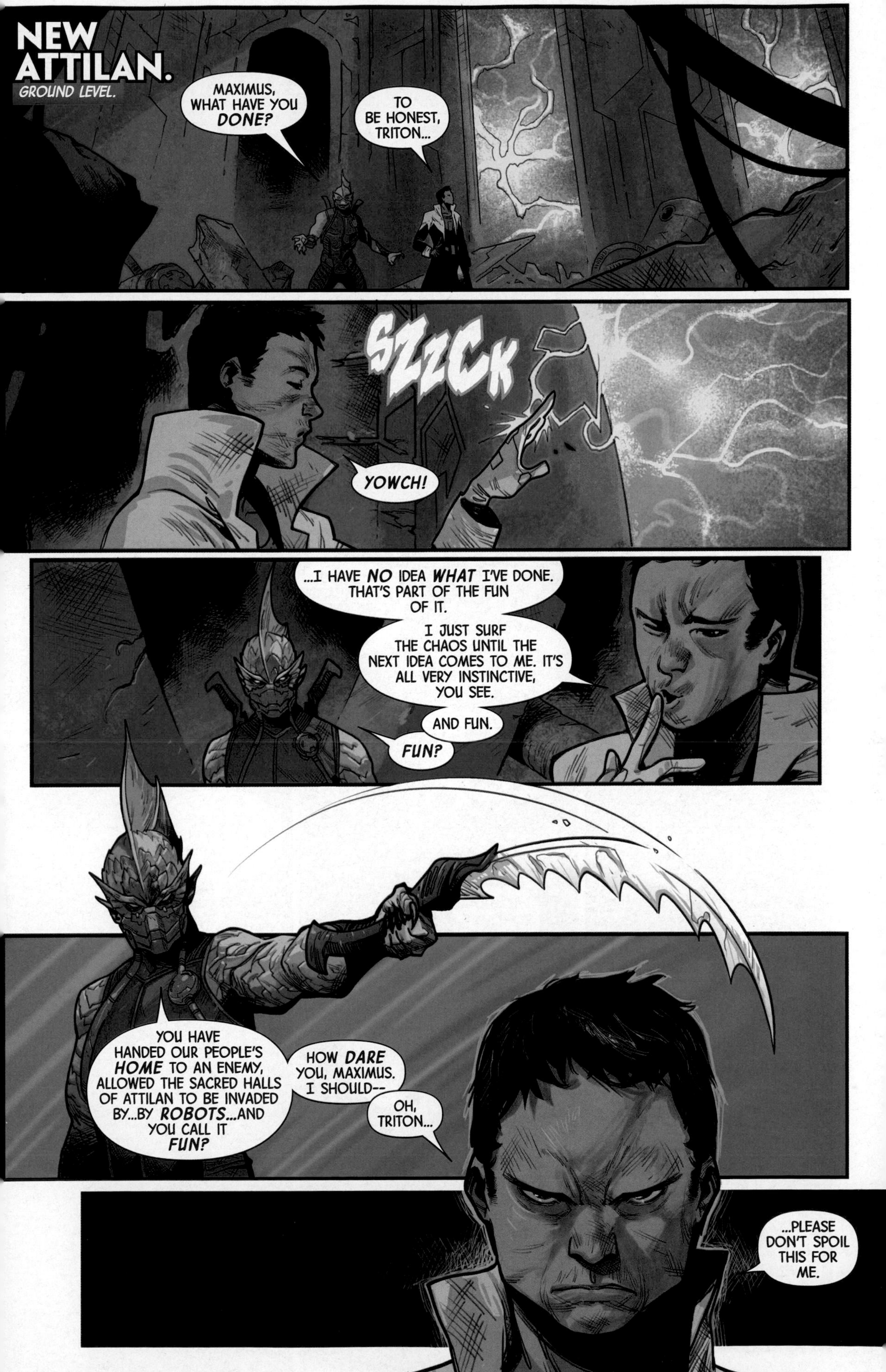
NEW ATTILAN.
GROUND LEVEL.
MAXIMUS, WHAT HAVE YOU DONE?
TO BE HONEST, TRITON...
SZZCK
YOWCH!
...I HAVE NO IDEA WHAT I'VE DONE. THAT'S PART OF THE FUN OF IT.
I JUST SURF THE CHAOS UNTIL THE NEXT IDEA COMES TO ME. IT'S ALL VERY INSTINCTIVE, YOU SEE.
AND FUN.
FUN?
YOU HAVE HANDED OUR PEOPLE'S HOME TO AN ENEMY, ALLOWED THE SACRED HALLS OF ATTILAN TO BE INVADED BY...BY ROBOTS...AND YOU CALL IT FUN?
HOW DARE YOU, MAXIMUS. I SHOULD--
OH, TRITON...
...PLEASE DON'T SPOIL THIS FOR ME.

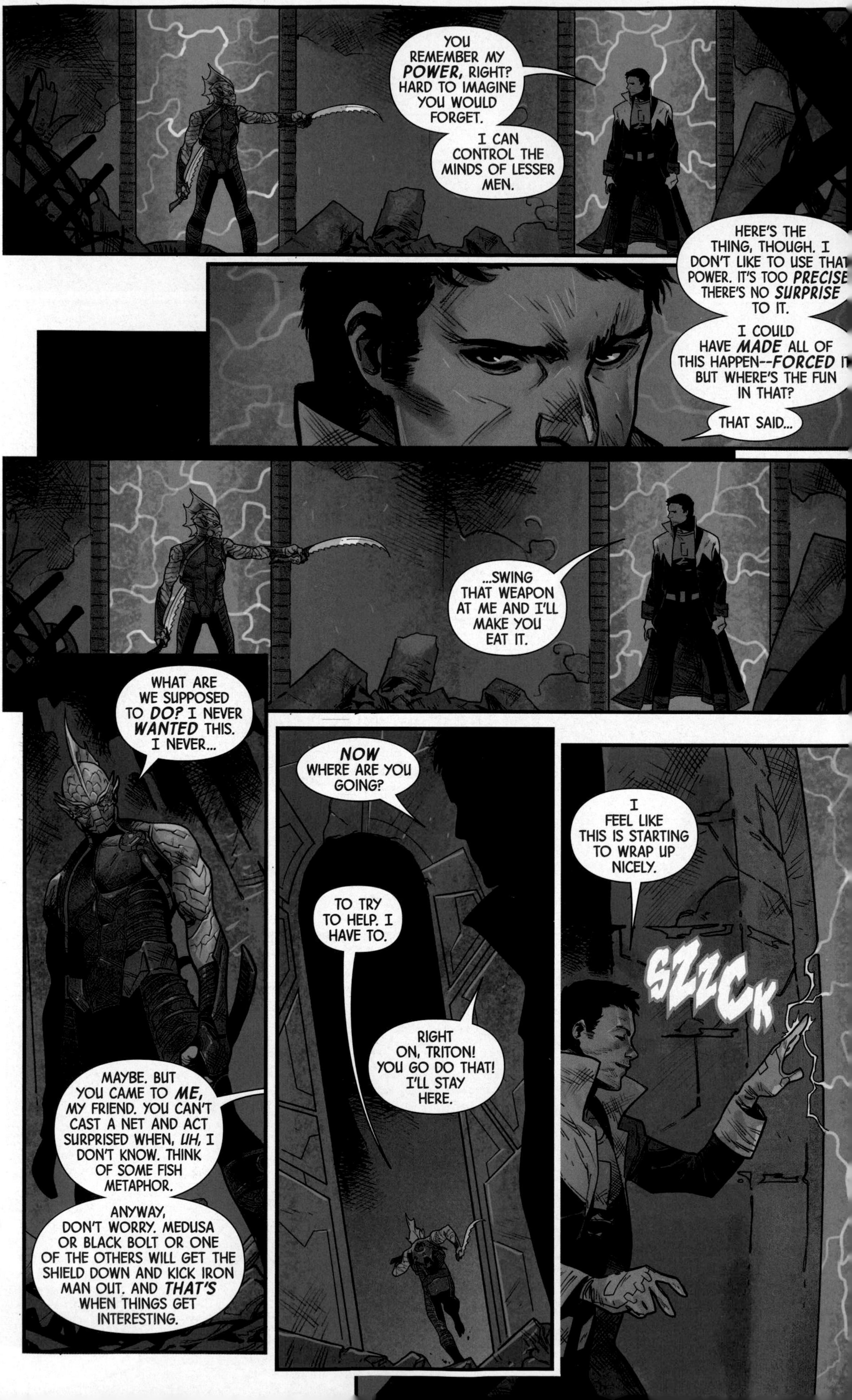

YOU REMEMBER MY POWER, RIGHT? HARD TO IMAGINE YOU WOULD FORGET.
I CAN CONTROL THE MINDS OF LESSER MEN.
HERE'S THE THING, THOUGH. I DON'T LIKE TO USE THAT POWER. IT'S TOO PRECISE. THERE'S NO SURPRISE TO IT.
I COULD HAVE MADE ALL OF THIS HAPPEN--FORCED IT, BUT WHERE'S THE FUN IN THAT?
THAT SAID...
...SWING THAT WEAPON AT ME AND I'LL MAKE YOU EAT IT.
WHAT ARE WE SUPPOSED TO DO? I NEVER WANTED THIS. I NEVER...
MAYBE. BUT YOU CAME TO ME, MY FRIEND. YOU CAN'T CAST A NET AND ACT SURPRISED WHEN, UH, I DON'T KNOW. THINK OF SOME FISH METAPHOR.
ANYWAY, DON'T WORRY. MEDUSA OR BLACK BOLT OR ONE OF THE OTHERS WILL GET THE SHIELD DOWN AND KICK IRON MAN OUT. AND THAT'S WHEN THINGS GET INTERESTING.
NOW WHERE ARE YOU GOING?
TO TRY TO HELP. I HAVE TO.
RIGHT ON, TRITON! YOU GO DO THAT! I'LL STAY HERE.
I FEEL LIKE THIS IS STARTING TO WRAP UP NICELY.
SZZCK

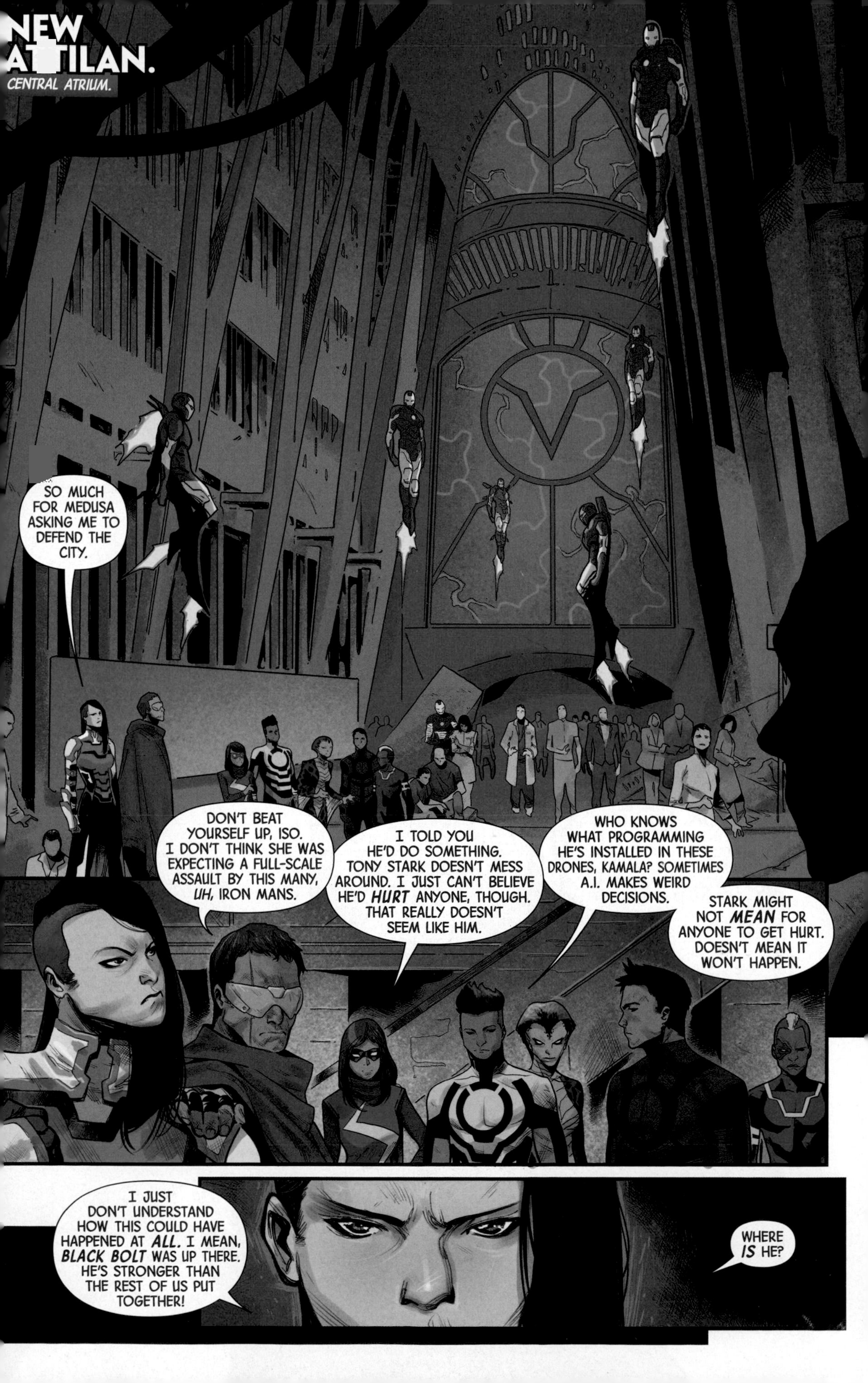
NEW
A TILAN.
CENTRAL ATRIUM.
SO MUCH FOR MEDUSA ASKING ME TO DEFEND THE CITY.
DON'T BEAT YOURSELF UP, ISO. I DON'T THINK SHE WAS EXPECTING A FULL-SCALE ASSAULT BY THIS MANY, UH, IRON MANS.
I TOLD YOU HE'D DO SOMETHING. TONY STARK DOESN'T MESS AROUND. I JUST CAN'T BELIEVE HE'D HURT ANYONE, THOUGH. THAT REALLY DOESN'T SEEM LIKE HIM.
WHO KNOWS WHAT PROGRAMMING HE'S INSTALLED IN THESE DRONES, KAMALA? SOMETIMES A.I. MAKES WEIRD DECISIONS.
STARK MIGHT NOT MEAN FOR ANYONE TO GET HURT. DOESN'T MEAN IT WON'T HAPPEN.
I JUST DON'T UNDERSTAND HOW THIS COULD HAVE HAPPENED AT ALL. I MEAN, BLACK BOLT WAS UP THERE. HE'S STRONGER THAN THE REST OF US PUT TOGETHER!
WHERE IS HE?

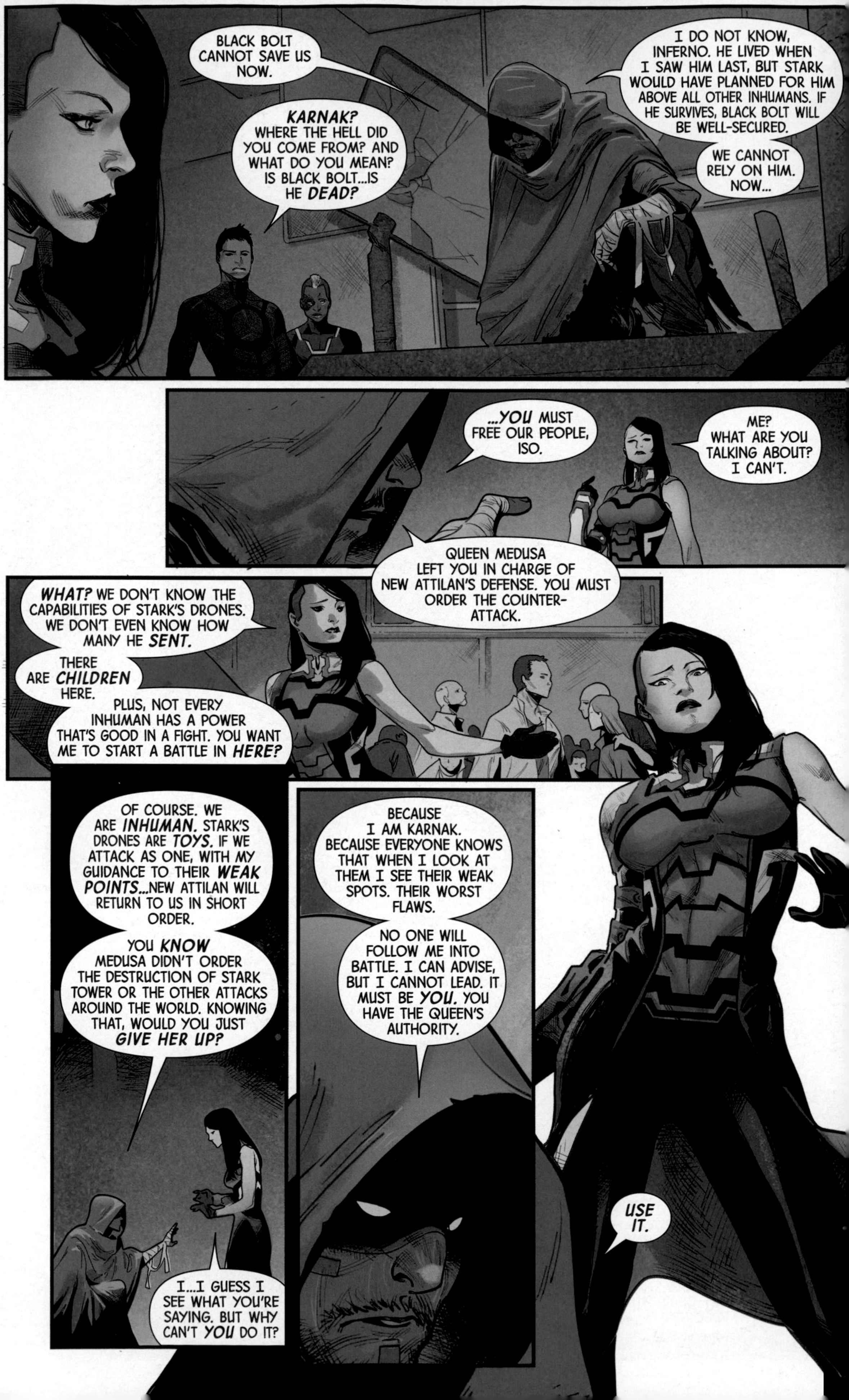
BLACK BOLT CANNOT SAVE US NOW.
KARNAK? WHERE THE HELL DID YOU COME FROM? AND WHAT DO YOU MEAN? IS BLACK BOLT...IS HE DEAD?
I DO NOT KNOW, INFERNO. HE LIVED WHEN I SAW HIM LAST, BUT STARK WOULD HAVE PLANNED FOR HIM ABOVE ALL OTHER INHUMANS. IF HE SURVIVES, BLACK BOLT WILL BE WELL-SECURED.
WE CANNOT RELY ON HIM. NOW...
...YOU MUST FREE OUR PEOPLE, ISO.
ME? WHAT ARE YOU TALKING ABOUT? I CAN'T.
QUEEN MEDUSA LEFT YOU IN CHARGE OF NEW ATTILAN'S DEFENSE. YOU MUST ORDER THE COUNTER-ATTACK.
WHAT? WE DON'T KNOW THE CAPABILITIES OF STARK'S DRONES. WE DON'T EVEN KNOW HOW MANY HE SENT.
THERE ARE CHILDREN HERE.
PLUS, NOT EVERY INHUMAN HAS A POWER THAT'S GOOD IN A FIGHT. YOU WANT ME TO START A BATTLE IN HERE?
OF COURSE. WE ARE INHUMAN. STARK'S DRONES ARE TOYS. IF WE ATTACK AS ONE, WITH MY GUIDANCE TO THEIR WEAK POINTS...NEW ATTILAN WILL RETURN TO US IN SHORT ORDER.
YOU KNOW MEDUSA DIDN'T ORDER THE DESTRUCTION OF STARK TOWER OR THE OTHER ATTACKS AROUND THE WORLD. KNOWING THAT, WOULD YOU JUST GIVE HER UP?
I...I GUESS I SEE WHAT YOU'RE SAYING. BUT WHY CAN'T YOU DO IT?
BECAUSE I AM KARNAK. BECAUSE EVERYONE KNOWS THAT WHEN I LOOK AT THEM I SEE THEIR WEAK SPOTS. THEIR WORST FLAWS.
NO ONE WILL FOLLOW ME INTO BATTLE. I CAN ADVISE, BUT I CANNOT LEAD. IT MUST BE YOU. YOU HAVE THE QUEEN'S AUTHORITY.
USE IT.

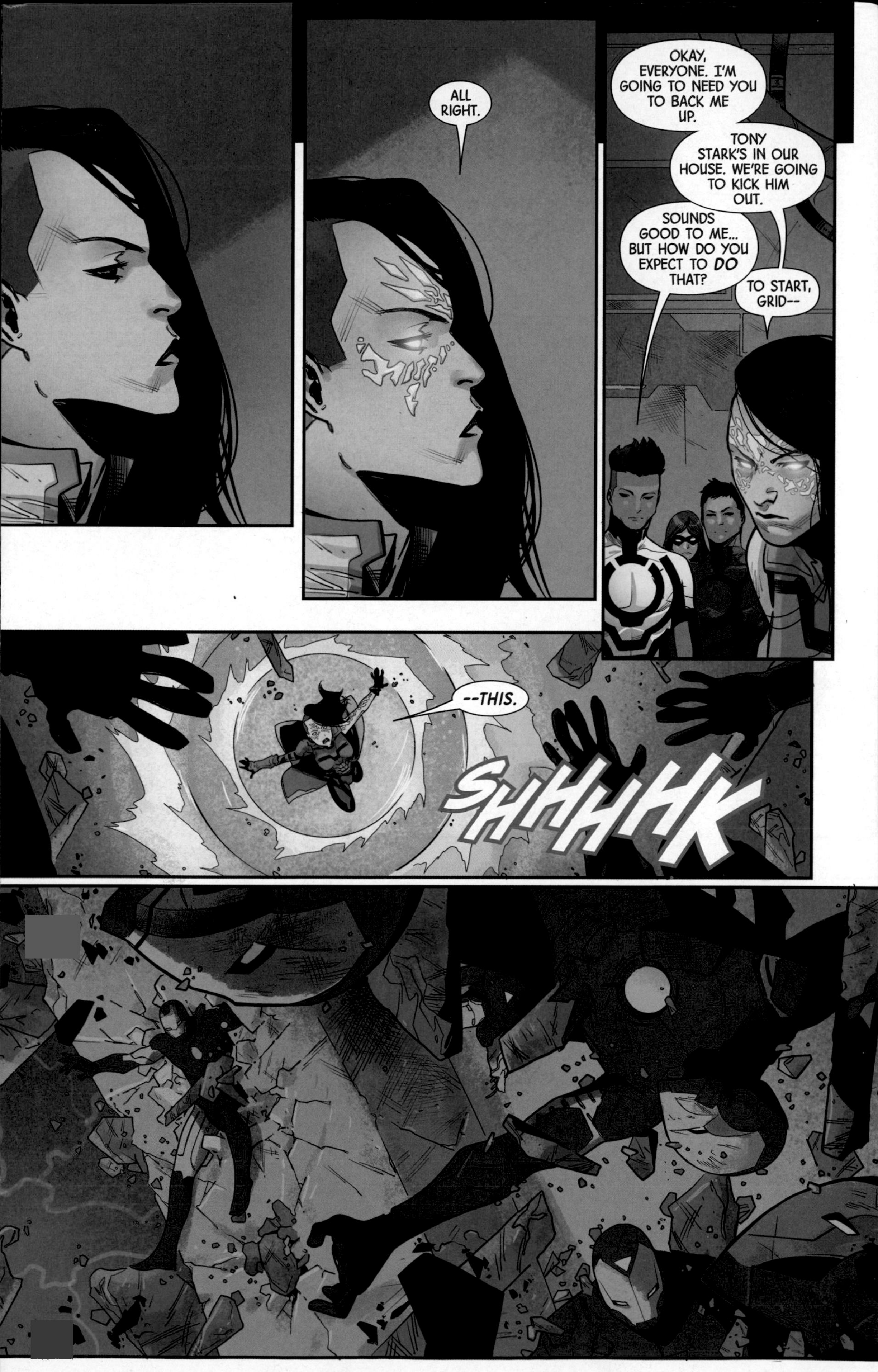
ALL RIGHT.
OKAY, EVERYONE. I'M GOING TO NEED YOU TO BACK ME UP.
TONY STARK'S IN OUR HOUSE. WE'RE GOING TO KICK HIM OUT.
SOUNDS GOOD TO ME... BUT HOW DO YOU EXPECT TO **DO** THAT?
TO START, GRID--
--THIS.
SHHHHK

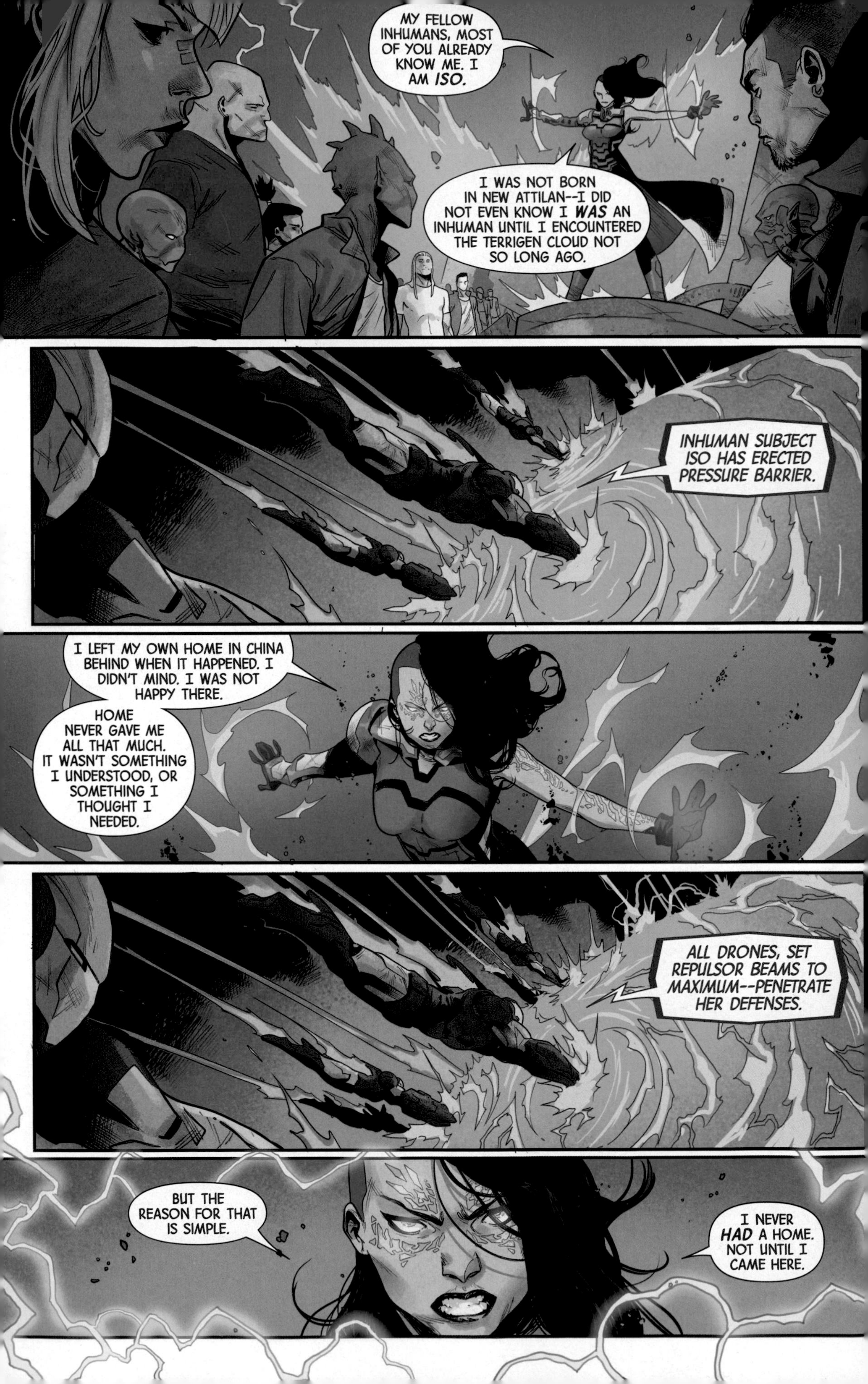
MY FELLOW INHUMANS, MOST OF YOU ALREADY KNOW ME. I AM ISO.
I WAS NOT BORN IN NEW ATTILAN--I DID NOT EVEN KNOW I WAS AN INHUMAN UNTIL I ENCOUNTERED THE TERRIGEN CLOUD NOT SO LONG AGO.
INHUMAN SUBJECT ISO HAS ERECTED PRESSURE BARRIER.
I LEFT MY OWN HOME IN CHINA BEHIND WHEN IT HAPPENED. I DIDN'T MIND. I WAS NOT HAPPY THERE.
HOME NEVER GAVE ME ALL THAT MUCH. IT WASN'T SOMETHING I UNDERSTOOD, OR SOMETHING I THOUGHT I NEEDED.
ALL DRONES, SET REPULSOR BEAMS TO MAXIMUM--PENETRATE HER DEFENSES.
BUT THE REASON FOR THAT IS SIMPLE.
I NEVER HAD A HOME. NOT UNTIL I CAME HERE.

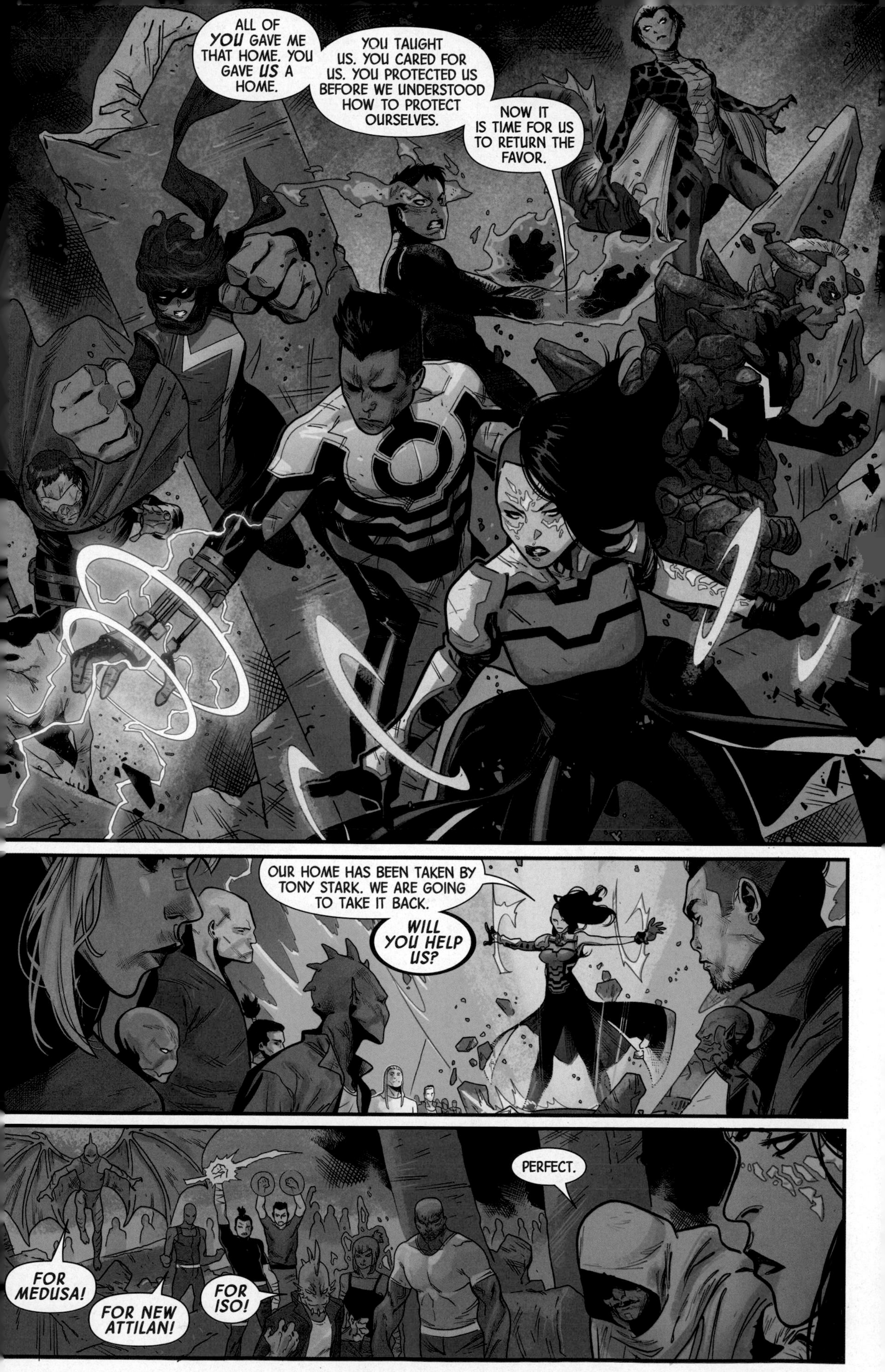
ALL OF YOU GAVE ME THAT HOME. YOU GAVE US A HOME.
YOU TAUGHT US. YOU CARED FOR US. YOU PROTECTED US BEFORE WE UNDERSTOOD HOW TO PROTECT OURSELVES.
NOW IT IS TIME FOR US TO RETURN THE FAVOR.
OUR HOME HAS BEEN TAKEN BY TONY STARK. WE ARE GOING TO TAKE IT BACK.
WILL YOU HELP US?
PERFECT.
FOR MEDUSA!
FOR NEW ATTILAN!
FOR ISO!

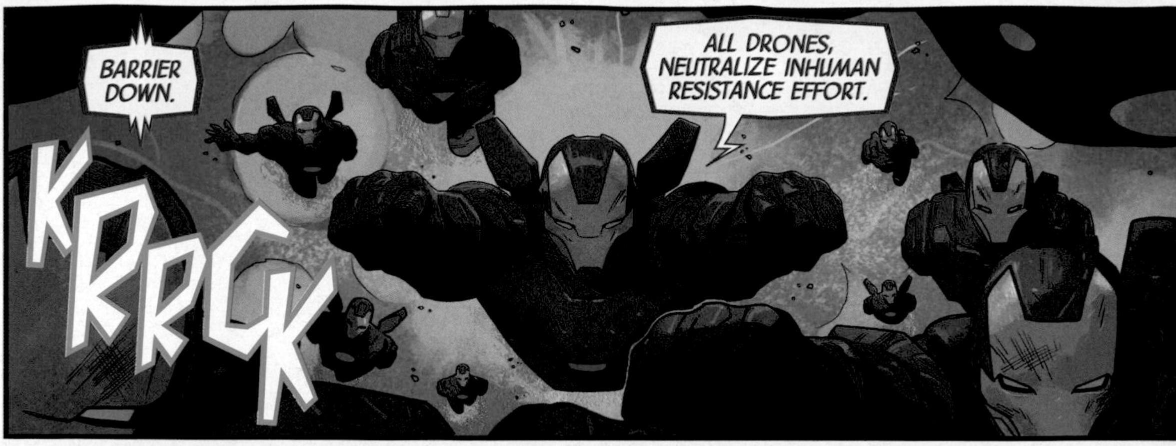
BARRIER DOWN.
ALL DRONES, NEUTRALIZE INHUMAN RESISTANCE EFFORT.
KRRCK

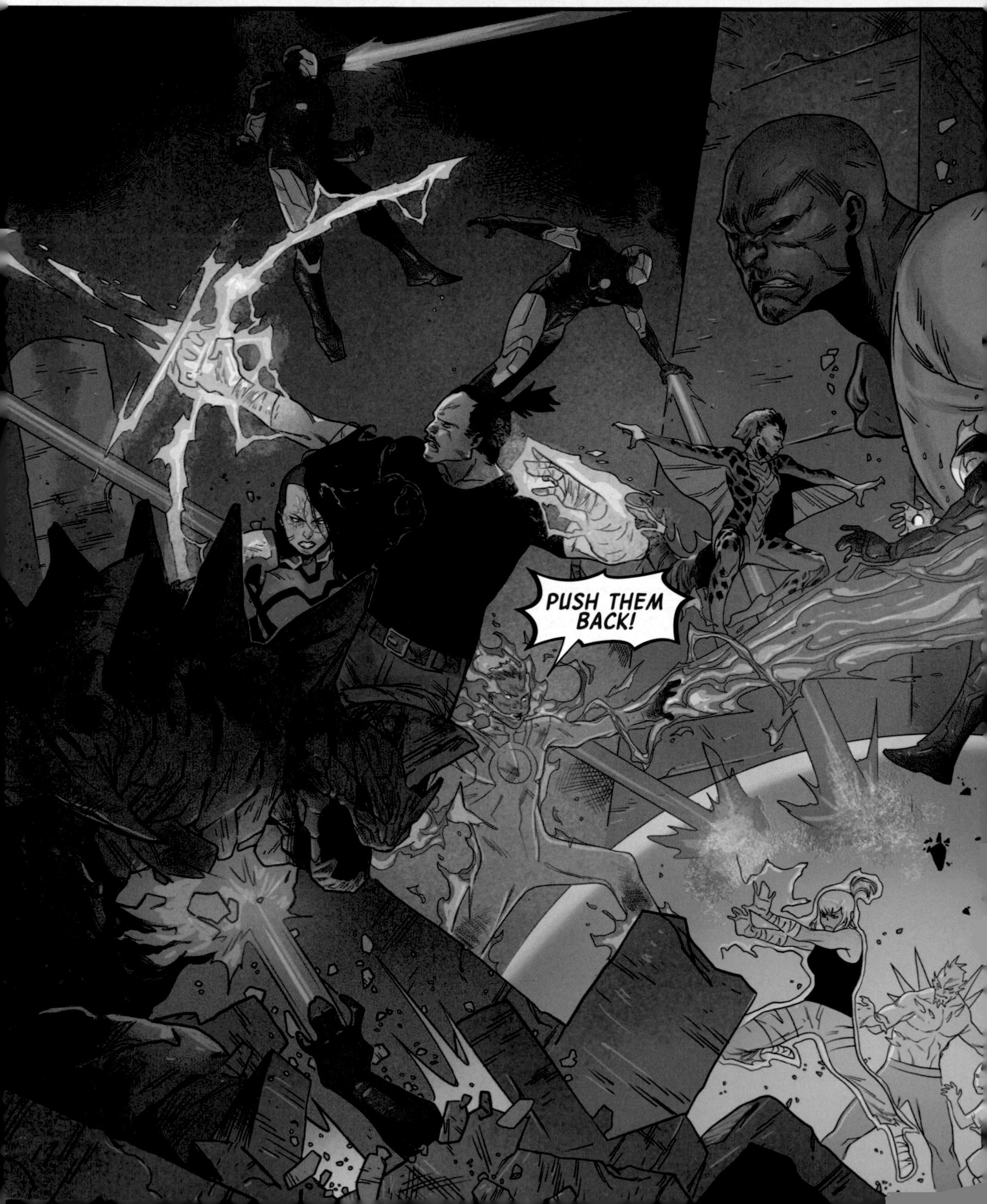
PUSH THEM BACK!

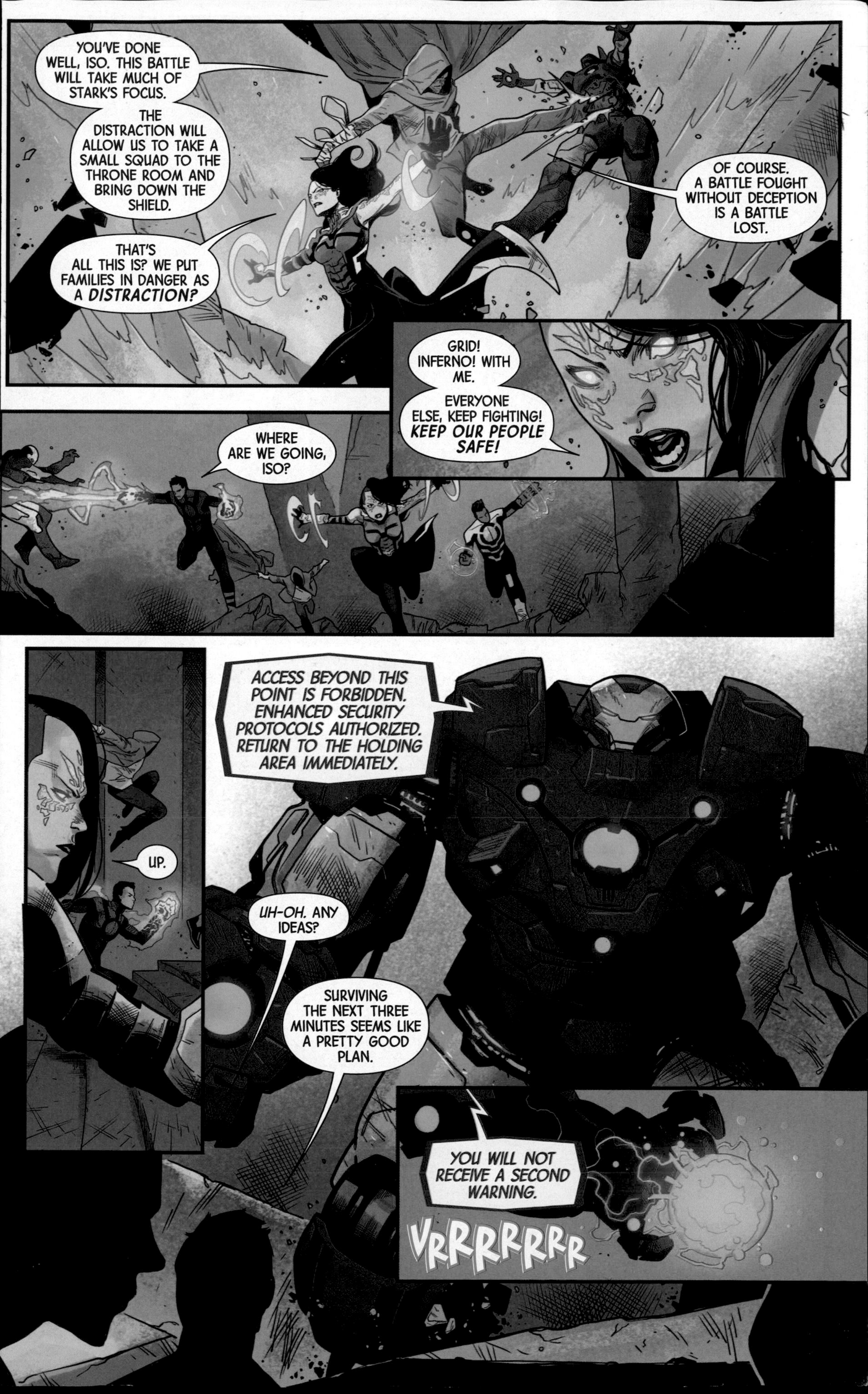

YOU'VE DONE WELL, ISO. THIS BATTLE WILL TAKE MUCH OF STARK'S FOCUS.
THE DISTRACTION WILL ALLOW US TO TAKE A SMALL SQUAD TO THE THRONE ROOM AND BRING DOWN THE SHIELD.
THAT'S ALL THIS IS? WE PUT FAMILIES IN DANGER AS A *DISTRACTION?*
OF COURSE. A BATTLE FOUGHT WITHOUT DECEPTION IS A BATTLE LOST.
GRID! INFERNO! WITH ME.
EVERYONE ELSE, KEEP FIGHTING! ***KEEP OUR PEOPLE SAFE!***
WHERE ARE WE GOING, ISO?
UP.
ACCESS BEYOND THIS POINT IS FORBIDDEN. ENHANCED SECURITY PROTOCOLS AUTHORIZED. RETURN TO THE HOLDING AREA IMMEDIATELY.
UH-OH. ANY IDEAS?
SURVIVING THE NEXT THREE MINUTES SEEMS LIKE A PRETTY GOOD PLAN.
YOU WILL NOT RECEIVE A SECOND WARNING.
VRRRRRRR

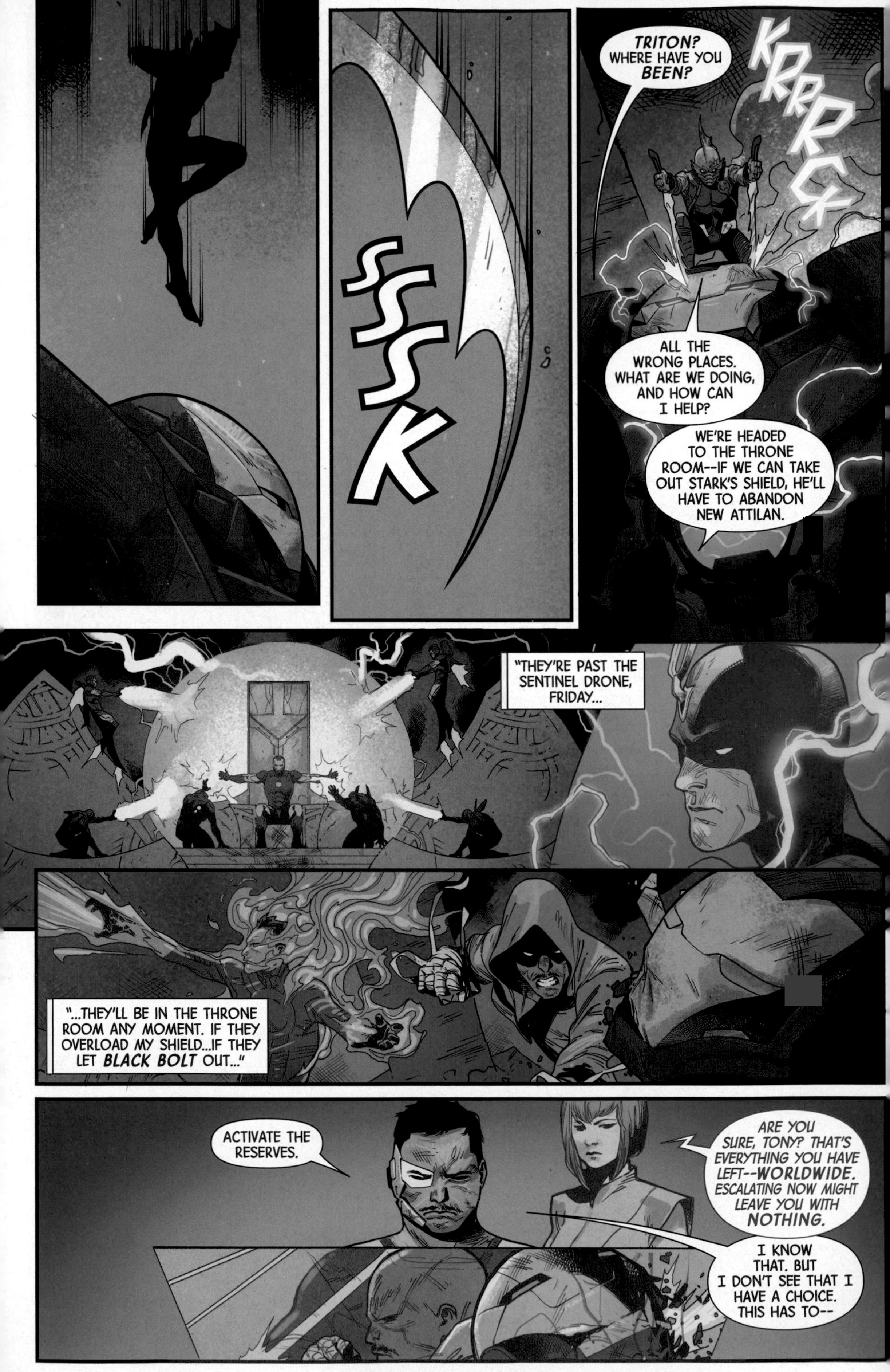
SSSK
TRITON? WHERE HAVE YOU BEEN?
KRRRCK
ALL THE WRONG PLACES. WHAT ARE WE DOING, AND HOW CAN I HELP?
WE'RE HEADED TO THE THRONE ROOM--IF WE CAN TAKE OUT STARK'S SHIELD, HE'LL HAVE TO ABANDON NEW ATTILAN.
"THEY'RE PAST THE SENTINEL DRONE, FRIDAY...
"...THEY'LL BE IN THE THRONE ROOM ANY MOMENT. IF THEY OVERLOAD MY SHIELD...IF THEY LET BLACK BOLT OUT..."
ACTIVATE THE RESERVES.
ARE YOU SURE, TONY? THAT'S EVERYTHING YOU HAVE LEFT--WORLDWIDE. ESCALATING NOW MIGHT LEAVE YOU WITH NOTHING.
I KNOW THAT. BUT I DON'T SEE THAT I HAVE A CHOICE. THIS HAS TO--

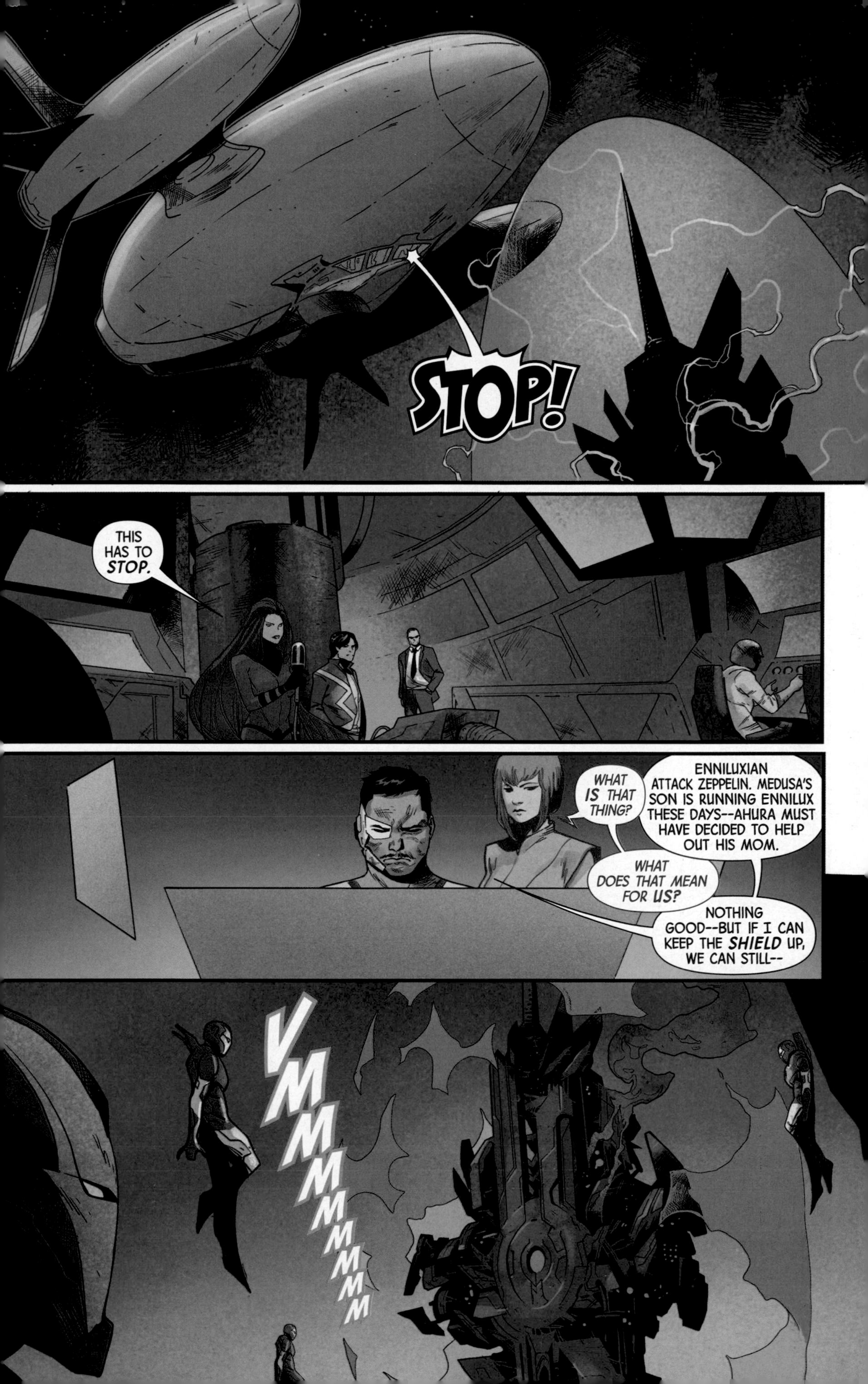
STOP!
THIS HAS TO STOP.
WHAT IS THAT THING?
ENNILUXIAN ATTACK ZEPPELIN. MEDUSA'S SON IS RUNNING ENNILUX THESE DAYS--AHURA MUST HAVE DECIDED TO HELP OUT HIS MOM.
WHAT DOES THAT MEAN FOR US?
NOTHING GOOD--BUT IF I CAN KEEP THE SHIELD UP, WE CAN STILL--
VMMMMMMMM

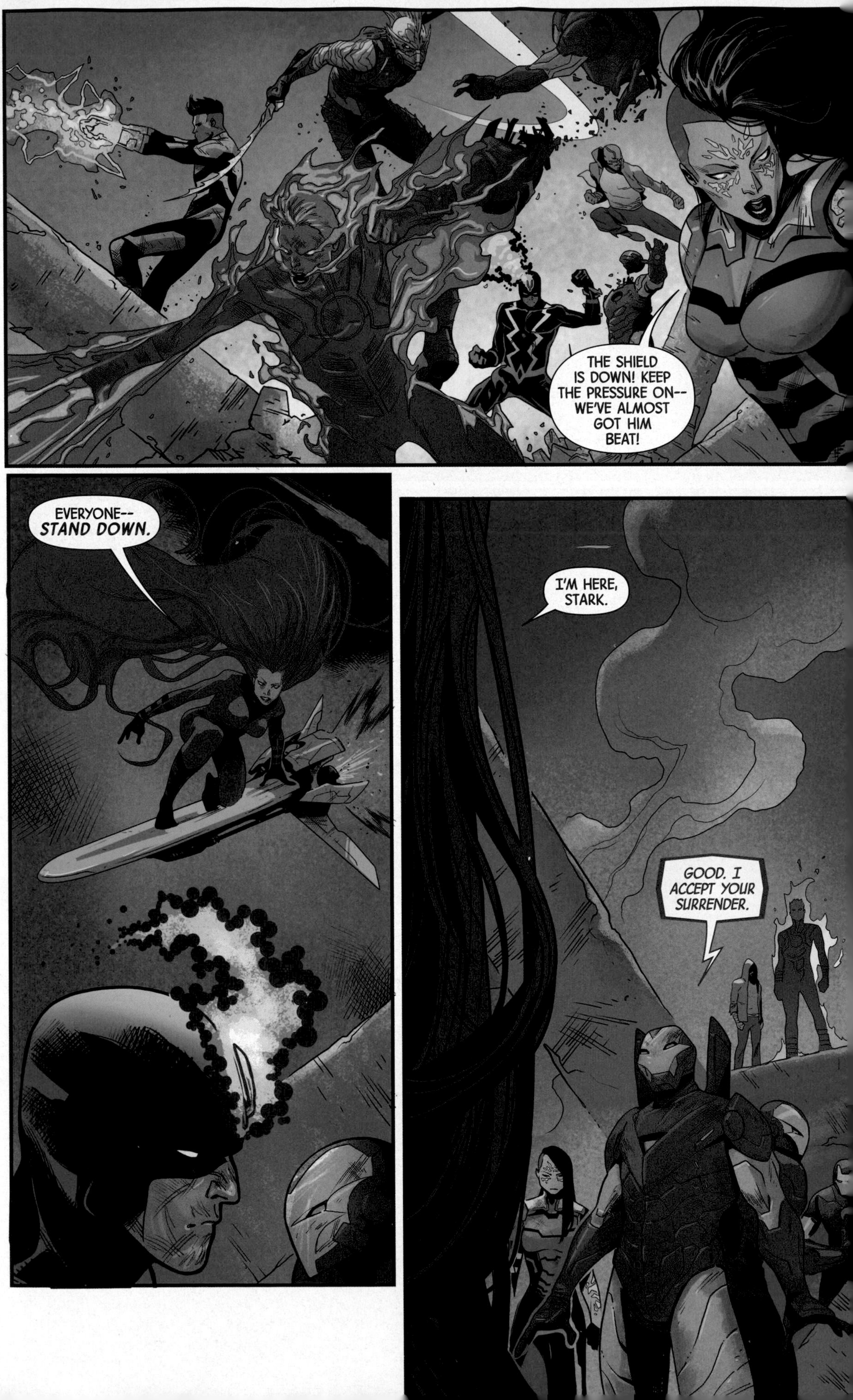
THE SHIELD IS DOWN! KEEP THE PRESSURE ON-- WE'VE ALMOST GOT HIM BEAT!
EVERYONE-- STAND DOWN.
I'M HERE, STARK.
GOOD. I ACCEPT YOUR SURRENDER.

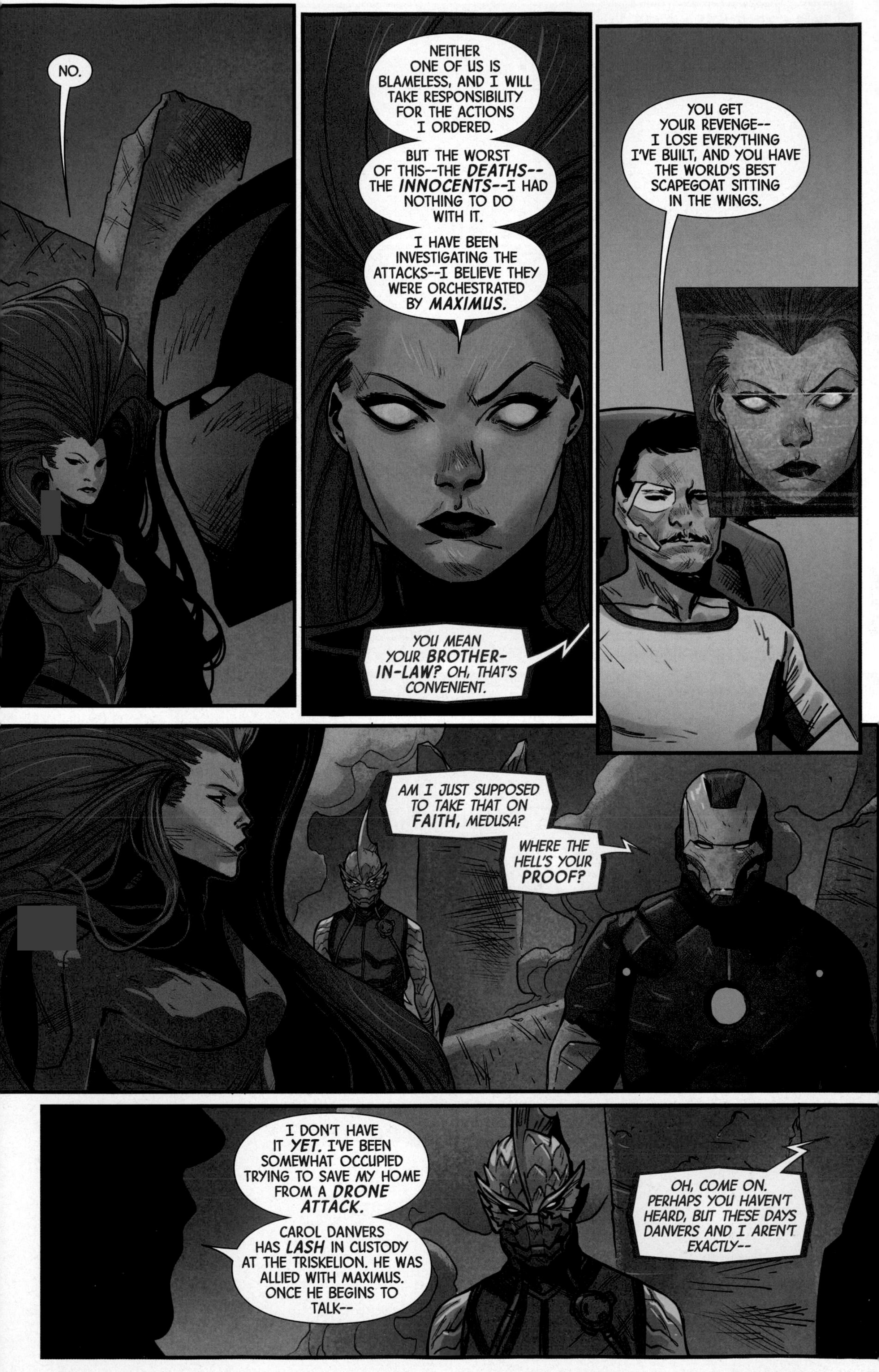
NO.
NEITHER ONE OF US IS BLAMELESS, AND I WILL TAKE RESPONSIBILITY FOR THE ACTIONS I ORDERED.
BUT THE WORST OF THIS--THE DEATHS--THE INNOCENTS--I HAD NOTHING TO DO WITH IT.
I HAVE BEEN INVESTIGATING THE ATTACKS--I BELIEVE THEY WERE ORCHESTRATED BY MAXIMUS.
YOU MEAN YOUR BROTHER-IN-LAW? OH, THAT'S CONVENIENT.
YOU GET YOUR REVENGE-- I LOSE EVERYTHING I'VE BUILT, AND YOU HAVE THE WORLD'S BEST SCAPEGOAT SITTING IN THE WINGS.
AM I JUST SUPPOSED TO TAKE THAT ON FAITH, MEDUSA?
WHERE THE HELL'S YOUR PROOF?
I DON'T HAVE IT YET. I'VE BEEN SOMEWHAT OCCUPIED TRYING TO SAVE MY HOME FROM A DRONE ATTACK.
CAROL DANVERS HAS LASH IN CUSTODY AT THE TRISKELION. HE WAS ALLIED WITH MAXIMUS. ONCE HE BEGINS TO TALK--
OH, COME ON. PERHAPS YOU HAVEN'T HEARD, BUT THESE DAYS DANVERS AND I AREN'T EXACTLY--

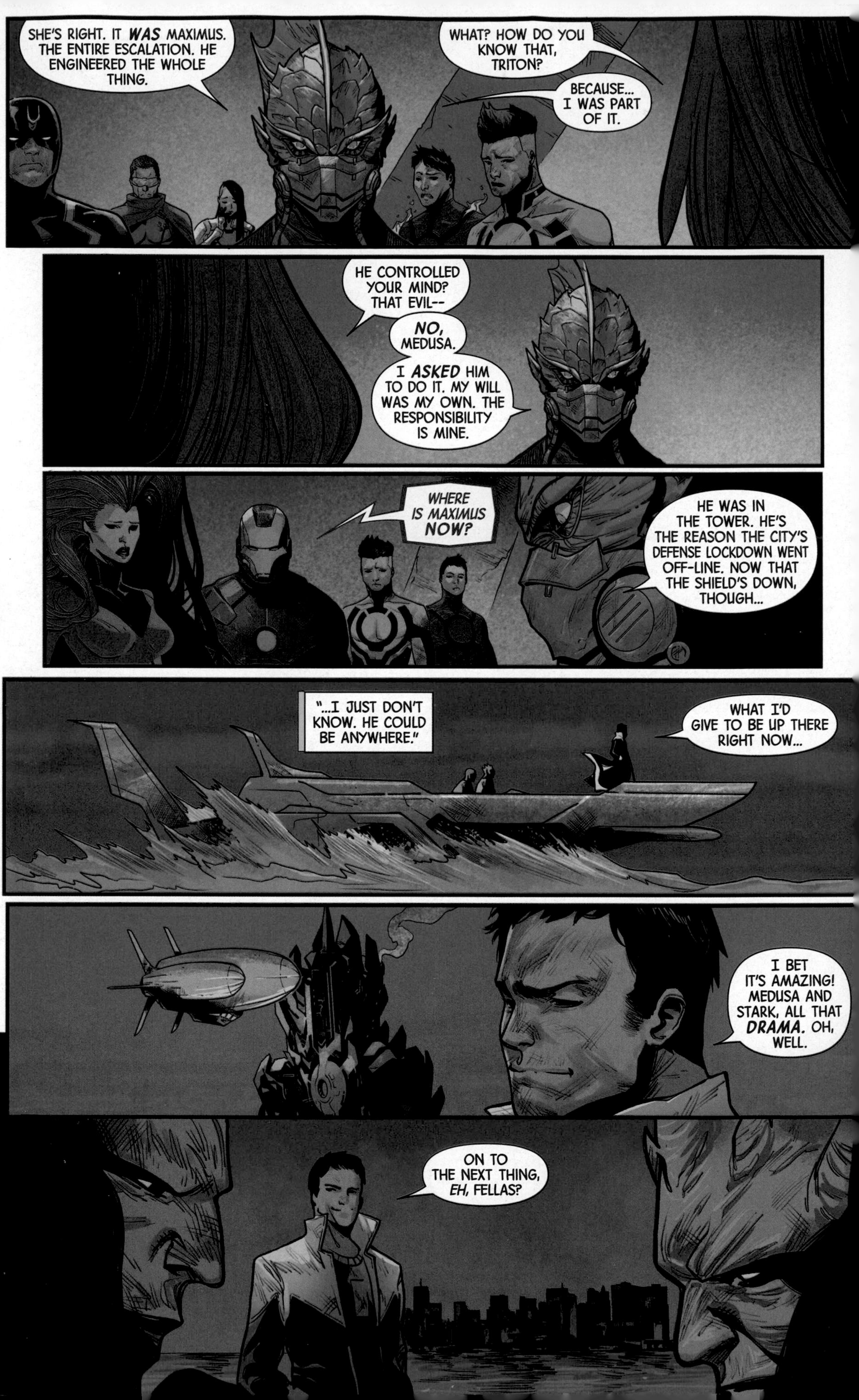
SHE'S RIGHT. IT WAS MAXIMUS. THE ENTIRE ESCALATION. HE ENGINEERED THE WHOLE THING.
WHAT? HOW DO YOU KNOW THAT, TRITON?
BECAUSE... I WAS PART OF IT.
HE CONTROLLED YOUR MIND? THAT EVIL--
NO, MEDUSA.
I ASKED HIM TO DO IT. MY WILL WAS MY OWN. THE RESPONSIBILITY IS MINE.
WHERE IS MAXIMUS NOW?
HE WAS IN THE TOWER. HE'S THE REASON THE CITY'S DEFENSE LOCKDOWN WENT OFF-LINE. NOW THAT THE SHIELD'S DOWN, THOUGH...
"...I JUST DON'T KNOW. HE COULD BE ANYWHERE."
WHAT I'D GIVE TO BE UP THERE RIGHT NOW...
I BET IT'S AMAZING! MEDUSA AND STARK, ALL THAT DRAMA. OH, WELL.
ON TO THE NEXT THING, EH, FELLAS?

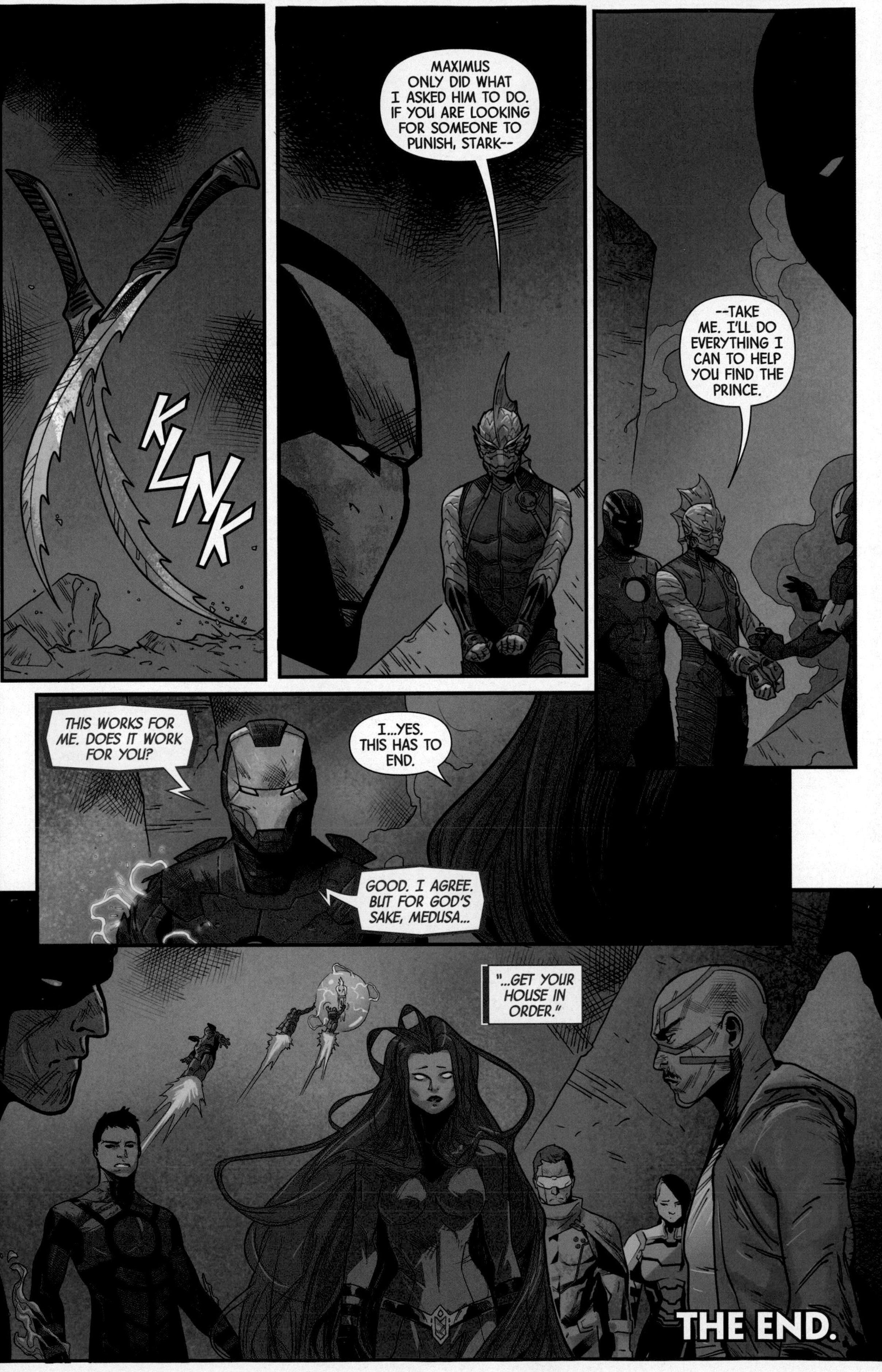

KLNK
MAXIMUS ONLY DID WHAT I ASKED HIM TO DO. IF YOU ARE LOOKING FOR SOMEONE TO PUNISH, STARK--
--TAKE ME. I'LL DO EVERYTHING I CAN TO HELP YOU FIND THE PRINCE.
THIS WORKS FOR ME. DOES IT WORK FOR YOU?
I...YES. THIS HAS TO END.
GOOD. I AGREE. BUT FOR GOD'S SAKE, MEDUSA...
"...GET YOUR HOUSE IN ORDER."
THE END.

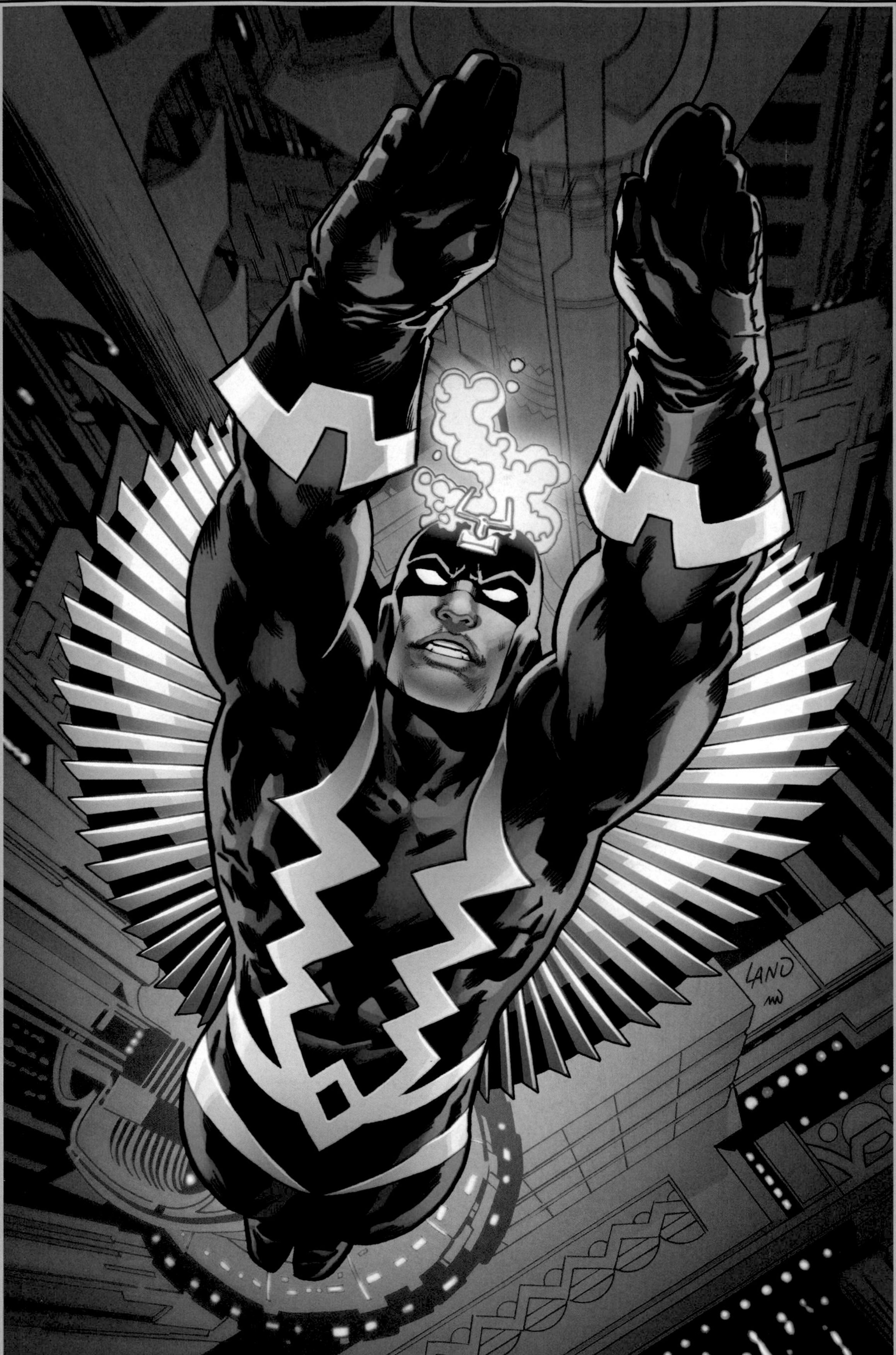

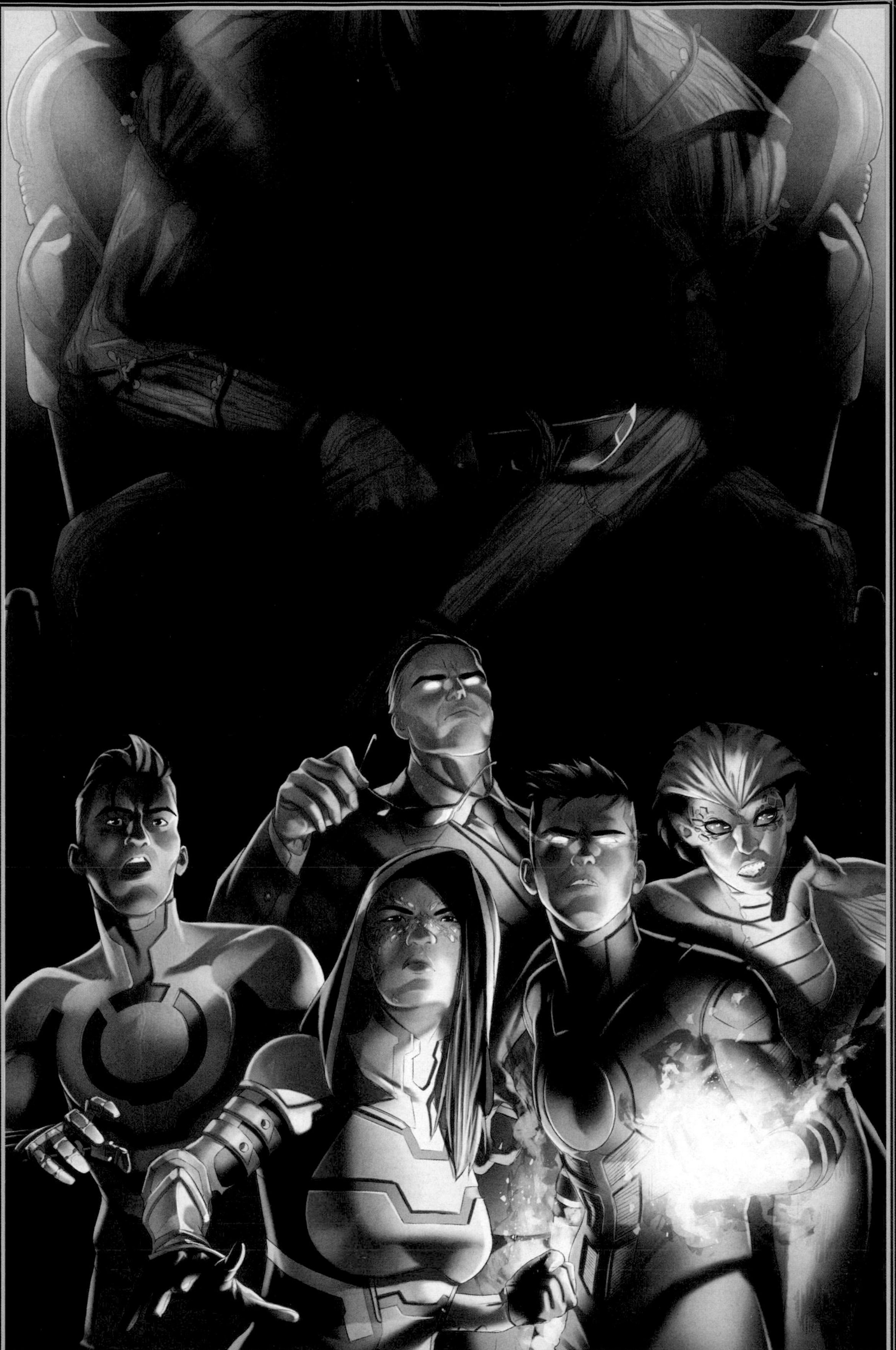

ANNUAL #1

Thousands of years ago aliens experimented on cavemen, supercharging their evolution, and then mysteriously left their experiments behind. These men and women built the city of Attilan and discovered a chemical called Terrigen that unlocked secret super-powers in their modified DNA, making them...

THE UNCANNY INHUMANS

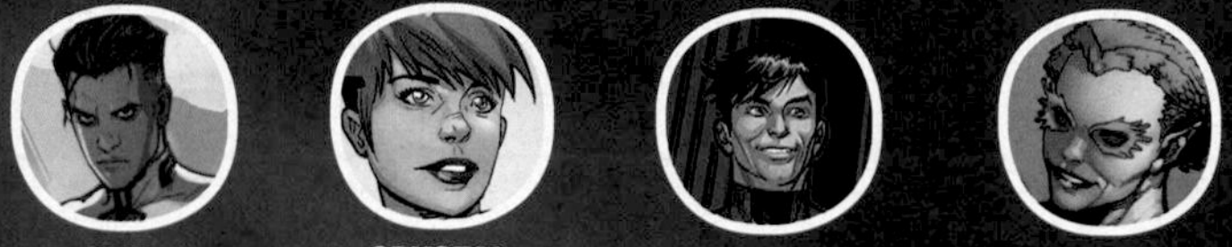

GRID CRYSTAL INFERNO NAJA

Months ago, the Terrigen Cloud passed through Mumbai, India, transforming civilians into Inhumans. Among those were famous movie star Ajay Roy, who was turned into a tree-like creature, and engineer Dinesh Deol, whose hands have been replaced by concentric rings of tangible electromagnetic waves. Since then, Dinesh has joined Queen Medusa and the Inhumans as Grid. Ajay Roy, however, hasn't been seen since that day...

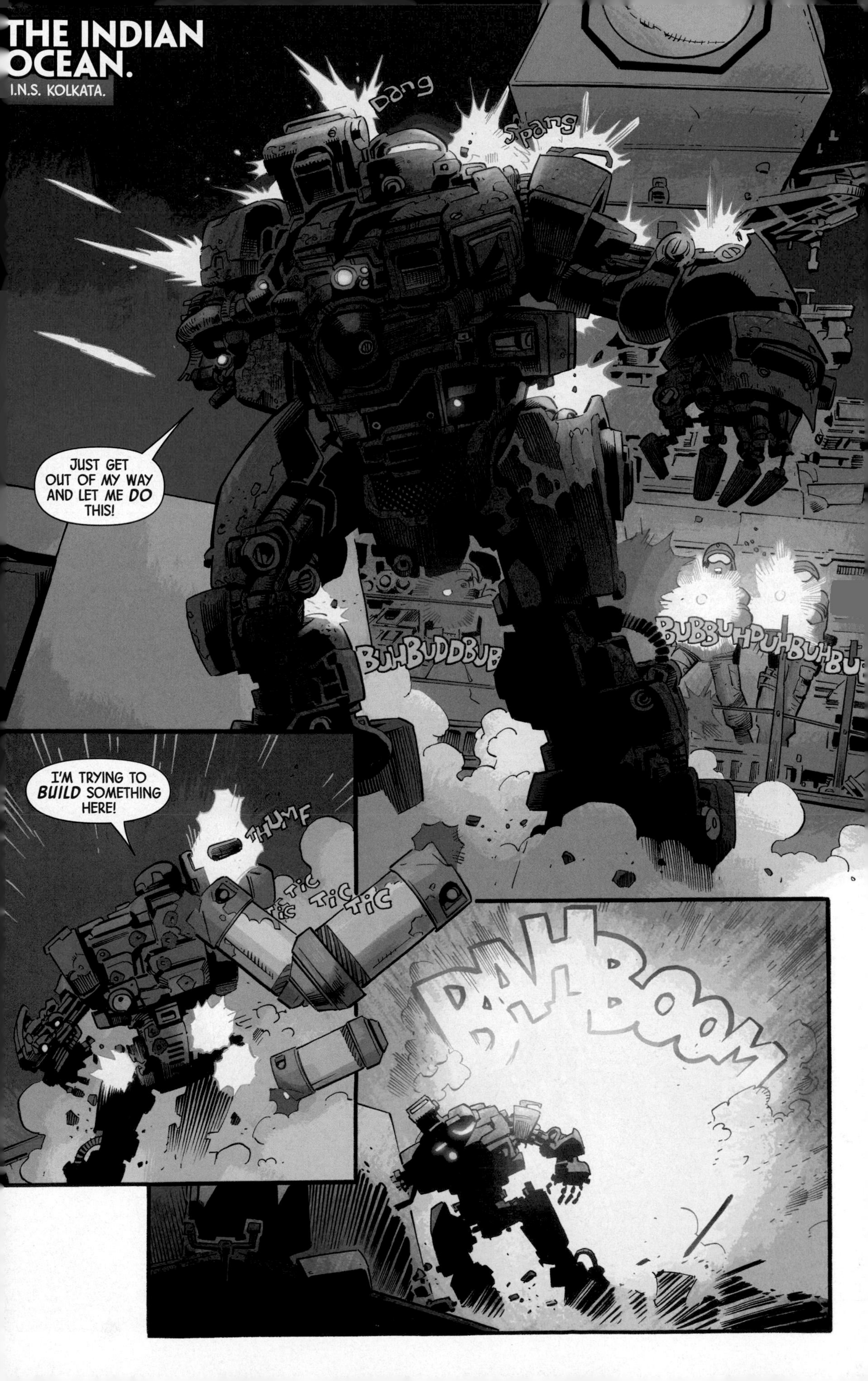
THE INDIAN OCEAN.
I.N.S. KOLKATA.
DANG
SPANG
JUST GET OUT OF MY WAY AND LET ME DO THIS!
BUHBUDDBUB
BUBBUHDUHBUHBU
I'M TRYING TO BUILD SOMETHING HERE!
THUMF
TIC TIC TIC TIC
BAHBOOM

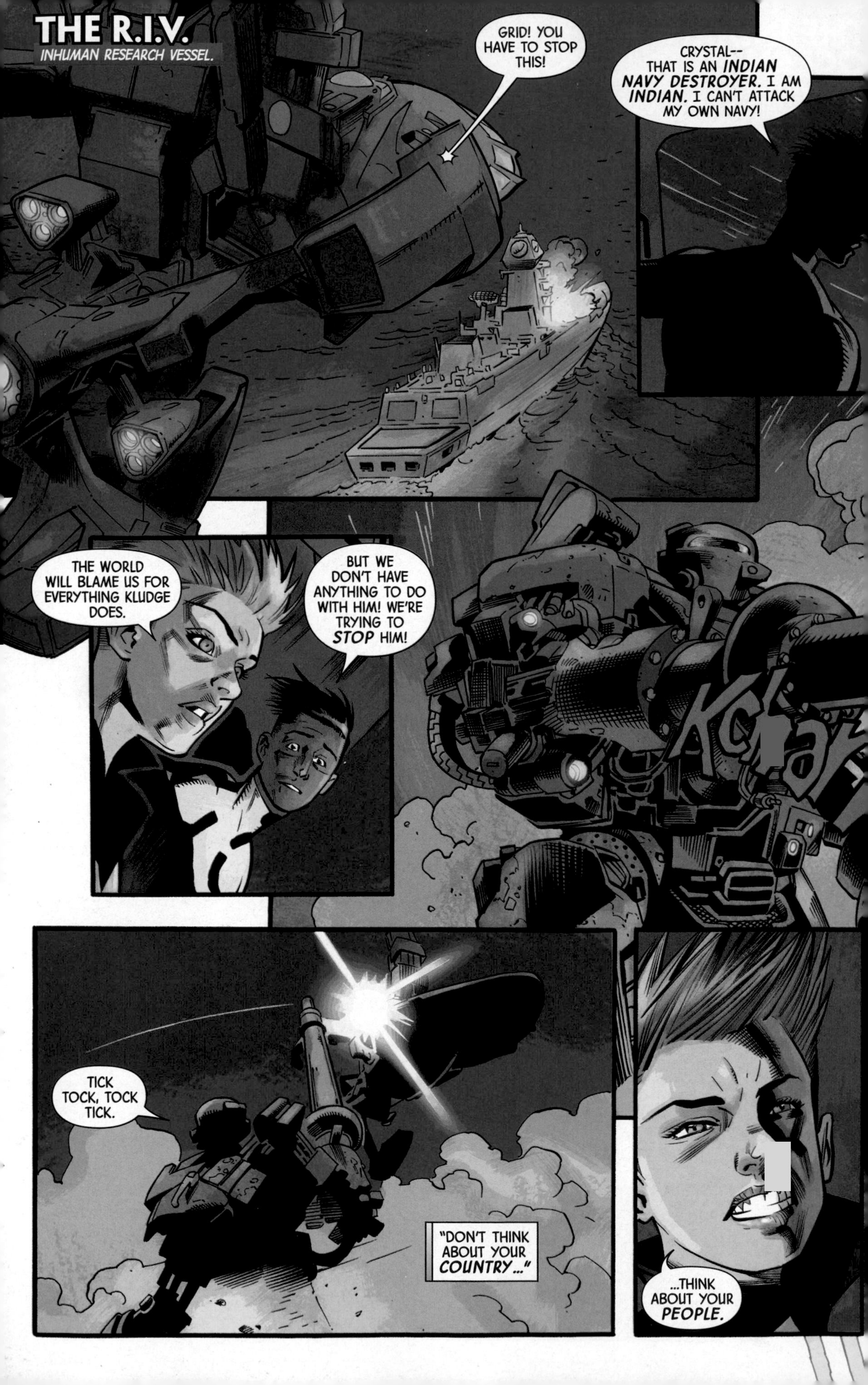
THE R.I.V.
INHUMAN RESEARCH VESSEL.
GRID! YOU HAVE TO STOP THIS!
CRYSTAL-- THAT IS AN INDIAN NAVY DESTROYER. I AM INDIAN. I CAN'T ATTACK MY OWN NAVY!
THE WORLD WILL BLAME US FOR EVERYTHING KLUDGE DOES.
BUT WE DON'T HAVE ANYTHING TO DO WITH HIM! WE'RE TRYING TO STOP HIM!
TICK TOCK, TOCK TICK.
"DON'T THINK ABOUT YOUR COUNTRY..."
...THINK ABOUT YOUR PEOPLE.

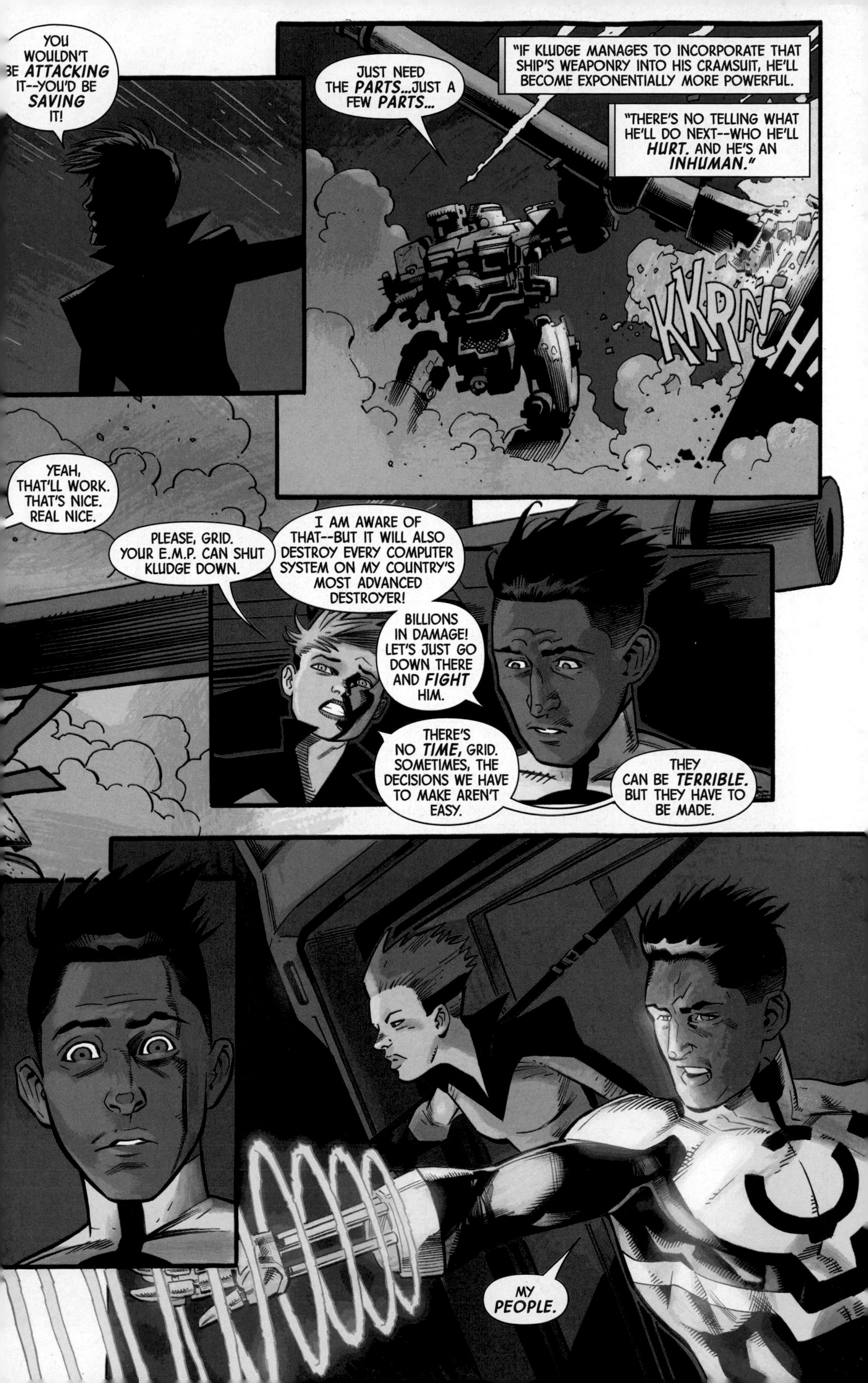

YOU WOULDN'T BE ATTACKING IT--YOU'D BE SAVING IT!
JUST NEED THE PARTS...JUST A FEW PARTS...
"IF KLUDGE MANAGES TO INCORPORATE THAT SHIP'S WEAPONRY INTO HIS CRAMSUIT, HE'LL BECOME EXPONENTIALLY MORE POWERFUL.
"THERE'S NO TELLING WHAT HE'LL DO NEXT--WHO HE'LL HURT. AND HE'S AN INHUMAN."
KKRNCH!
YEAH, THAT'LL WORK. THAT'S NICE. REAL NICE.
PLEASE, GRID. YOUR E.M.P. CAN SHUT KLUDGE DOWN.
I AM AWARE OF THAT--BUT IT WILL ALSO DESTROY EVERY COMPUTER SYSTEM ON MY COUNTRY'S MOST ADVANCED DESTROYER!
BILLIONS IN DAMAGE! LET'S JUST GO DOWN THERE AND FIGHT HIM.
THERE'S NO TIME, GRID. SOMETIMES, THE DECISIONS WE HAVE TO MAKE AREN'T EASY.
THEY CAN BE TERRIBLE. BUT THEY HAVE TO BE MADE.
MY PEOPLE.

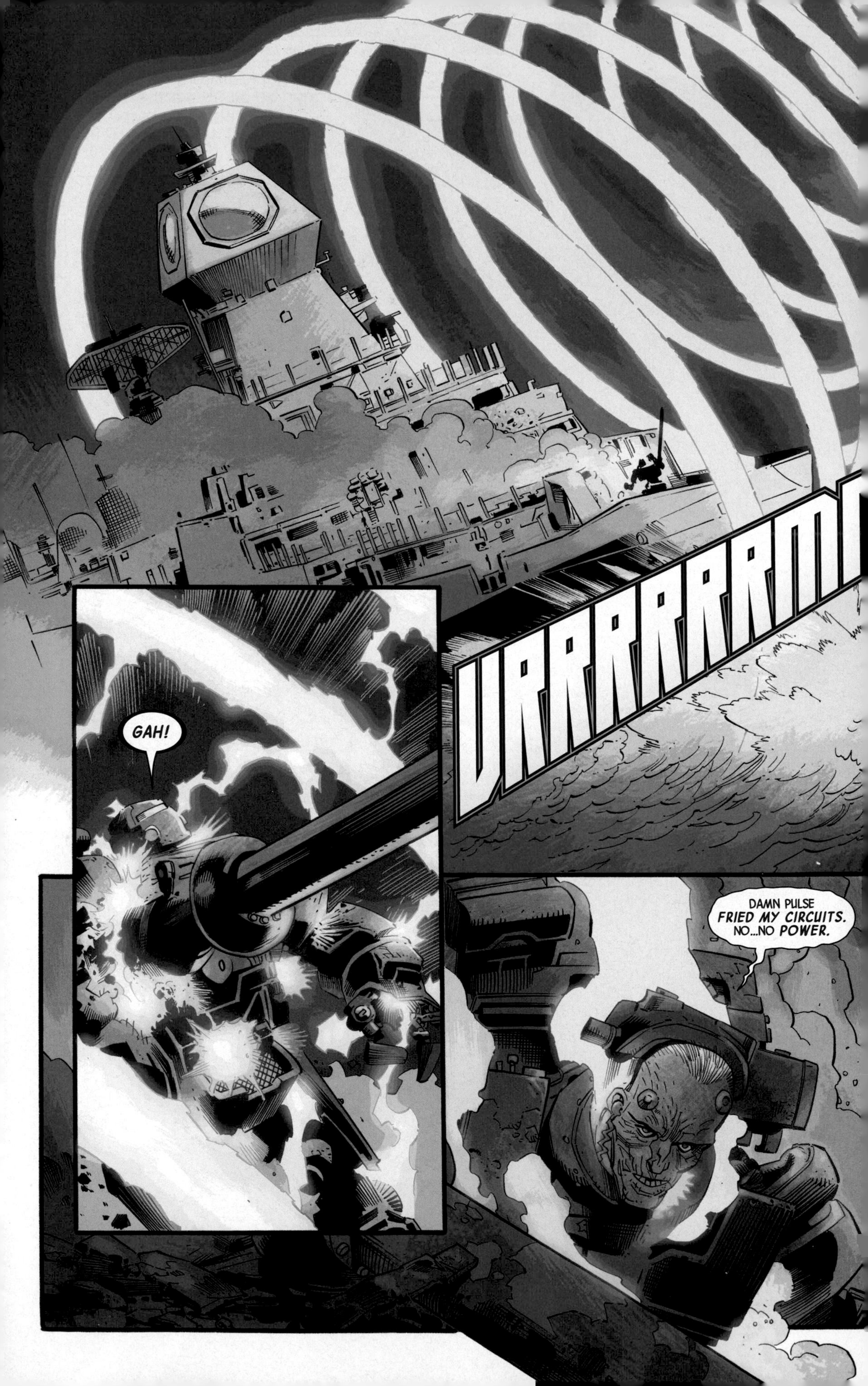
VRRRRRRM
GAH!
DAMN PULSE
FRIED MY CIRCUITS.
NO...NO POWER.

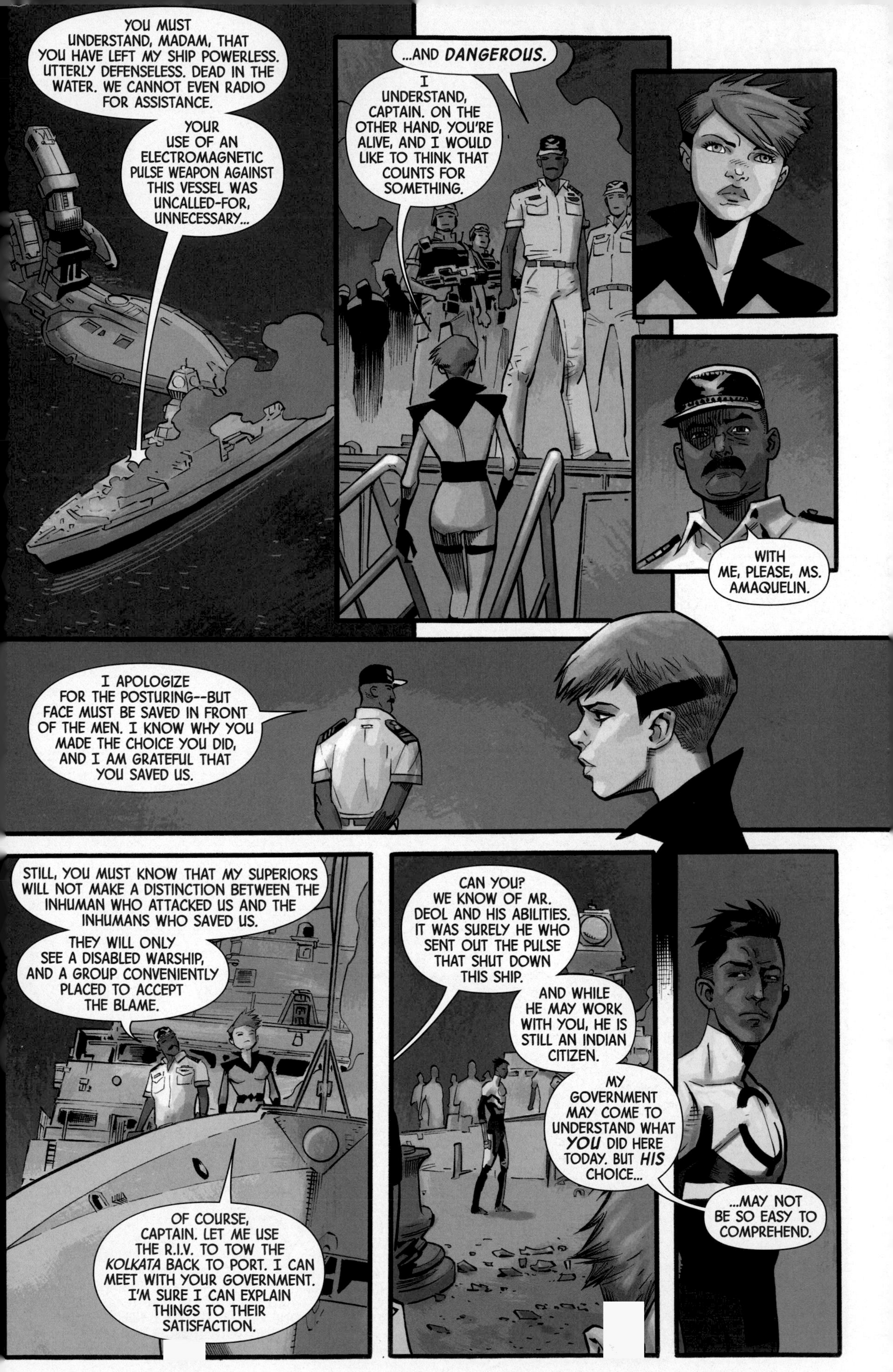
YOU MUST UNDERSTAND, MADAM, THAT YOU HAVE LEFT MY SHIP POWERLESS. UTTERLY DEFENSELESS. DEAD IN THE WATER. WE CANNOT EVEN RADIO FOR ASSISTANCE.
YOUR USE OF AN ELECTROMAGNETIC PULSE WEAPON AGAINST THIS VESSEL WAS UNCALLED-FOR, UNNECESSARY...
...AND DANGEROUS.
I UNDERSTAND, CAPTAIN. ON THE OTHER HAND, YOU'RE ALIVE, AND I WOULD LIKE TO THINK THAT COUNTS FOR SOMETHING.
WITH ME, PLEASE, MS. AMAQUELIN.
I APOLOGIZE FOR THE POSTURING--BUT FACE MUST BE SAVED IN FRONT OF THE MEN. I KNOW WHY YOU MADE THE CHOICE YOU DID, AND I AM GRATEFUL THAT YOU SAVED US.
STILL, YOU MUST KNOW THAT MY SUPERIORS WILL NOT MAKE A DISTINCTION BETWEEN THE INHUMAN WHO ATTACKED US AND THE INHUMANS WHO SAVED US.
THEY WILL ONLY SEE A DISABLED WARSHIP, AND A GROUP CONVENIENTLY PLACED TO ACCEPT THE BLAME.
OF COURSE, CAPTAIN. LET ME USE THE R.I.V. TO TOW THE KOLKATA BACK TO PORT. I CAN MEET WITH YOUR GOVERNMENT. I'M SURE I CAN EXPLAIN THINGS TO THEIR SATISFACTION.
CAN YOU? WE KNOW OF MR. DEOL AND HIS ABILITIES. IT WAS SURELY HE WHO SENT OUT THE PULSE THAT SHUT DOWN THIS SHIP.
AND WHILE HE MAY WORK WITH YOU, HE IS STILL AN INDIAN CITIZEN.
MY GOVERNMENT MAY COME TO UNDERSTAND WHAT YOU DID HERE TODAY. BUT HIS CHOICE...
...MAY NOT BE SO EASY TO COMPREHEND.

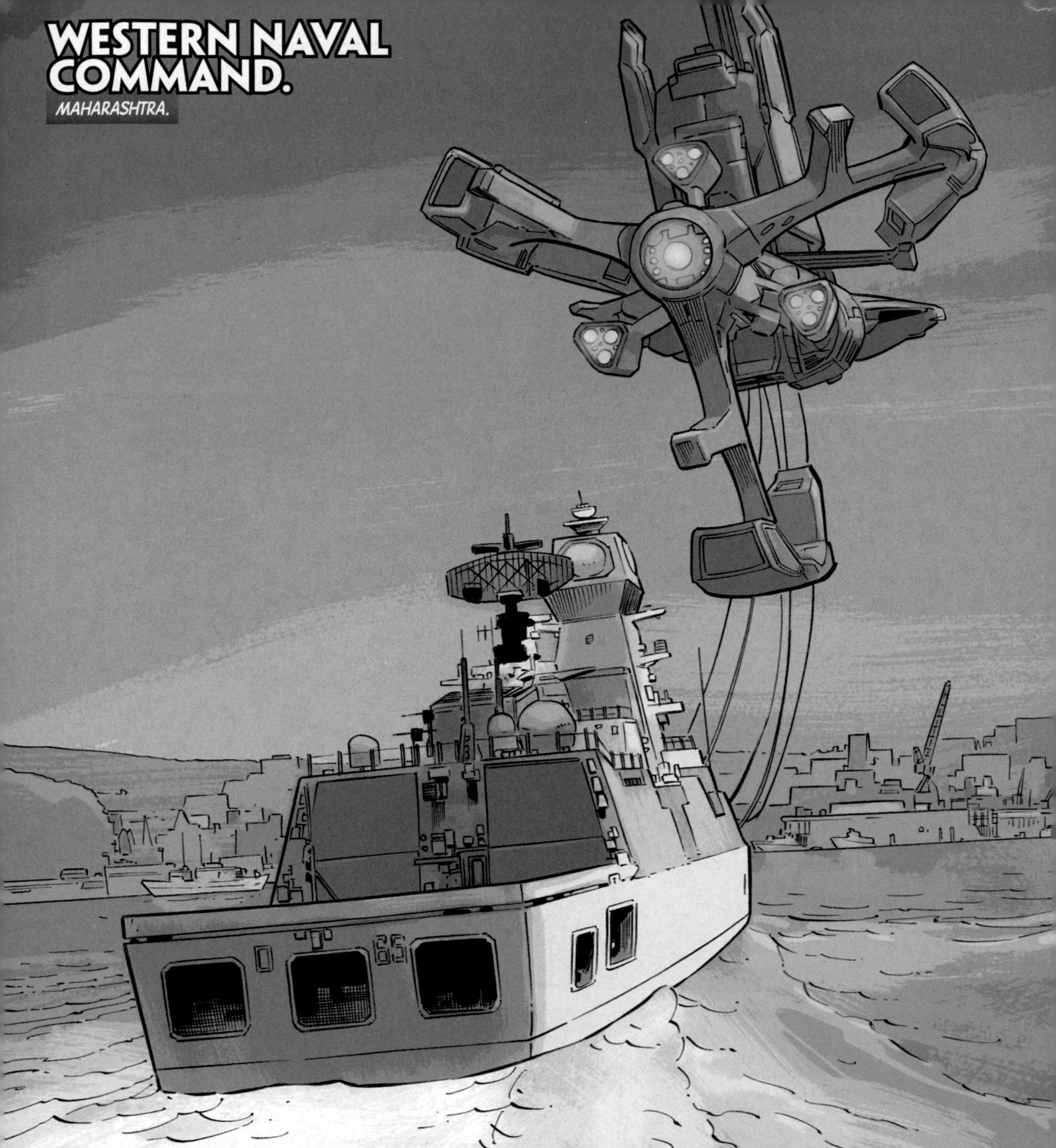
WESTERN NAVAL COMMAND.
MAHARASHTRA.

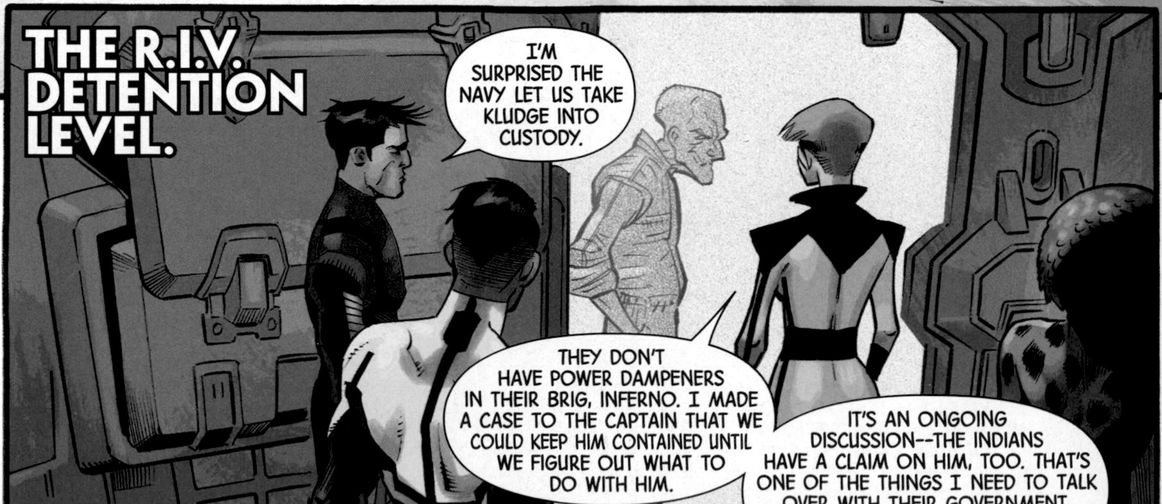
THE R.I.V. DETENTION LEVEL.
I'M SURPRISED THE NAVY LET US TAKE KLUDGE INTO CUSTODY.
THEY DON'T HAVE POWER DAMPENERS IN THEIR BRIG, INFERNO. I MADE A CASE TO THE CAPTAIN THAT WE COULD KEEP HIM CONTAINED UNTIL WE FIGURE OUT WHAT TO DO WITH HIM.
IT'S AN ONGOING DISCUSSION--THE INDIANS HAVE A CLAIM ON HIM, TOO. THAT'S ONE OF THE THINGS I NEED TO TALK OVER WITH THEIR GOVERNMENT.

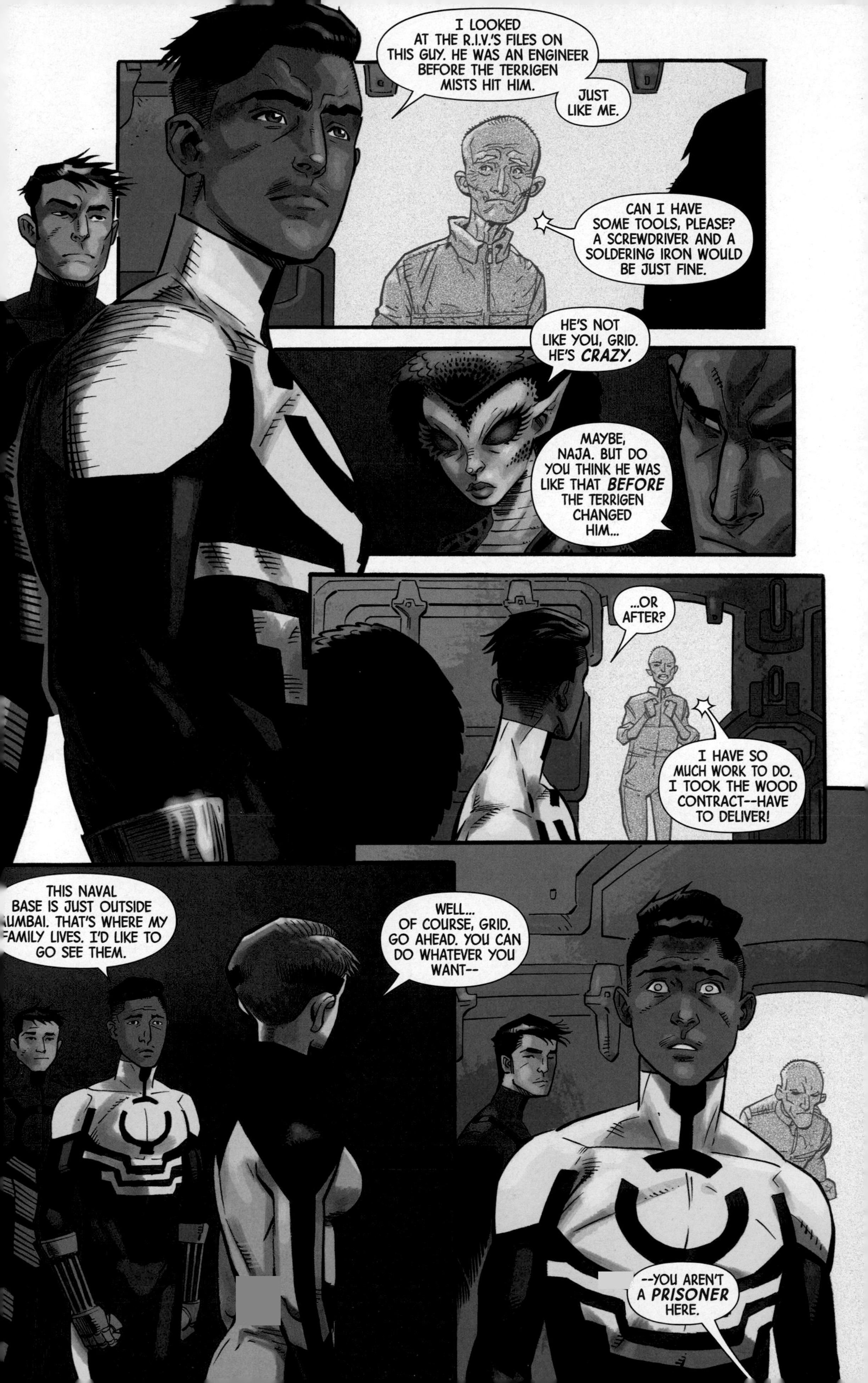
I LOOKED AT THE R.I.V.'S FILES ON THIS GUY. HE WAS AN ENGINEER BEFORE THE TERRIGEN MISTS HIT HIM.
JUST LIKE ME.
CAN I HAVE SOME TOOLS, PLEASE? A SCREWDRIVER AND A SOLDERING IRON WOULD BE JUST FINE.
HE'S NOT LIKE YOU, GRID. HE'S CRAZY.
MAYBE, NAJA. BUT DO YOU THINK HE WAS LIKE THAT BEFORE THE TERRIGEN CHANGED HIM...
...OR AFTER?
I HAVE SO MUCH WORK TO DO. I TOOK THE WOOD CONTRACT--HAVE TO DELIVER!
THIS NAVAL BASE IS JUST OUTSIDE UMBAI. THAT'S WHERE MY FAMILY LIVES. I'D LIKE TO GO SEE THEM.
WELL... OF COURSE, GRID. GO AHEAD. YOU CAN DO WHATEVER YOU WANT--
--YOU AREN'T A PRISONER HERE.

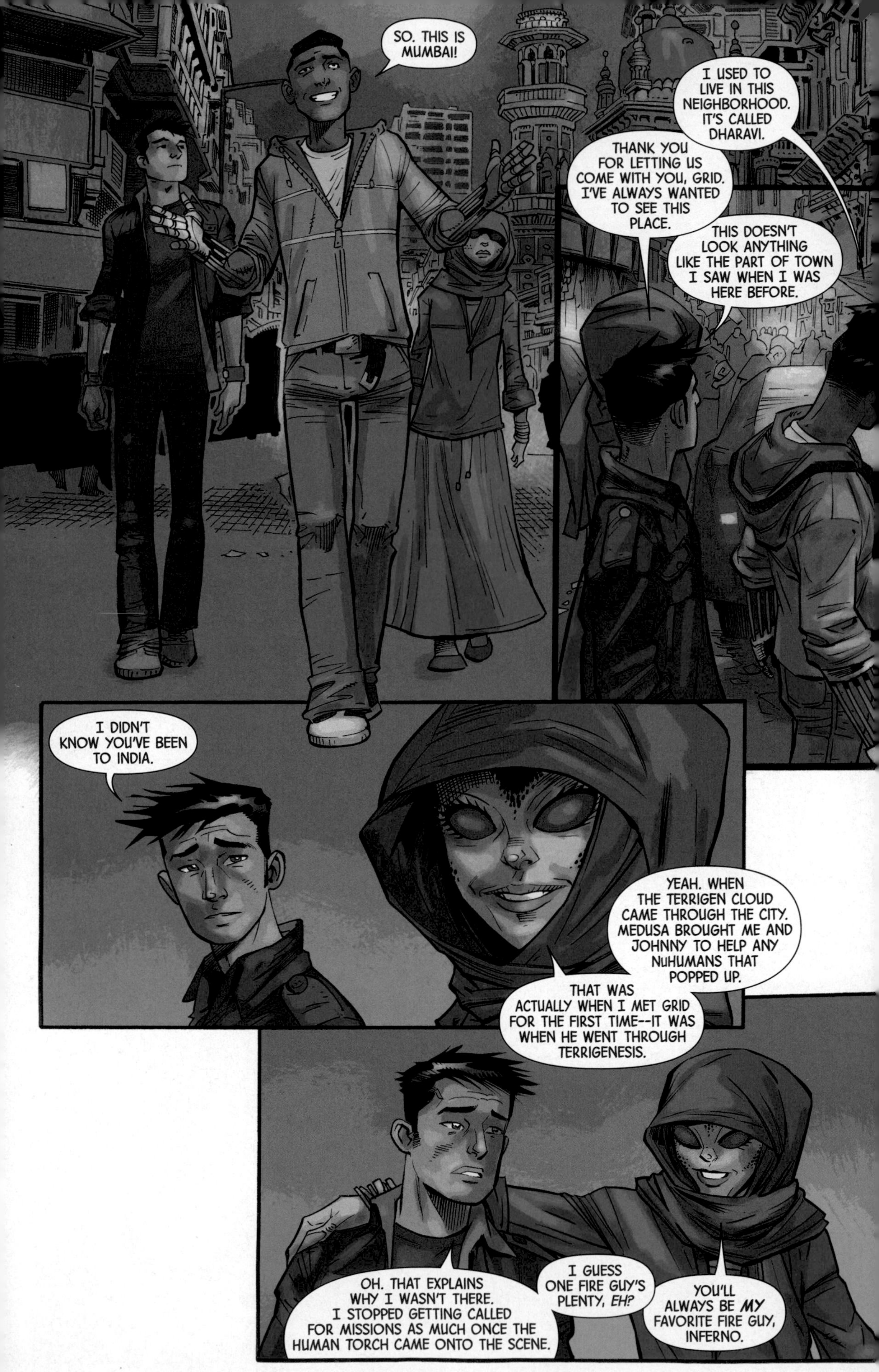
SO. THIS IS MUMBAI!
I USED TO LIVE IN THIS NEIGHBORHOOD. IT'S CALLED DHARAVI.
THANK YOU FOR LETTING US COME WITH YOU, GRID. I'VE ALWAYS WANTED TO SEE THIS PLACE.
THIS DOESN'T LOOK ANYTHING LIKE THE PART OF TOWN I SAW WHEN I WAS HERE BEFORE.
I DIDN'T KNOW YOU'VE BEEN TO INDIA.
YEAH. WHEN THE TERRIGEN CLOUD CAME THROUGH THE CITY. MEDUSA BROUGHT ME AND JOHNNY TO HELP ANY NUHUMANS THAT POPPED UP.
THAT WAS ACTUALLY WHEN I MET GRID FOR THE FIRST TIME--IT WAS WHEN HE WENT THROUGH TERRIGENESIS.
OH. THAT EXPLAINS WHY I WASN'T THERE. I STOPPED GETTING CALLED FOR MISSIONS AS MUCH ONCE THE HUMAN TORCH CAME ONTO THE SCENE.
I GUESS ONE FIRE GUY'S PLENTY, *EH?*
YOU'LL ALWAYS BE *MY* FAVORITE FIRE GUY, INFERNO.

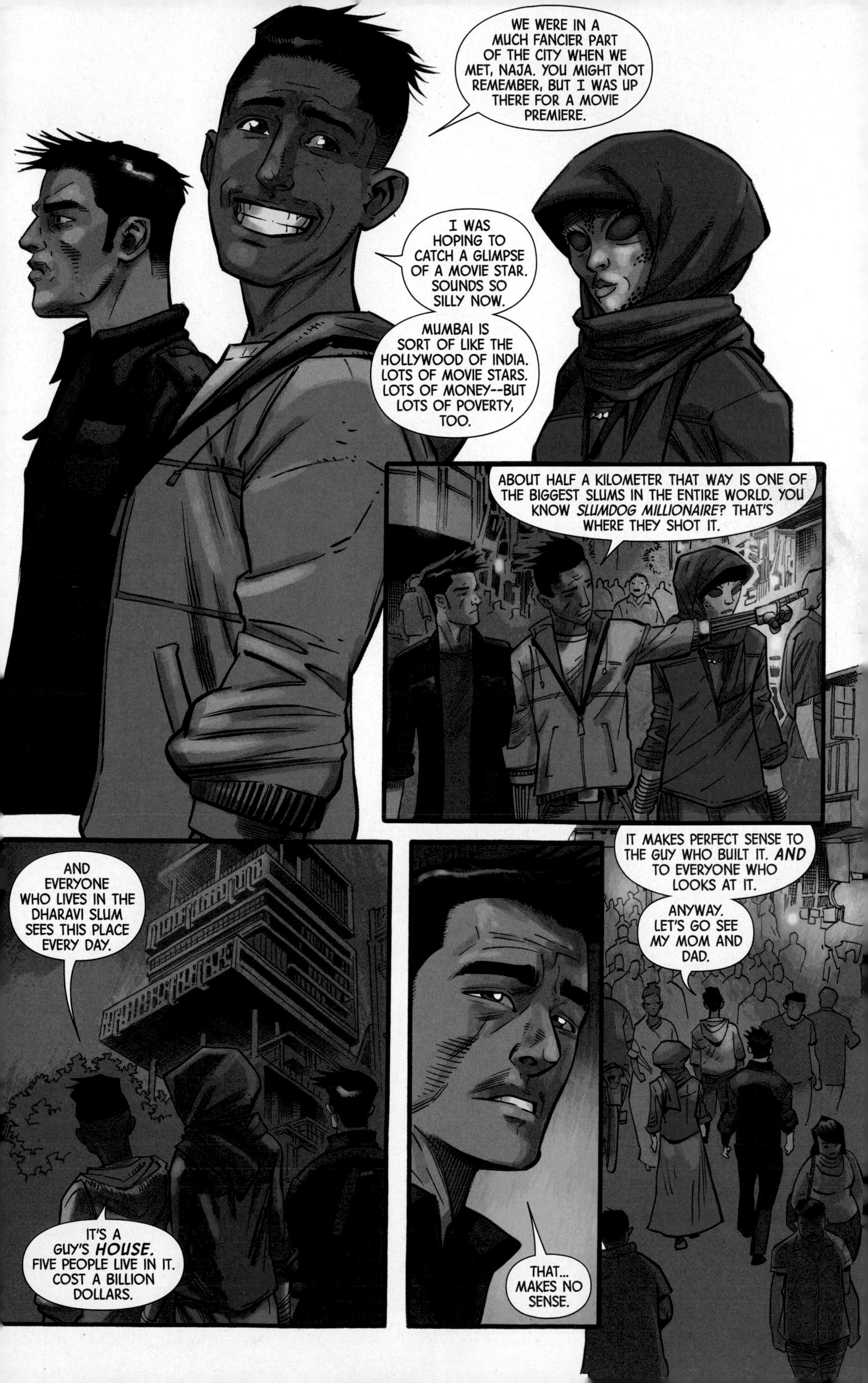
WE WERE IN A MUCH FANCIER PART OF THE CITY WHEN WE MET, NAJA. YOU MIGHT NOT REMEMBER, BUT I WAS UP THERE FOR A MOVIE PREMIERE.
I WAS HOPING TO CATCH A GLIMPSE OF A MOVIE STAR. SOUNDS SO SILLY NOW.
MUMBAI IS SORT OF LIKE THE HOLLYWOOD OF INDIA. LOTS OF MOVIE STARS. LOTS OF MONEY--BUT LOTS OF POVERTY, TOO.
ABOUT HALF A KILOMETER THAT WAY IS ONE OF THE BIGGEST SLUMS IN THE ENTIRE WORLD. YOU KNOW *SLUMDOG MILLIONAIRE*? THAT'S WHERE THEY SHOT IT.
AND EVERYONE WHO LIVES IN THE DHARAVI SLUM SEES THIS PLACE EVERY DAY.
IT'S A GUY'S **HOUSE.** FIVE PEOPLE LIVE IN IT. COST A BILLION DOLLARS.
THAT... MAKES NO SENSE.
IT MAKES PERFECT SENSE TO THE GUY WHO BUILT IT. ***AND*** TO EVERYONE WHO LOOKS AT IT.
ANYWAY. LET'S GO SEE MY MOM AND DAD.

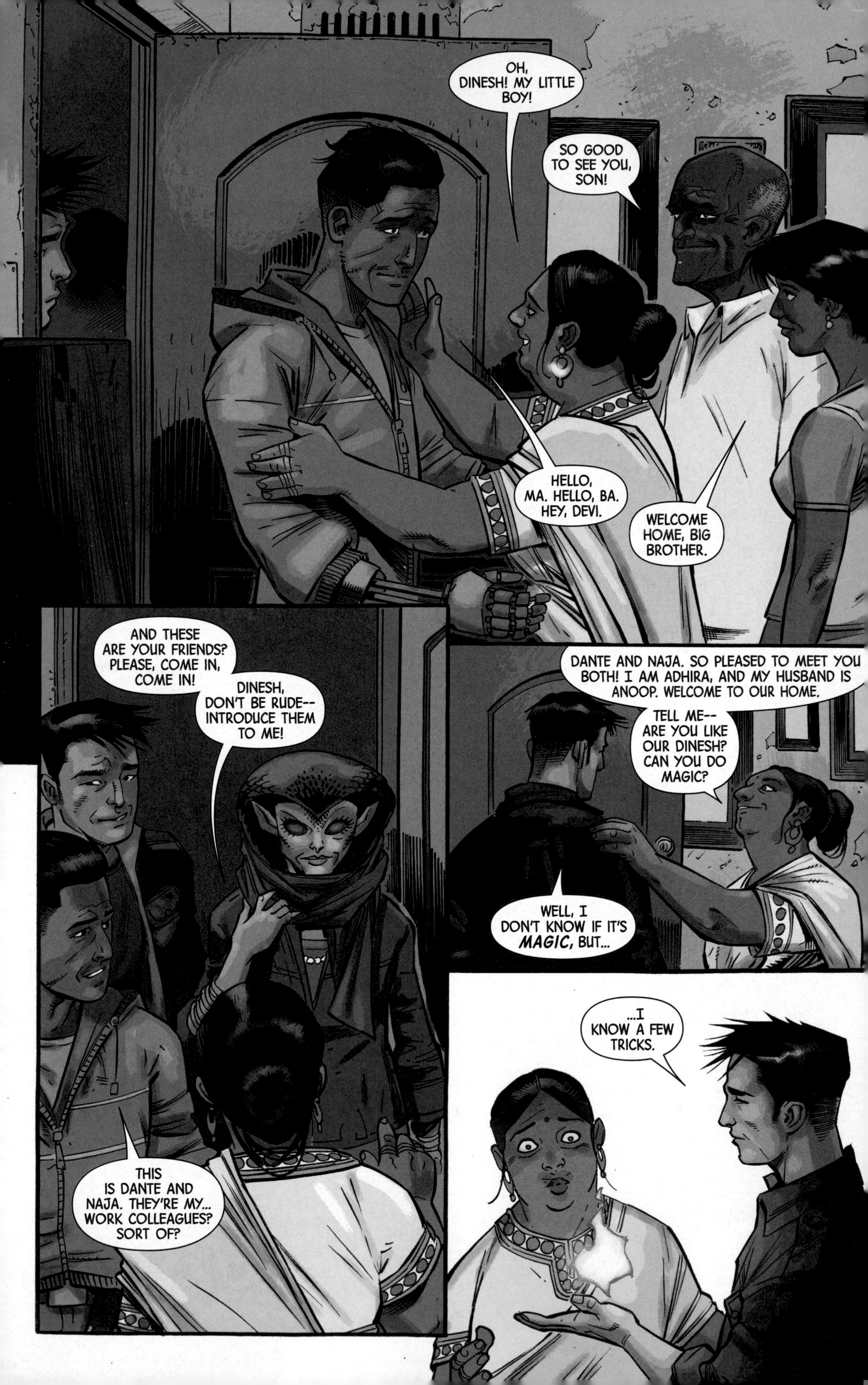
OH, DINESH! MY LITTLE BOY!
SO GOOD TO SEE YOU, SON!
HELLO, MA. HELLO, BA. HEY, DEVI.
WELCOME HOME, BIG BROTHER.
AND THESE ARE YOUR FRIENDS? PLEASE, COME IN, COME IN!
DINESH, DON'T BE RUDE--INTRODUCE THEM TO ME!
THIS IS DANTE AND NAJA. THEY'RE MY... WORK COLLEAGUES? SORT OF?
DANTE AND NAJA. SO PLEASED TO MEET YOU BOTH! I AM ADHIRA, AND MY HUSBAND IS ANOOP. WELCOME TO OUR HOME.
TELL ME--ARE YOU LIKE OUR DINESH? CAN YOU DO MAGIC?
WELL, I DON'T KNOW IF IT'S *MAGIC*, BUT...
...I KNOW A FEW TRICKS.

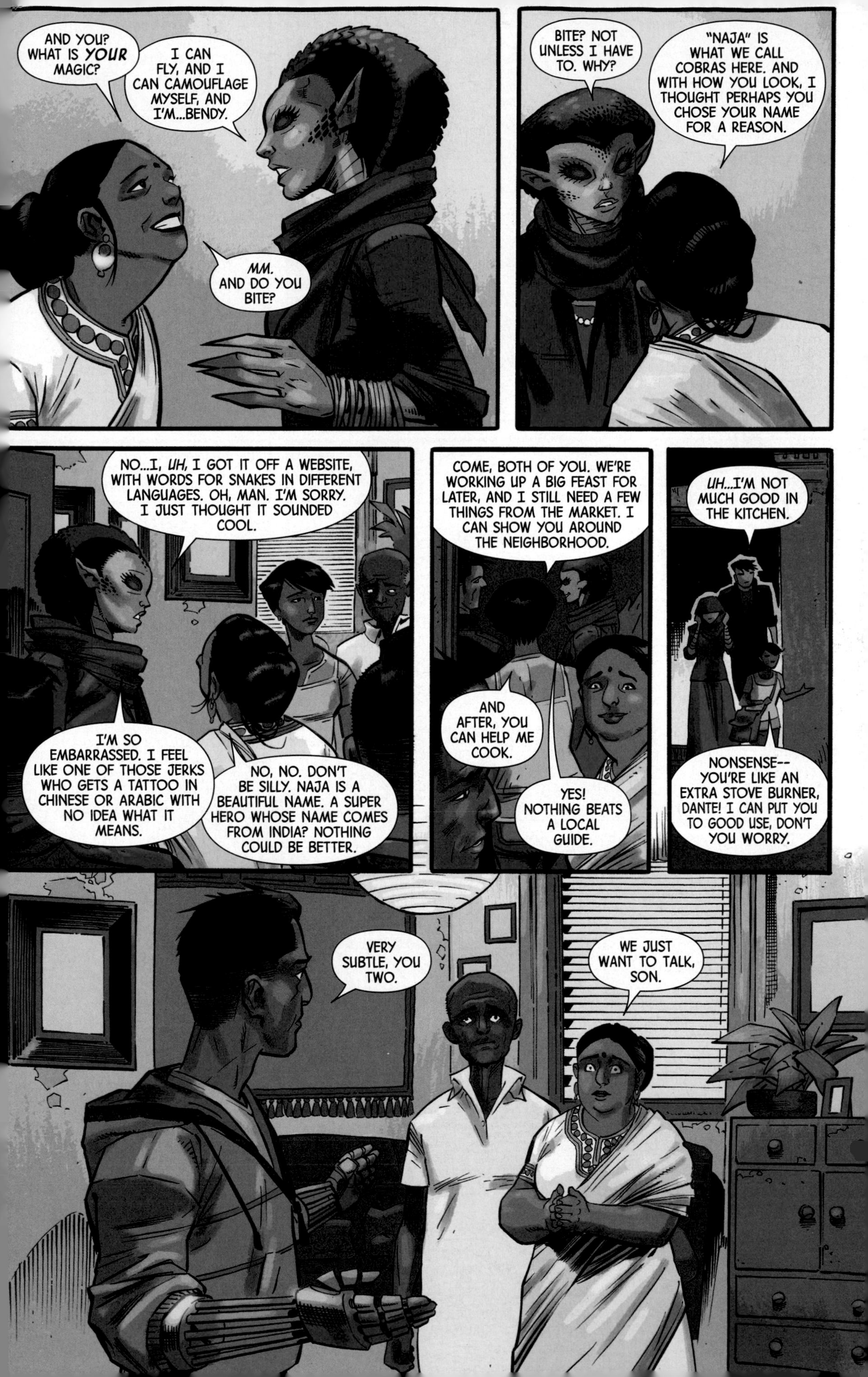
AND YOU? WHAT IS YOUR MAGIC?
I CAN FLY, AND I CAN CAMOUFLAGE MYSELF, AND I'M...BENDY.
MM. AND DO YOU BITE?
BITE? NOT UNLESS I HAVE TO. WHY?
"NAJA" IS WHAT WE CALL COBRAS HERE. AND WITH HOW YOU LOOK, I THOUGHT PERHAPS YOU CHOSE YOUR NAME FOR A REASON.
NO...I, UH, I GOT IT OFF A WEBSITE, WITH WORDS FOR SNAKES IN DIFFERENT LANGUAGES. OH, MAN. I'M SORRY. I JUST THOUGHT IT SOUNDED COOL.
I'M SO EMBARRASSED. I FEEL LIKE ONE OF THOSE JERKS WHO GETS A TATTOO IN CHINESE OR ARABIC WITH NO IDEA WHAT IT MEANS.
NO, NO. DON'T BE SILLY. NAJA IS A BEAUTIFUL NAME. A SUPER HERO WHOSE NAME COMES FROM INDIA? NOTHING COULD BE BETTER.
COME, BOTH OF YOU. WE'RE WORKING UP A BIG FEAST FOR LATER, AND I STILL NEED A FEW THINGS FROM THE MARKET. I CAN SHOW YOU AROUND THE NEIGHBORHOOD.
AND AFTER, YOU CAN HELP ME COOK.
YES! NOTHING BEATS A LOCAL GUIDE.
UH...I'M NOT MUCH GOOD IN THE KITCHEN.
NONSENSE-- YOU'RE LIKE AN EXTRA STOVE BURNER, DANTE! I CAN PUT YOU TO GOOD USE, DON'T YOU WORRY.
VERY SUBTLE, YOU TWO.
WE JUST WANT TO TALK, SON.

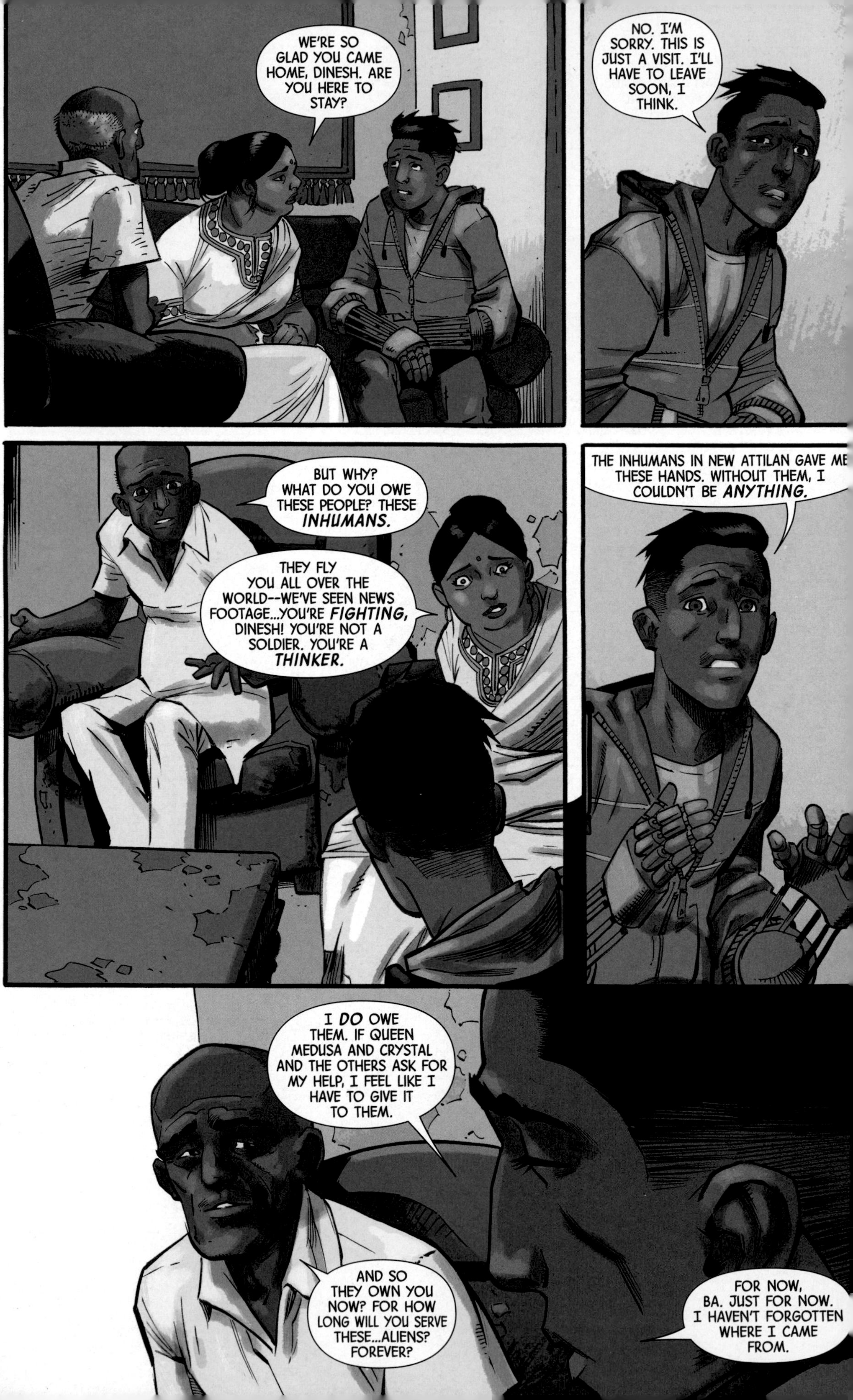
WE'RE SO GLAD YOU CAME HOME, DINESH. ARE YOU HERE TO STAY?
NO. I'M SORRY. THIS IS JUST A VISIT. I'LL HAVE TO LEAVE SOON, I THINK.
BUT WHY? WHAT DO YOU OWE THESE PEOPLE? THESE INHUMANS.
THEY FLY YOU ALL OVER THE WORLD--WE'VE SEEN NEWS FOOTAGE...YOU'RE FIGHTING, DINESH! YOU'RE NOT A SOLDIER. YOU'RE A THINKER.
THE INHUMANS IN NEW ATTILAN GAVE ME THESE HANDS. WITHOUT THEM, I COULDN'T BE ANYTHING.
I DO OWE THEM. IF QUEEN MEDUSA AND CRYSTAL AND THE OTHERS ASK FOR MY HELP, I FEEL LIKE I HAVE TO GIVE IT TO THEM.
AND SO THEY OWN YOU NOW? FOR HOW LONG WILL YOU SERVE THESE...ALIENS? FOREVER?
FOR NOW, BA. JUST FOR NOW. I HAVEN'T FORGOTTEN WHERE I CAME FROM.

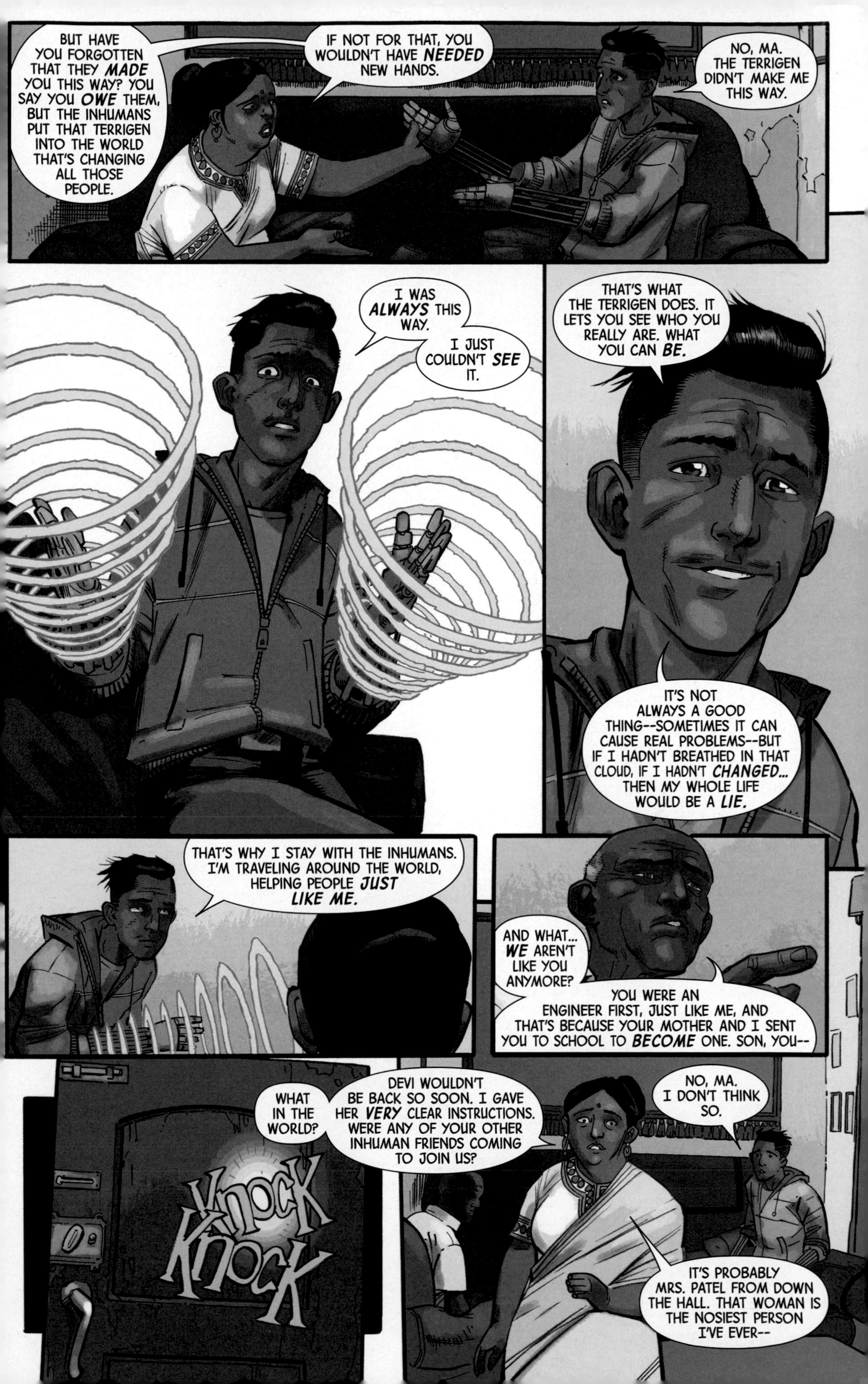
BUT HAVE YOU FORGOTTEN THAT THEY MADE YOU THIS WAY? YOU SAY YOU OWE THEM, BUT THE INHUMANS PUT THAT TERRIGEN INTO THE WORLD THAT'S CHANGING ALL THOSE PEOPLE.
IF NOT FOR THAT, YOU WOULDN'T HAVE NEEDED NEW HANDS.
NO, MA. THE TERRIGEN DIDN'T MAKE ME THIS WAY.
I WAS ALWAYS THIS WAY.
I JUST COULDN'T SEE IT.
THAT'S WHAT THE TERRIGEN DOES. IT LETS YOU SEE WHO YOU REALLY ARE. WHAT YOU CAN BE.
IT'S NOT ALWAYS A GOOD THING--SOMETIMES IT CAN CAUSE REAL PROBLEMS--BUT IF I HADN'T BREATHED IN THAT CLOUD, IF I HADN'T CHANGED... THEN MY WHOLE LIFE WOULD BE A LIE.
THAT'S WHY I STAY WITH THE INHUMANS. I'M TRAVELING AROUND THE WORLD, HELPING PEOPLE JUST LIKE ME.
AND WHAT... WE AREN'T LIKE YOU ANYMORE?
YOU WERE AN ENGINEER FIRST, JUST LIKE ME, AND THAT'S BECAUSE YOUR MOTHER AND I SENT YOU TO SCHOOL TO BECOME ONE. SON, YOU--
KNOCK KNOCK
WHAT IN THE WORLD?
DEVI WOULDN'T BE BACK SO SOON. I GAVE HER VERY CLEAR INSTRUCTIONS. WERE ANY OF YOUR OTHER INHUMAN FRIENDS COMING TO JOIN US?
NO, MA. I DON'T THINK SO.
IT'S PROBABLY MRS. PATEL FROM DOWN THE HALL. THAT WOMAN IS THE NOSIEST PERSON I'VE EVER--

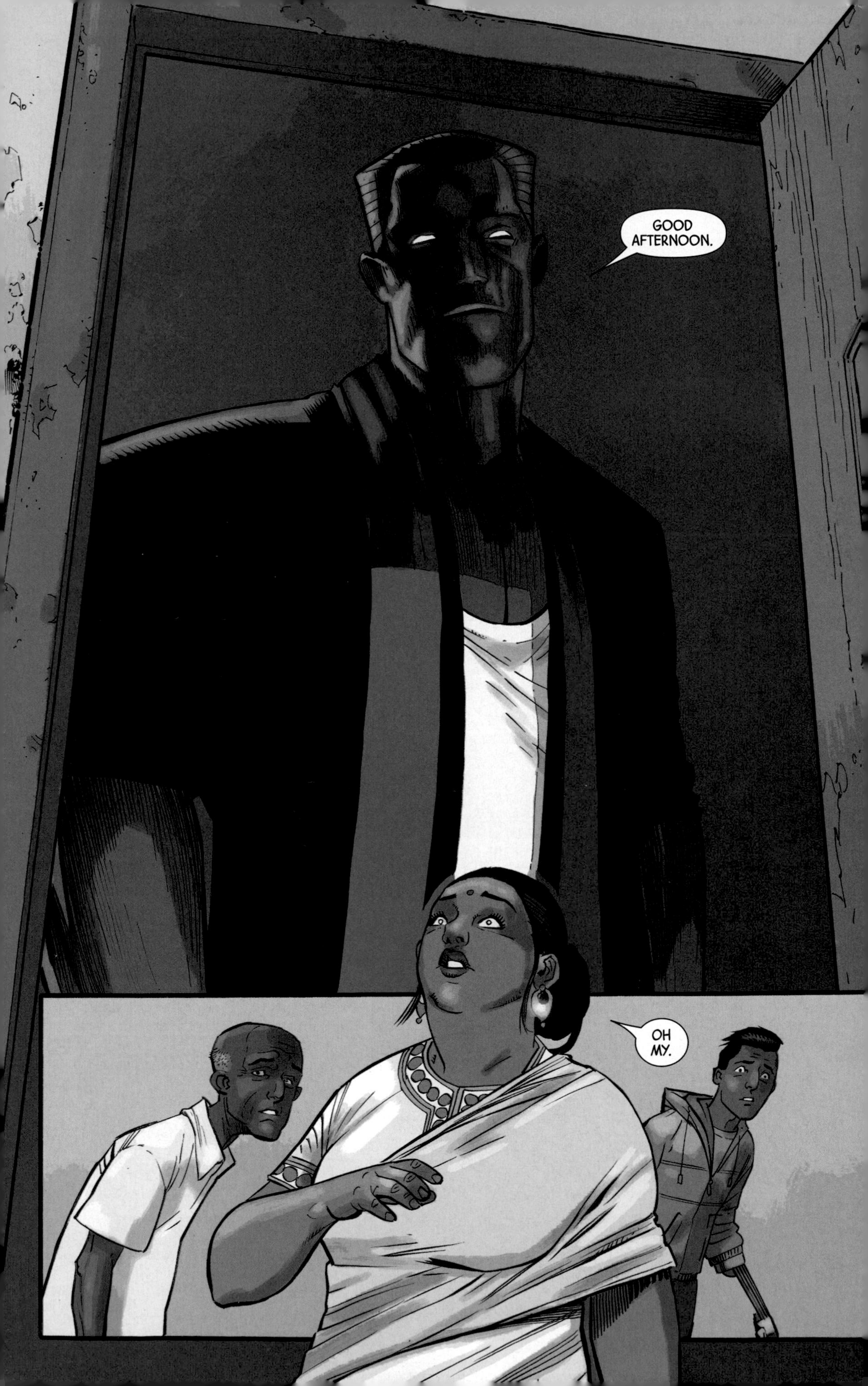
GOOD AFTERNOON.
OH MY.

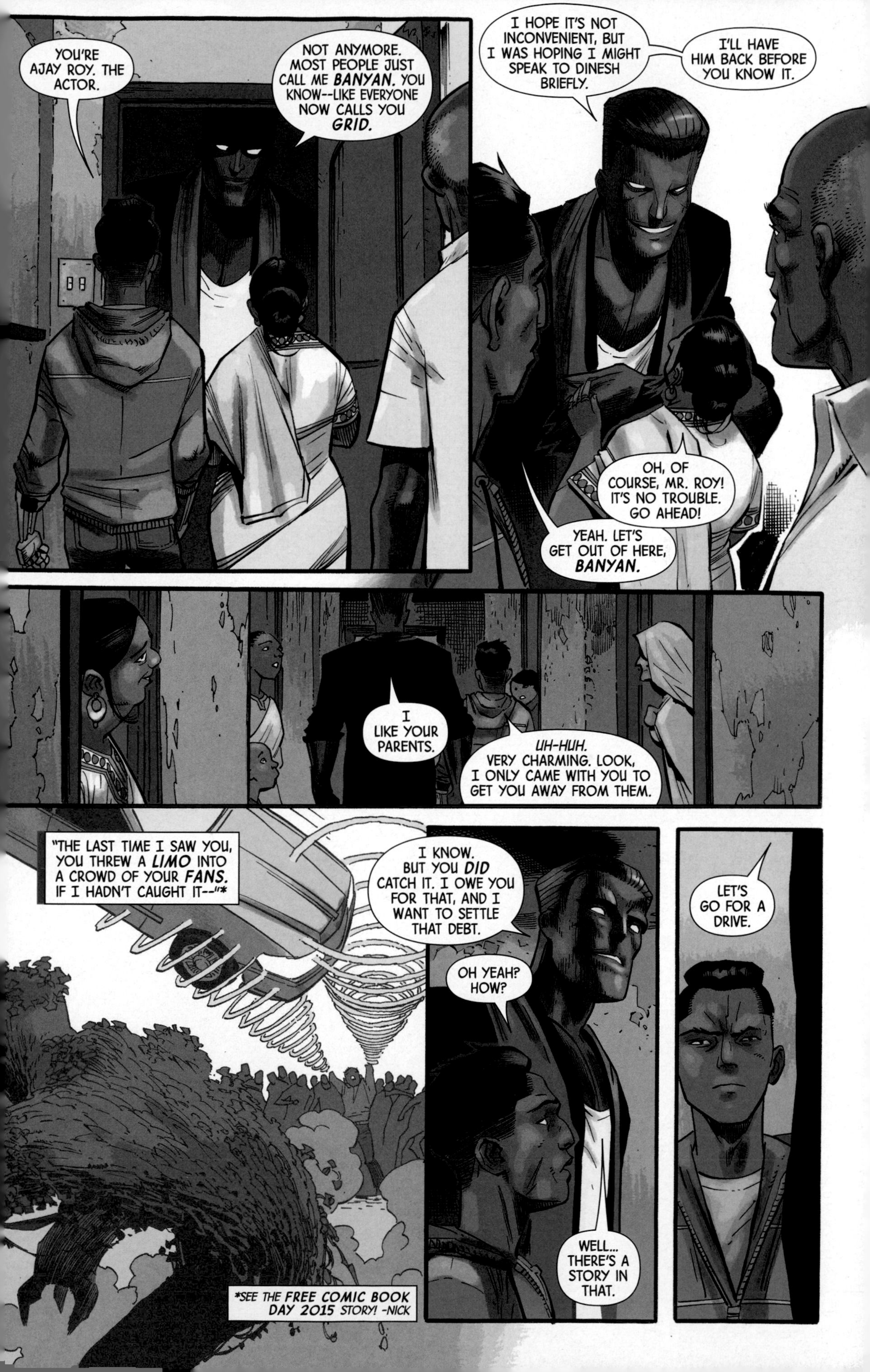
YOU'RE AJAY ROY. THE ACTOR.
NOT ANYMORE. MOST PEOPLE JUST CALL ME BANYAN. YOU KNOW--LIKE EVERYONE NOW CALLS YOU GRID.
I HOPE IT'S NOT INCONVENIENT, BUT I WAS HOPING I MIGHT SPEAK TO DINESH BRIEFLY.
I'LL HAVE HIM BACK BEFORE YOU KNOW IT.
OH, OF COURSE, MR. ROY! IT'S NO TROUBLE. GO AHEAD!
YEAH. LET'S GET OUT OF HERE, BANYAN.
I LIKE YOUR PARENTS.
UH-HUH. VERY CHARMING. LOOK, I ONLY CAME WITH YOU TO GET YOU AWAY FROM THEM.
"THE LAST TIME I SAW YOU, YOU THREW A LIMO INTO A CROWD OF YOUR FANS. IF I HADN'T CAUGHT IT--"*
I KNOW. BUT YOU DID CATCH IT. I OWE YOU FOR THAT, AND I WANT TO SETTLE THAT DEBT.
OH YEAH? HOW?
WELL... THERE'S A STORY IN THAT.
LET'S GO FOR A DRIVE.
*SEE THE FREE COMIC BOOK DAY 2015 STORY! -NICK

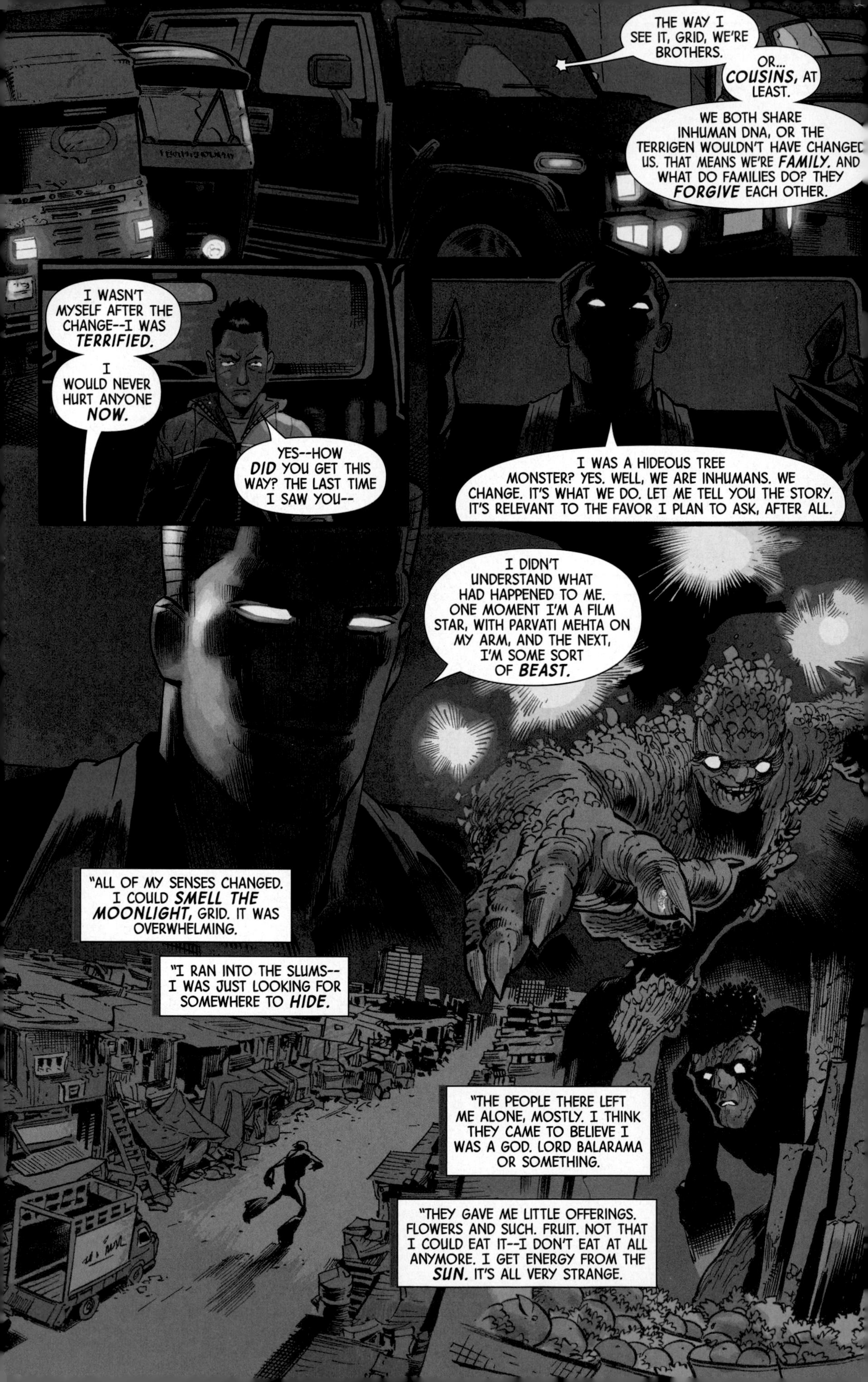
THE WAY I SEE IT, GRID, WE'RE BROTHERS.
OR... COUSINS, AT LEAST.
WE BOTH SHARE INHUMAN DNA, OR THE TERRIGEN WOULDN'T HAVE CHANGED US. THAT MEANS WE'RE FAMILY. AND WHAT DO FAMILIES DO? THEY FORGIVE EACH OTHER.
I WASN'T MYSELF AFTER THE CHANGE--I WAS TERRIFIED.
I WOULD NEVER HURT ANYONE NOW.
YES--HOW DID YOU GET THIS WAY? THE LAST TIME I SAW YOU--
I WAS A HIDEOUS TREE MONSTER? YES. WELL, WE ARE INHUMANS. WE CHANGE. IT'S WHAT WE DO. LET ME TELL YOU THE STORY. IT'S RELEVANT TO THE FAVOR I PLAN TO ASK, AFTER ALL.
I DIDN'T UNDERSTAND WHAT HAD HAPPENED TO ME. ONE MOMENT I'M A FILM STAR, WITH PARVATI MEHTA ON MY ARM, AND THE NEXT, I'M SOME SORT OF BEAST.
"ALL OF MY SENSES CHANGED. I COULD SMELL THE MOONLIGHT, GRID. IT WAS OVERWHELMING.
"I RAN INTO THE SLUMS-- I WAS JUST LOOKING FOR SOMEWHERE TO HIDE.
"THE PEOPLE THERE LEFT ME ALONE, MOSTLY. I THINK THEY CAME TO BELIEVE I WAS A GOD. LORD BALARAMA OR SOMETHING.
"THEY GAVE ME LITTLE OFFERINGS. FLOWERS AND SUCH. FRUIT. NOT THAT I COULD EAT IT--I DON'T EAT AT ALL ANYMORE. I GET ENERGY FROM THE SUN. IT'S ALL VERY STRANGE.

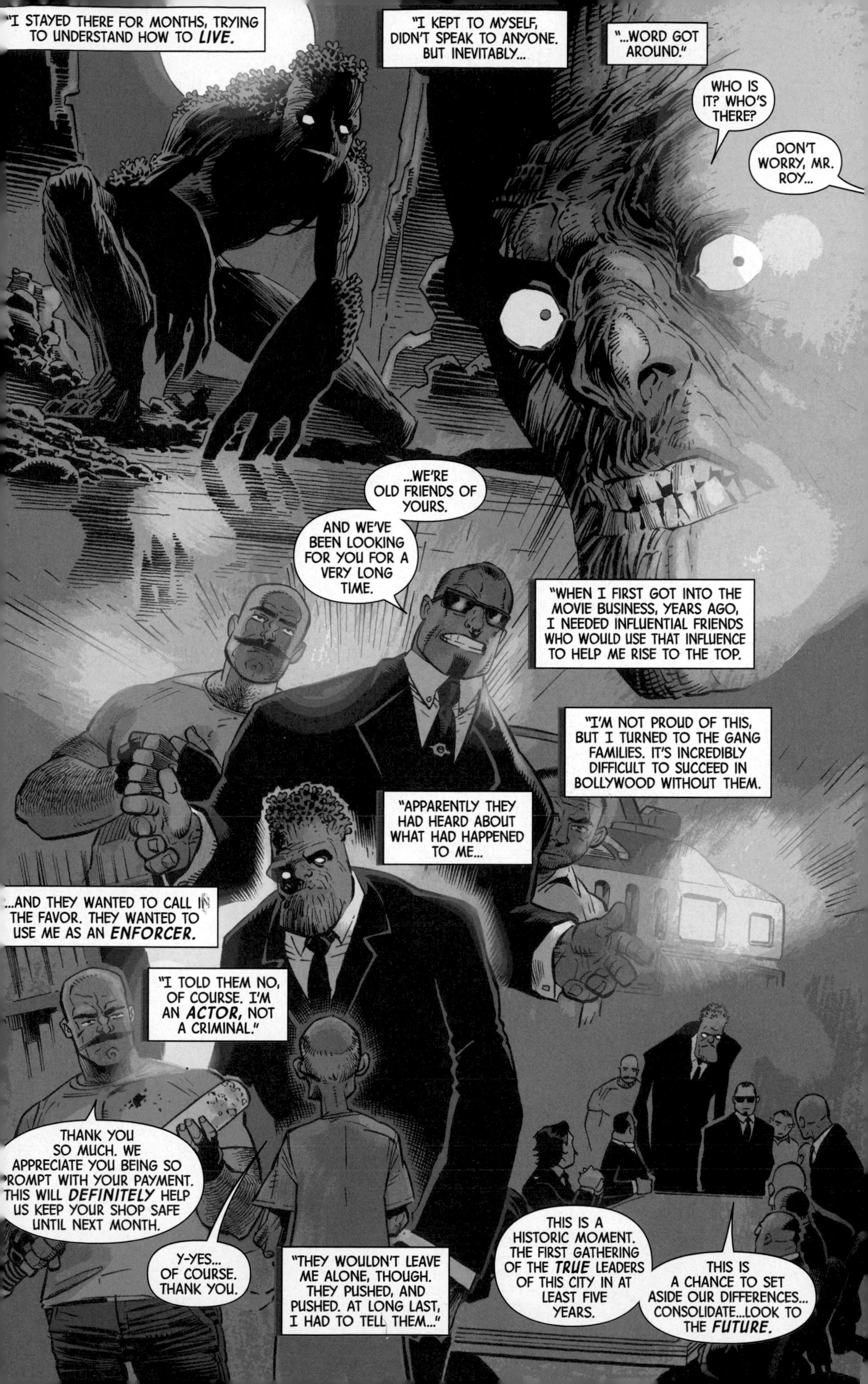
"I STAYED THERE FOR MONTHS, TRYING TO UNDERSTAND HOW TO LIVE.
"I KEPT TO MYSELF, DIDN'T SPEAK TO ANYONE. BUT INEVITABLY...
"...WORD GOT AROUND."
WHO IS IT? WHO'S THERE?
DON'T WORRY, MR. ROY...
...WE'RE OLD FRIENDS OF YOURS.
AND WE'VE BEEN LOOKING FOR YOU FOR A VERY LONG TIME.
"WHEN I FIRST GOT INTO THE MOVIE BUSINESS, YEARS AGO, I NEEDED INFLUENTIAL FRIENDS WHO WOULD USE THAT INFLUENCE TO HELP ME RISE TO THE TOP.
"I'M NOT PROUD OF THIS, BUT I TURNED TO THE GANG FAMILIES. IT'S INCREDIBLY DIFFICULT TO SUCCEED IN BOLLYWOOD WITHOUT THEM.
"APPARENTLY THEY HAD HEARD ABOUT WHAT HAD HAPPENED TO ME...
...AND THEY WANTED TO CALL IN THE FAVOR. THEY WANTED TO USE ME AS AN ENFORCER.
"I TOLD THEM NO, OF COURSE. I'M AN ACTOR, NOT A CRIMINAL."
THANK YOU SO MUCH. WE APPRECIATE YOU BEING SO PROMPT WITH YOUR PAYMENT. THIS WILL DEFINITELY HELP US KEEP YOUR SHOP SAFE UNTIL NEXT MONTH.
Y-YES... OF COURSE. THANK YOU.
"THEY WOULDN'T LEAVE ME ALONE, THOUGH. THEY PUSHED, AND PUSHED. AT LONG LAST, I HAD TO TELL THEM..."
THIS IS A HISTORIC MOMENT. THE FIRST GATHERING OF THE TRUE LEADERS OF THIS CITY IN AT LEAST FIVE YEARS.
THIS IS A CHANCE TO SET ASIDE OUR DIFFERENCES... CONSOLIDATE...LOOK TO THE FUTURE.

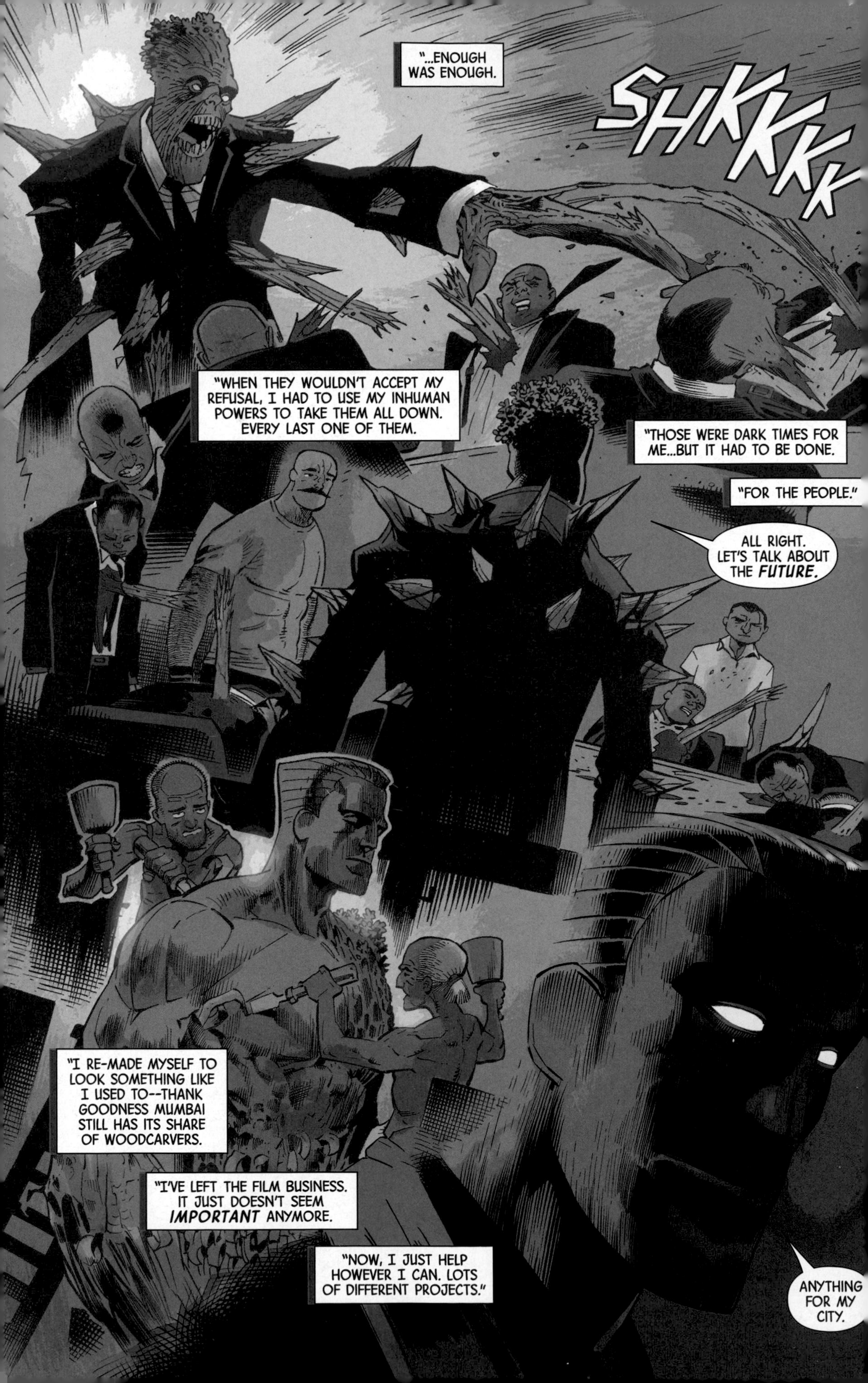
"...ENOUGH WAS ENOUGH.
SHKKKK
"WHEN THEY WOULDN'T ACCEPT MY REFUSAL, I HAD TO USE MY INHUMAN POWERS TO TAKE THEM ALL DOWN. EVERY LAST ONE OF THEM.
"THOSE WERE DARK TIMES FOR ME...BUT IT HAD TO BE DONE.
"FOR THE PEOPLE."
ALL RIGHT. LET'S TALK ABOUT THE *FUTURE.*
"I RE-MADE MYSELF TO LOOK SOMETHING LIKE I USED TO--THANK GOODNESS MUMBAI STILL HAS ITS SHARE OF WOODCARVERS.
"I'VE LEFT THE FILM BUSINESS. IT JUST DOESN'T SEEM *IMPORTANT* ANYMORE.
"NOW, I JUST HELP HOWEVER I CAN. LOTS OF DIFFERENT PROJECTS."
ANYTHING FOR MY CITY.

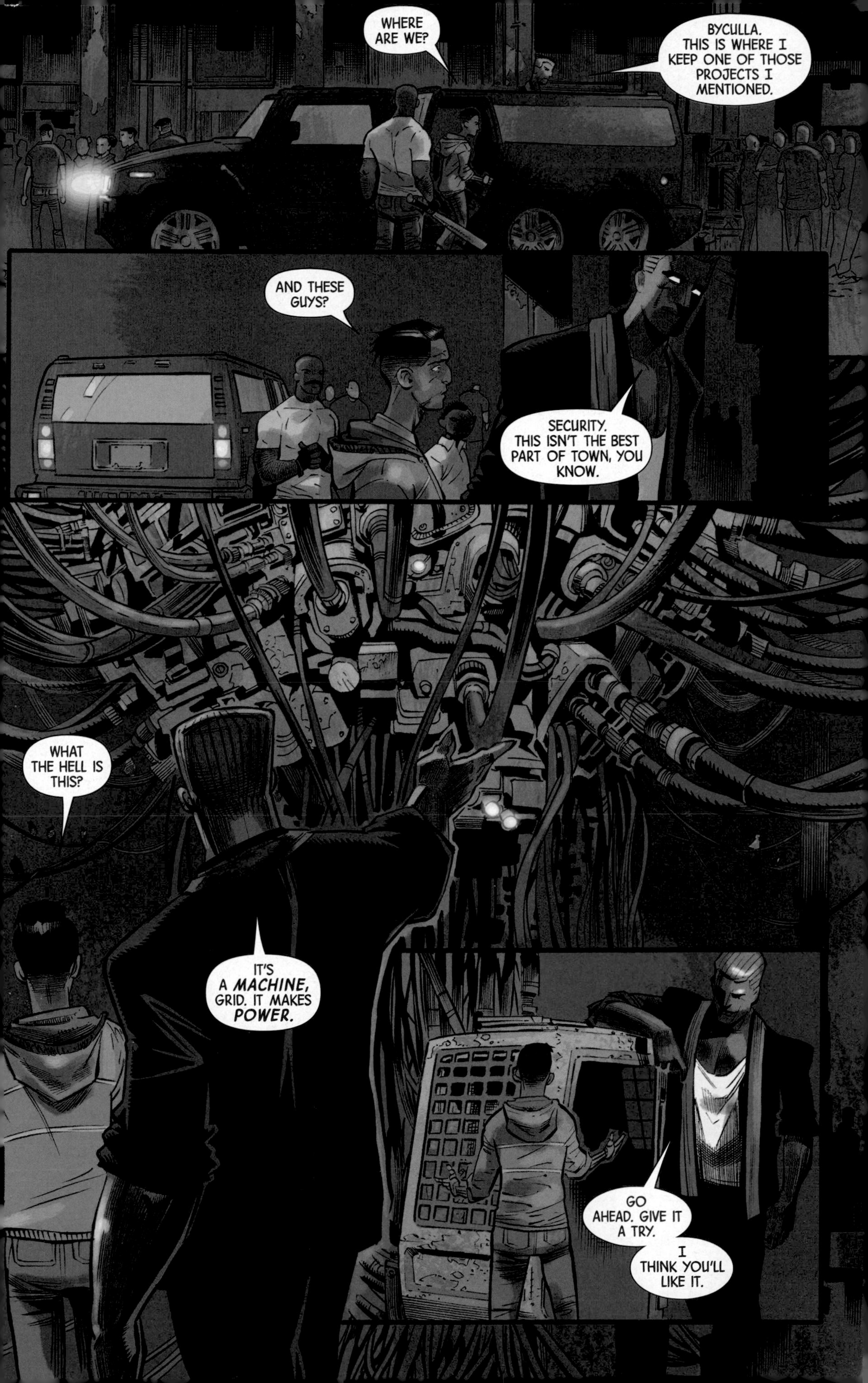
WHERE ARE WE?
BYCULLA. THIS IS WHERE I KEEP ONE OF THOSE PROJECTS I MENTIONED.
AND THESE GUYS?
SECURITY. THIS ISN'T THE BEST PART OF TOWN, YOU KNOW.
WHAT THE HELL IS THIS?
IT'S A *MACHINE*, GRID. IT MAKES **POWER.**
GO AHEAD. GIVE IT A TRY.
I THINK YOU'LL LIKE IT.

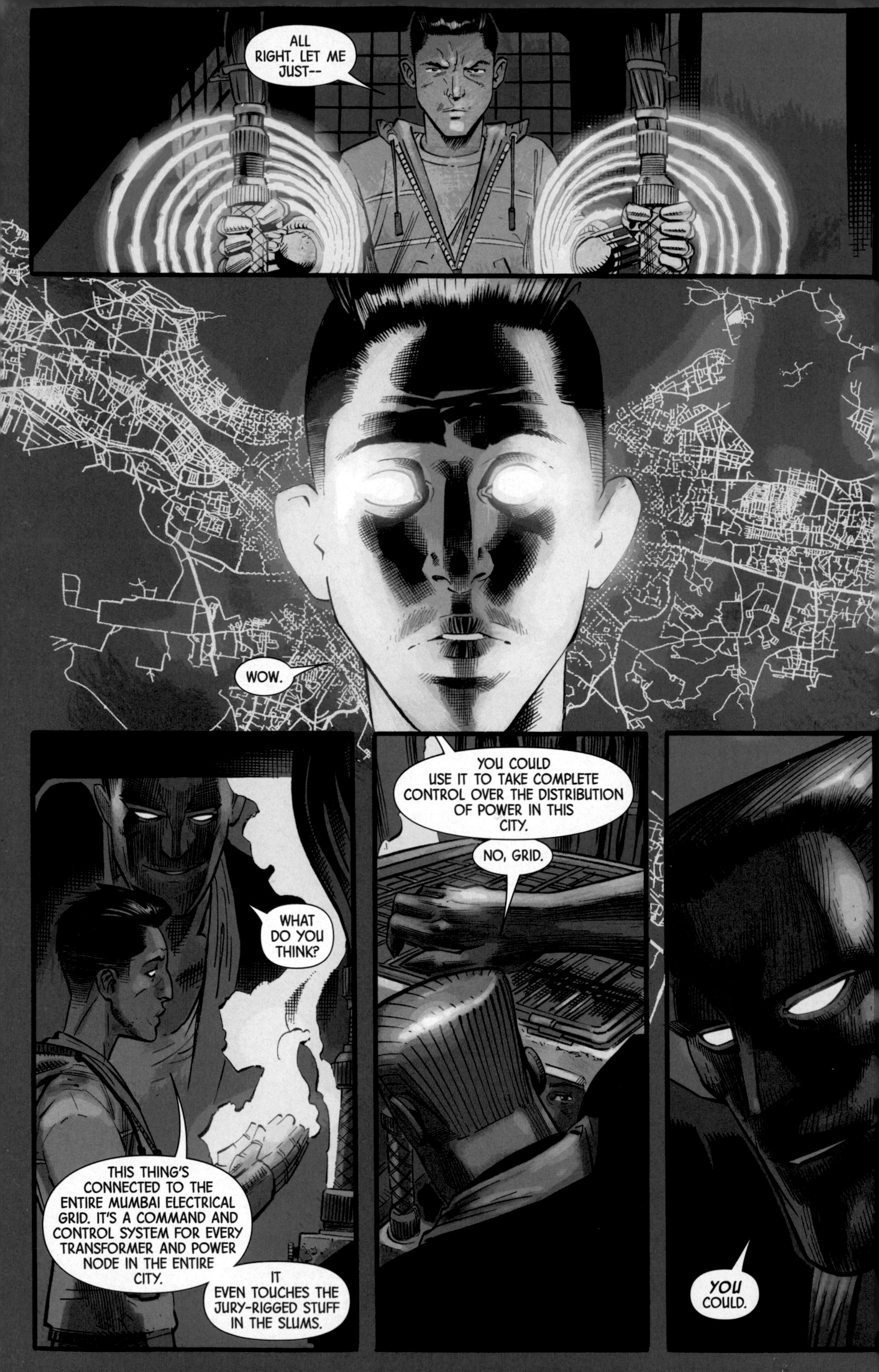
ALL RIGHT. LET ME JUST--
WOW.
WHAT DO YOU THINK?
THIS THING'S CONNECTED TO THE ENTIRE MUMBAI ELECTRICAL GRID. IT'S A COMMAND AND CONTROL SYSTEM FOR EVERY TRANSFORMER AND POWER NODE IN THE ENTIRE CITY.
IT EVEN TOUCHES THE JURY-RIGGED STUFF IN THE SLUMS.
YOU COULD USE IT TO TAKE COMPLETE CONTROL OVER THE DISTRIBUTION OF POWER IN THIS CITY.
NO, GRID.
YOU COULD.

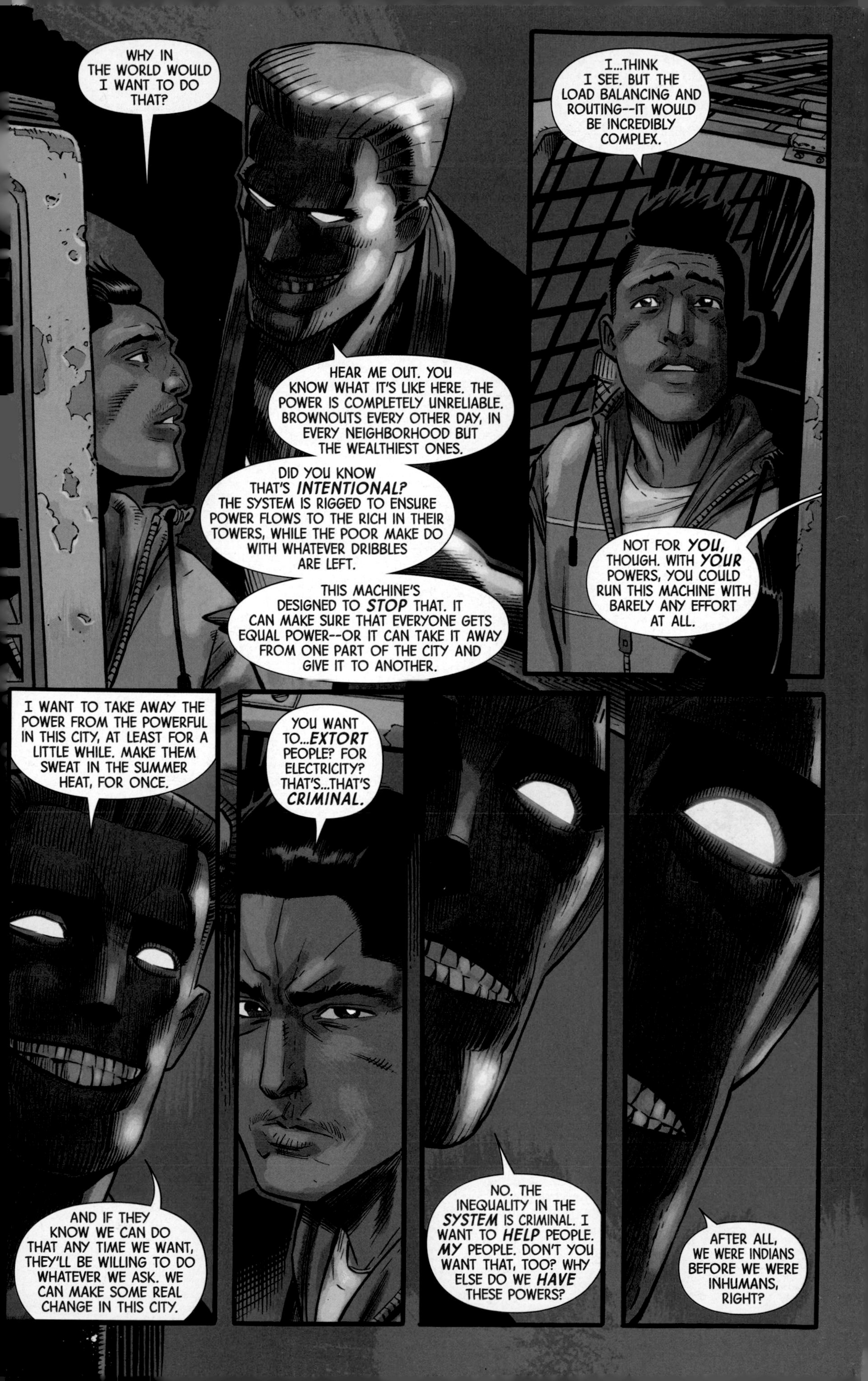
WHY IN THE WORLD WOULD I WANT TO DO THAT?
HEAR ME OUT. YOU KNOW WHAT IT'S LIKE HERE. THE POWER IS COMPLETELY UNRELIABLE. BROWNOUTS EVERY OTHER DAY, IN EVERY NEIGHBORHOOD BUT THE WEALTHIEST ONES.
DID YOU KNOW THAT'S INTENTIONAL? THE SYSTEM IS RIGGED TO ENSURE POWER FLOWS TO THE RICH IN THEIR TOWERS, WHILE THE POOR MAKE DO WITH WHATEVER DRIBBLES ARE LEFT.
THIS MACHINE'S DESIGNED TO STOP THAT. IT CAN MAKE SURE THAT EVERYONE GETS EQUAL POWER--OR IT CAN TAKE IT AWAY FROM ONE PART OF THE CITY AND GIVE IT TO ANOTHER.
I...THINK I SEE. BUT THE LOAD BALANCING AND ROUTING--IT WOULD BE INCREDIBLY COMPLEX.
NOT FOR YOU, THOUGH. WITH YOUR POWERS, YOU COULD RUN THIS MACHINE WITH BARELY ANY EFFORT AT ALL.
I WANT TO TAKE AWAY THE POWER FROM THE POWERFUL IN THIS CITY, AT LEAST FOR A LITTLE WHILE. MAKE THEM SWEAT IN THE SUMMER HEAT, FOR ONCE.
AND IF THEY KNOW WE CAN DO THAT ANY TIME WE WANT, THEY'LL BE WILLING TO DO WHATEVER WE ASK. WE CAN MAKE SOME REAL CHANGE IN THIS CITY.
YOU WANT TO...EXTORT PEOPLE? FOR ELECTRICITY? THAT'S...THAT'S CRIMINAL.
NO. THE INEQUALITY IN THE SYSTEM IS CRIMINAL. I WANT TO HELP PEOPLE. MY PEOPLE. DON'T YOU WANT THAT, TOO? WHY ELSE DO WE HAVE THESE POWERS?
AFTER ALL, WE WERE INDIANS BEFORE WE WERE INHUMANS, RIGHT?

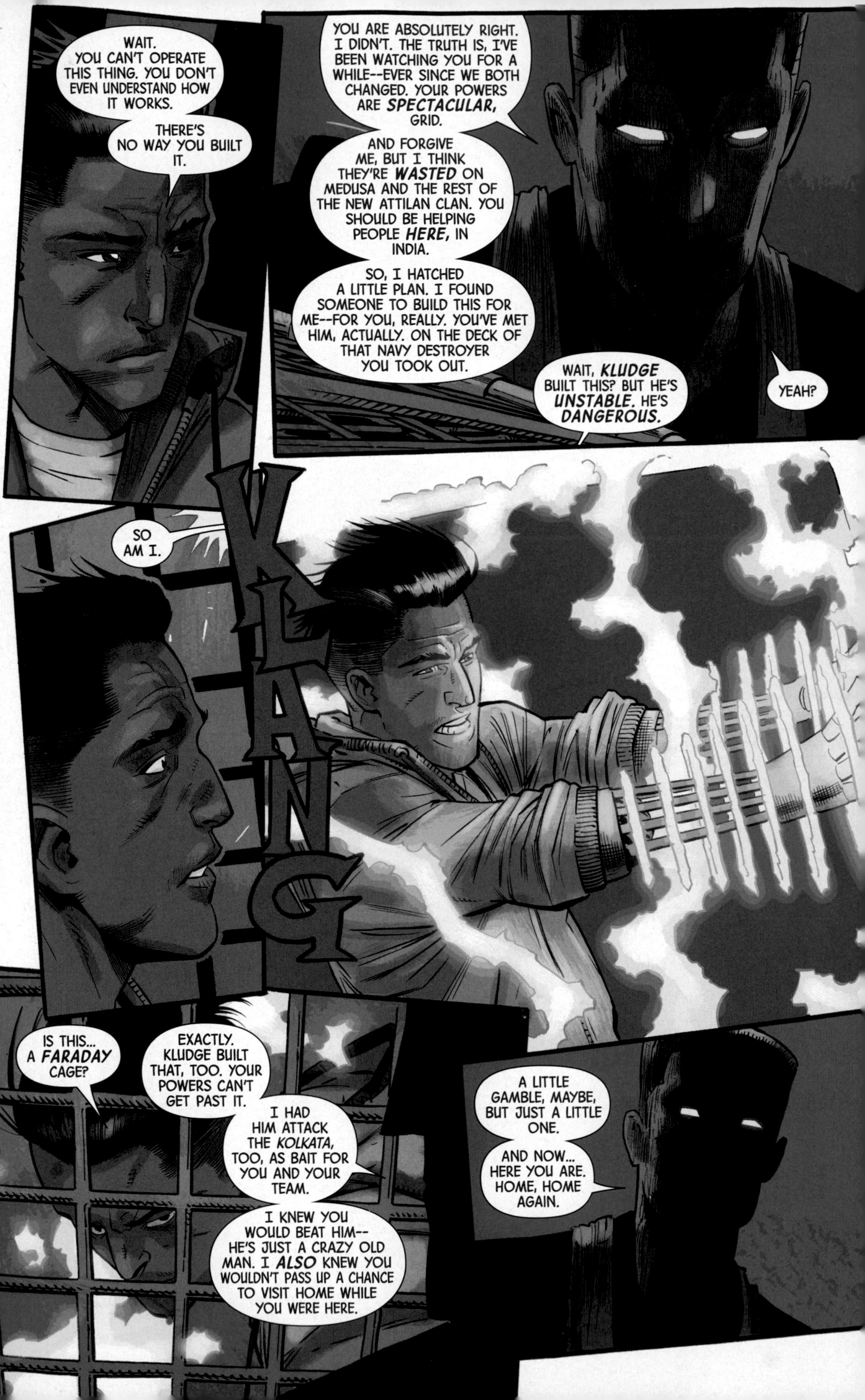
WAIT. YOU CAN'T OPERATE THIS THING. YOU DON'T EVEN UNDERSTAND HOW IT WORKS.
THERE'S NO WAY YOU BUILT IT.
YOU ARE ABSOLUTELY RIGHT. I DIDN'T. THE TRUTH IS, I'VE BEEN WATCHING YOU FOR A WHILE--EVER SINCE WE BOTH CHANGED. YOUR POWERS ARE SPECTACULAR, GRID.
AND FORGIVE ME, BUT I THINK THEY'RE WASTED ON MEDUSA AND THE REST OF THE NEW ATTILAN CLAN. YOU SHOULD BE HELPING PEOPLE HERE, IN INDIA.
SO, I HATCHED A LITTLE PLAN. I FOUND SOMEONE TO BUILD THIS FOR ME--FOR YOU, REALLY. YOU'VE MET HIM, ACTUALLY. ON THE DECK OF THAT NAVY DESTROYER YOU TOOK OUT.
WAIT, KLUDGE BUILT THIS? BUT HE'S UNSTABLE. HE'S DANGEROUS.
YEAH?
SO AM I.
KLANG
IS THIS... A FARADAY CAGE?
EXACTLY. KLUDGE BUILT THAT, TOO. YOUR POWERS CAN'T GET PAST IT.
I HAD HIM ATTACK THE KOLKATA, TOO, AS BAIT FOR YOU AND YOUR TEAM.
I KNEW YOU WOULD BEAT HIM--HE'S JUST A CRAZY OLD MAN. I ALSO KNEW YOU WOULDN'T PASS UP A CHANCE TO VISIT HOME WHILE YOU WERE HERE.
A LITTLE GAMBLE, MAYBE, BUT JUST A LITTLE ONE.
AND NOW... HERE YOU ARE. HOME, HOME AGAIN.

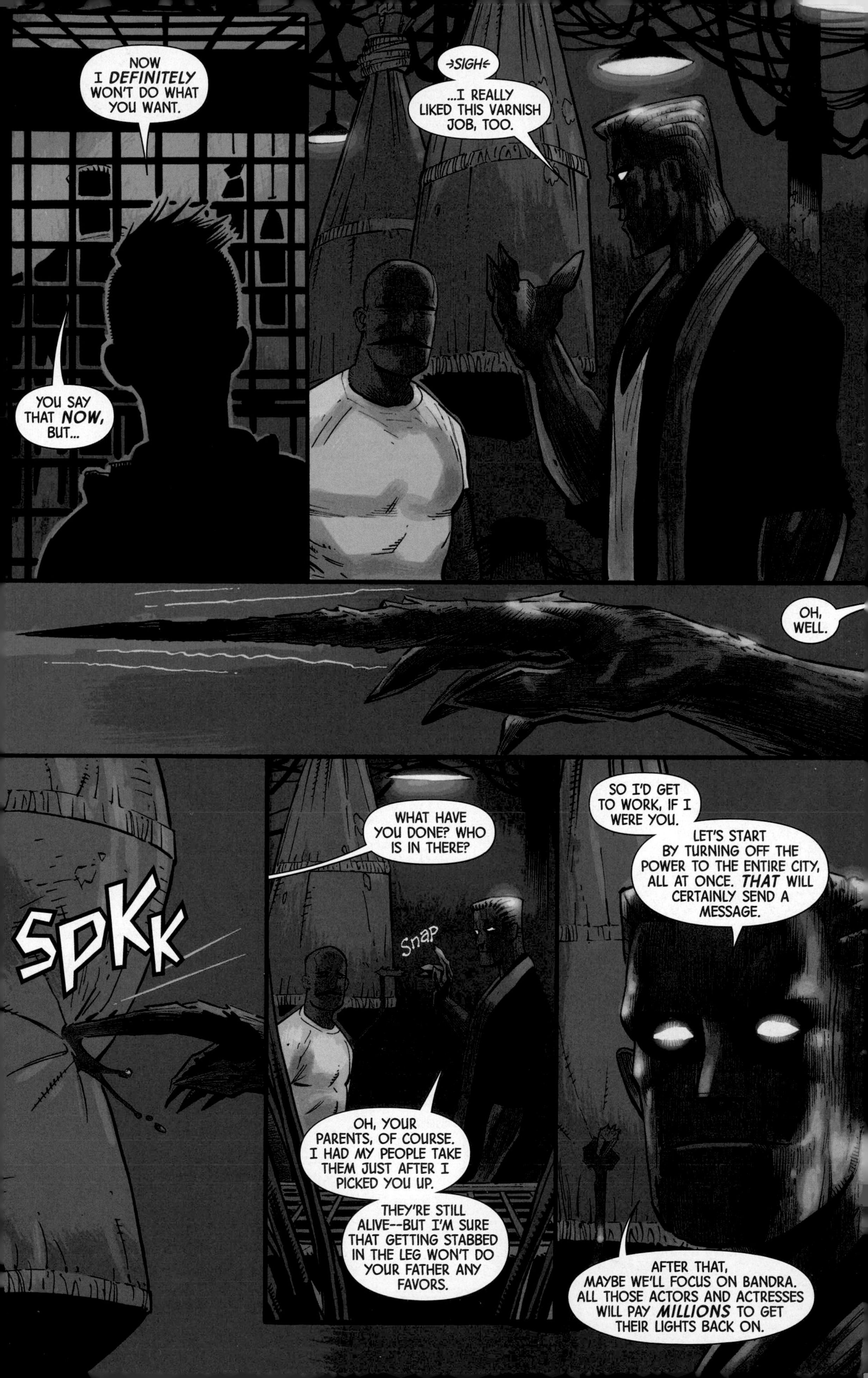
NOW I DEFINITELY WON'T DO WHAT YOU WANT.
YOU SAY THAT NOW, BUT...
SIGH
...I REALLY LIKED THIS VARNISH JOB, TOO.
OH, WELL.
SPKK
WHAT HAVE YOU DONE? WHO IS IN THERE?
SNAP
OH, YOUR PARENTS, OF COURSE. I HAD MY PEOPLE TAKE THEM JUST AFTER I PICKED YOU UP.
THEY'RE STILL ALIVE--BUT I'M SURE THAT GETTING STABBED IN THE LEG WON'T DO YOUR FATHER ANY FAVORS.
SO I'D GET TO WORK, IF I WERE YOU.
LET'S START BY TURNING OFF THE POWER TO THE ENTIRE CITY, ALL AT ONCE. THAT WILL CERTAINLY SEND A MESSAGE.
AFTER THAT, MAYBE WE'LL FOCUS ON BANDRA. ALL THOSE ACTORS AND ACTRESSES WILL PAY MILLIONS TO GET THEIR LIGHTS BACK ON.

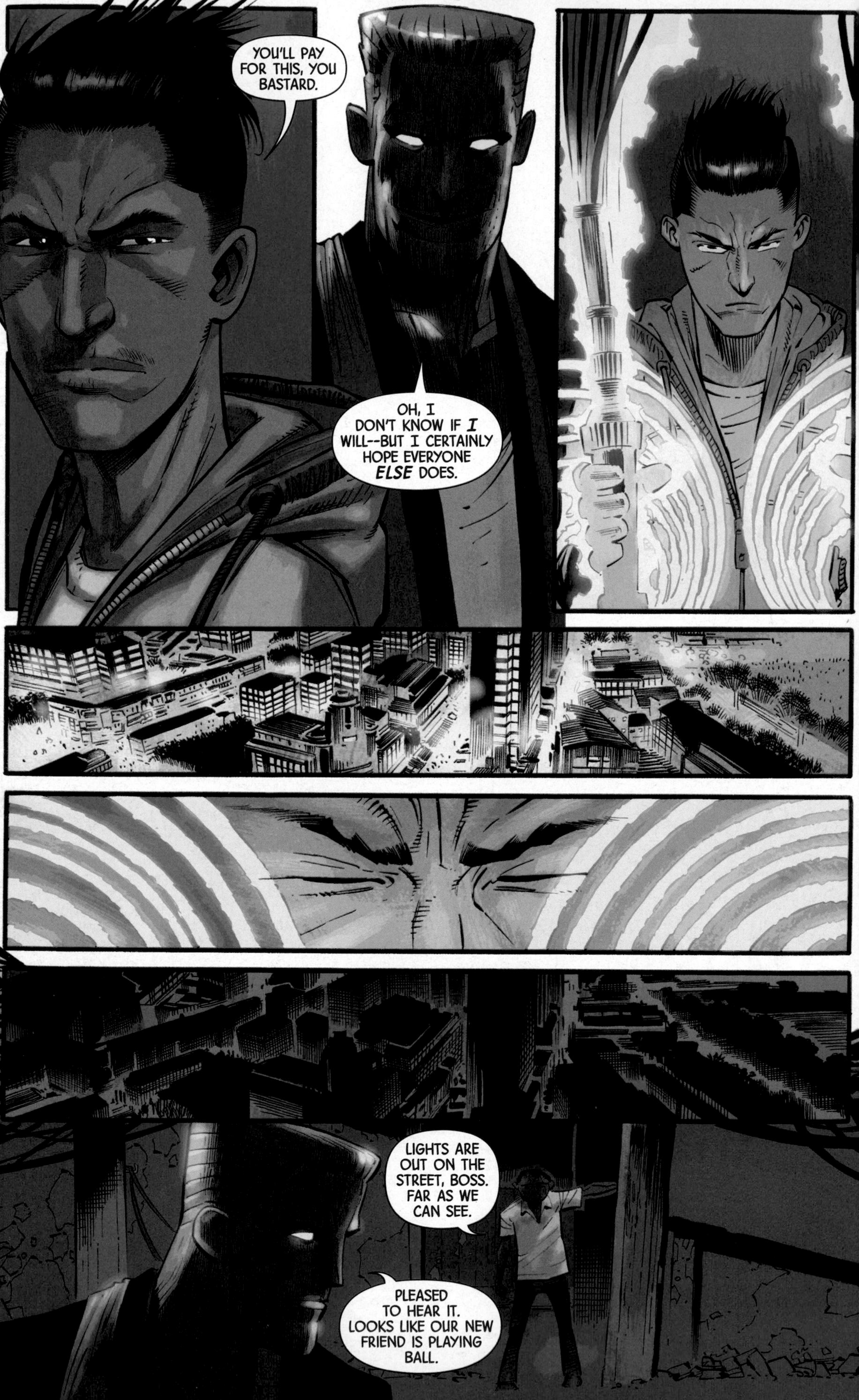
YOU'LL PAY FOR THIS, YOU BASTARD.
OH, I DON'T KNOW IF *I* WILL--BUT I CERTAINLY HOPE EVERYONE *ELSE* DOES.
LIGHTS ARE OUT ON THE STREET, BOSS. FAR AS WE CAN SEE.
PLEASED TO HEAR IT. LOOKS LIKE OUR NEW FRIEND IS PLAYING BALL.

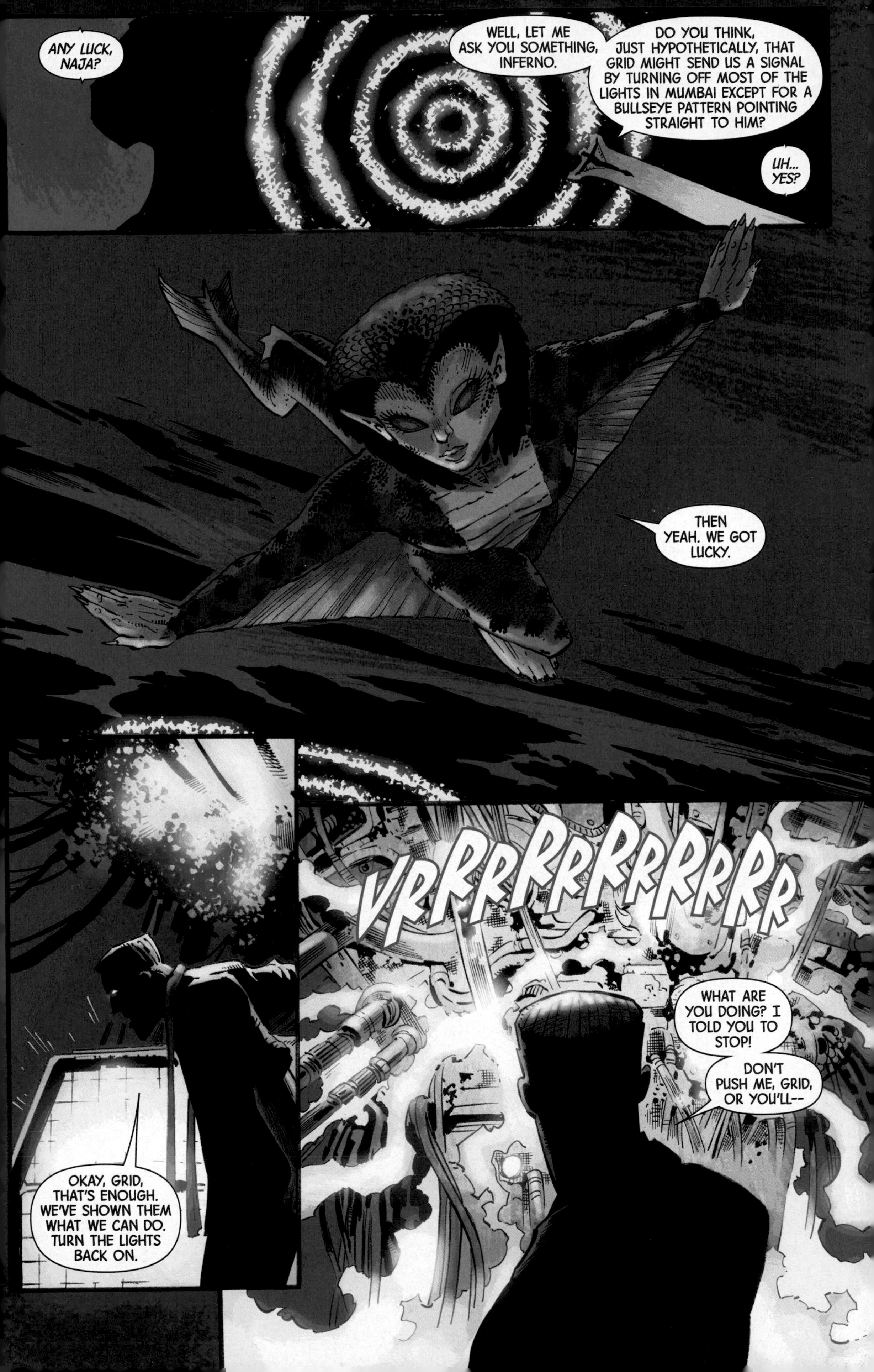
ANY LUCK, NAJA?
WELL, LET ME ASK YOU SOMETHING, INFERNO.
DO YOU THINK, JUST HYPOTHETICALLY, THAT GRID MIGHT SEND US A SIGNAL BY TURNING OFF MOST OF THE LIGHTS IN MUMBAI EXCEPT FOR A BULLSEYE PATTERN POINTING STRAIGHT TO HIM?
UH... YES?
THEN YEAH. WE GOT LUCKY.
OKAY, GRID, THAT'S ENOUGH. WE'VE SHOWN THEM WHAT WE CAN DO. TURN THE LIGHTS BACK ON.
VRRRRRRRRRRR
WHAT ARE YOU DOING? I TOLD YOU TO STOP!
DON'T PUSH ME, GRID, OR YOU'LL--

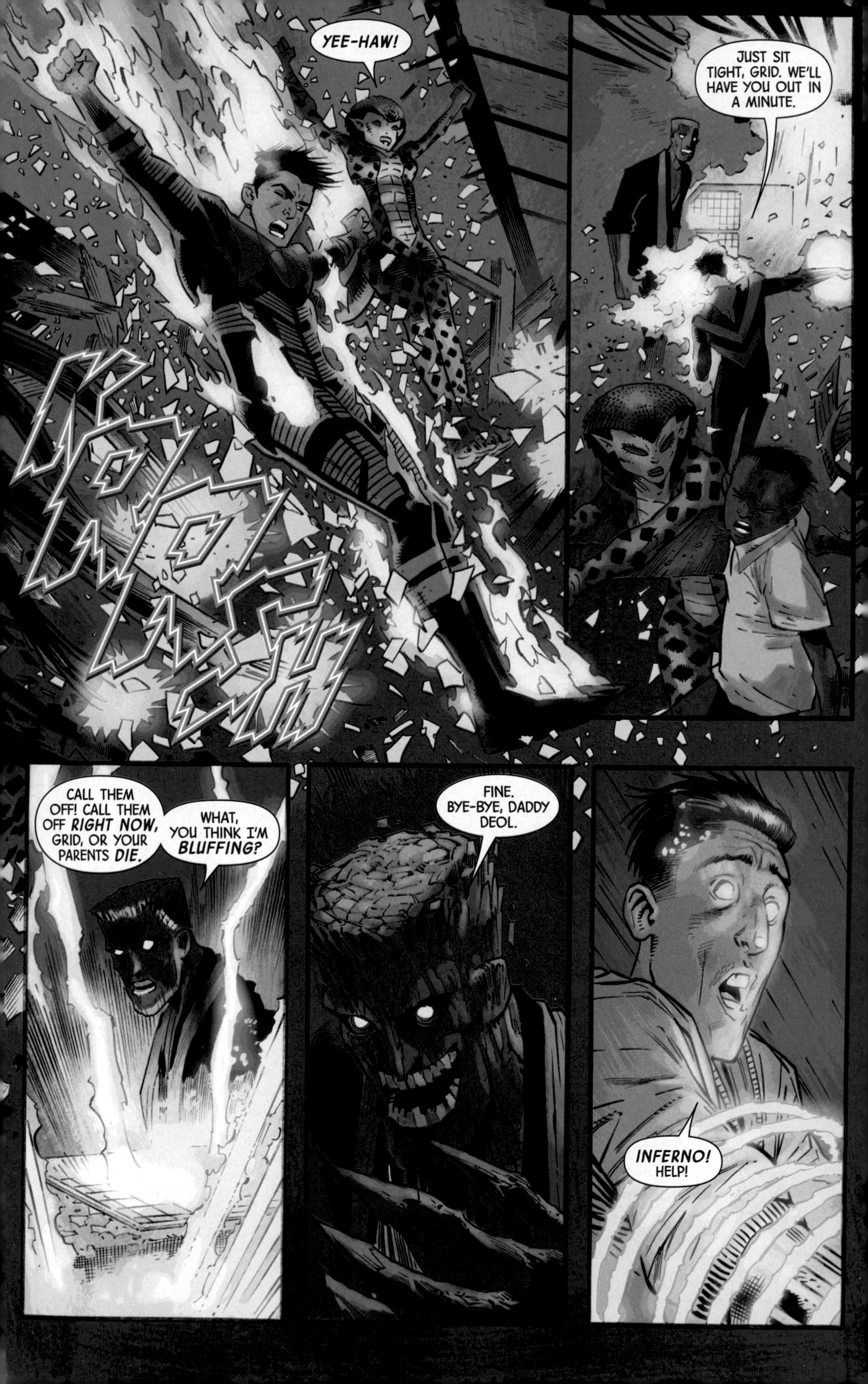
YEE-HAW!
JUST SIT TIGHT, GRID. WE'LL HAVE YOU OUT IN A MINUTE.
CALL THEM OFF! CALL THEM OFF *RIGHT NOW*, GRID, OR YOUR PARENTS *DIE*.
WHAT, YOU THINK I'M *BLUFFING*?
FINE. BYE-BYE, DADDY DEOL.
INFERNO! HELP!

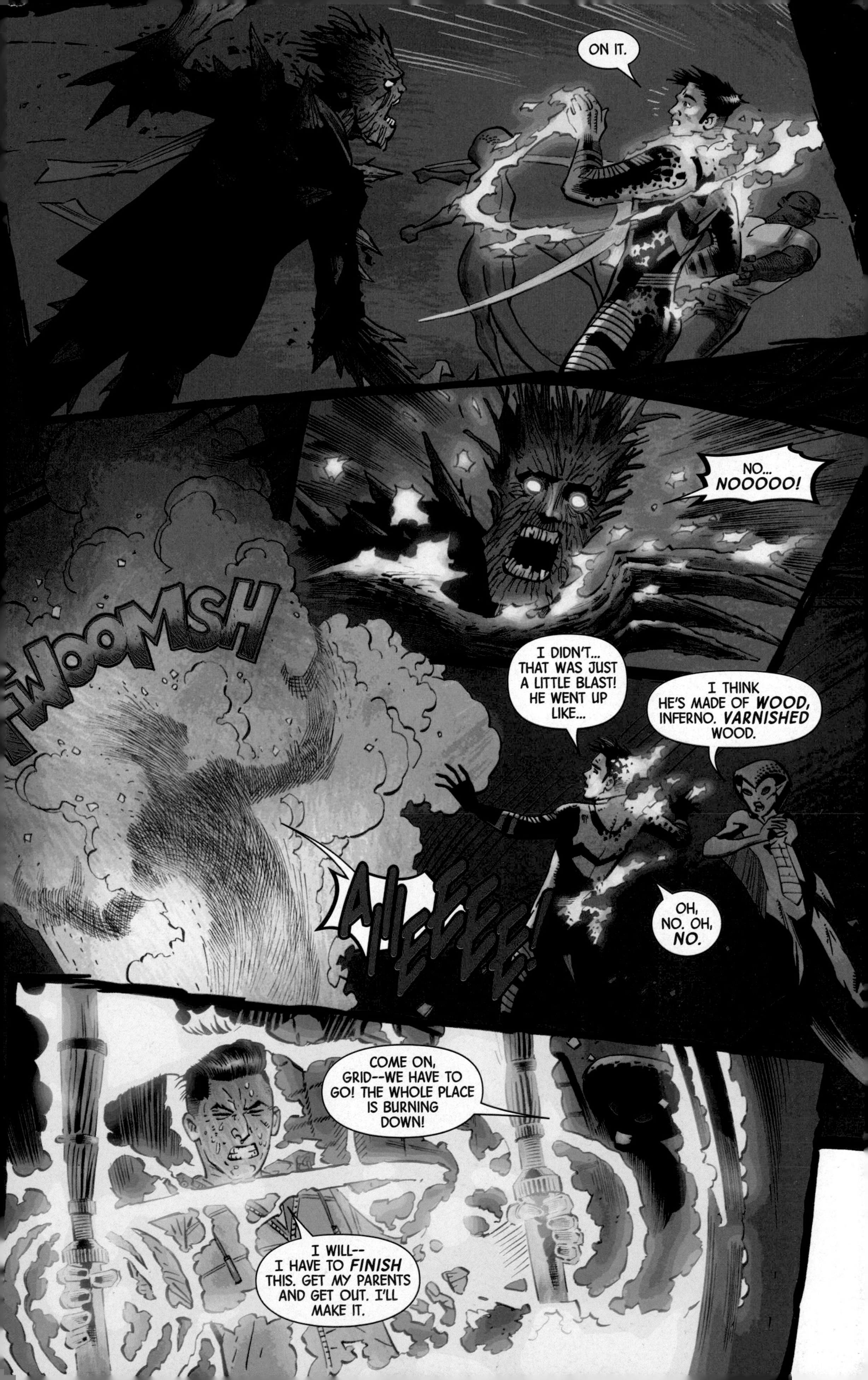
ON IT.
NO... NOOOOO!
WOOMSH
I DIDN'T... THAT WAS JUST A LITTLE BLAST! HE WENT UP LIKE...
I THINK HE'S MADE OF WOOD, INFERNO. VARNISHED WOOD.
AIIEEEE!
OH, NO. OH, NO.
COME ON, GRID--WE HAVE TO GO! THE WHOLE PLACE IS BURNING DOWN!
I WILL-- I HAVE TO FINISH THIS. GET MY PARENTS AND GET OUT. I'LL MAKE IT.

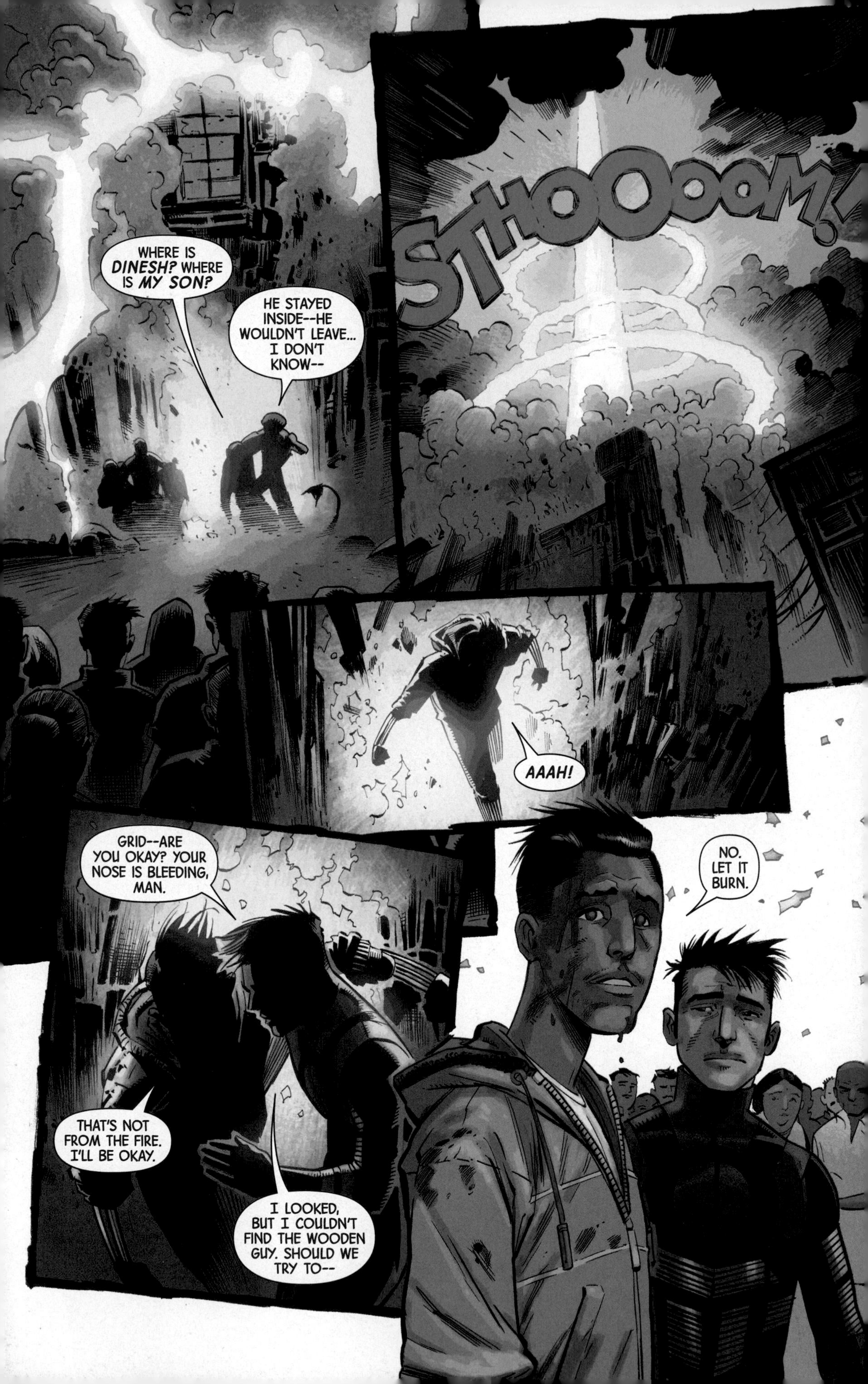
WHERE IS DINESH? WHERE IS MY SON?
HE STAYED INSIDE--HE WOULDN'T LEAVE... I DON'T KNOW--
STHOOOoom!
AAAH!
GRID--ARE YOU OKAY? YOUR NOSE IS BLEEDING, MAN.
THAT'S NOT FROM THE FIRE. I'LL BE OKAY.
I LOOKED, BUT I COULDN'T FIND THE WOODEN GUY. SHOULD WE TRY TO--
NO. LET IT BURN.

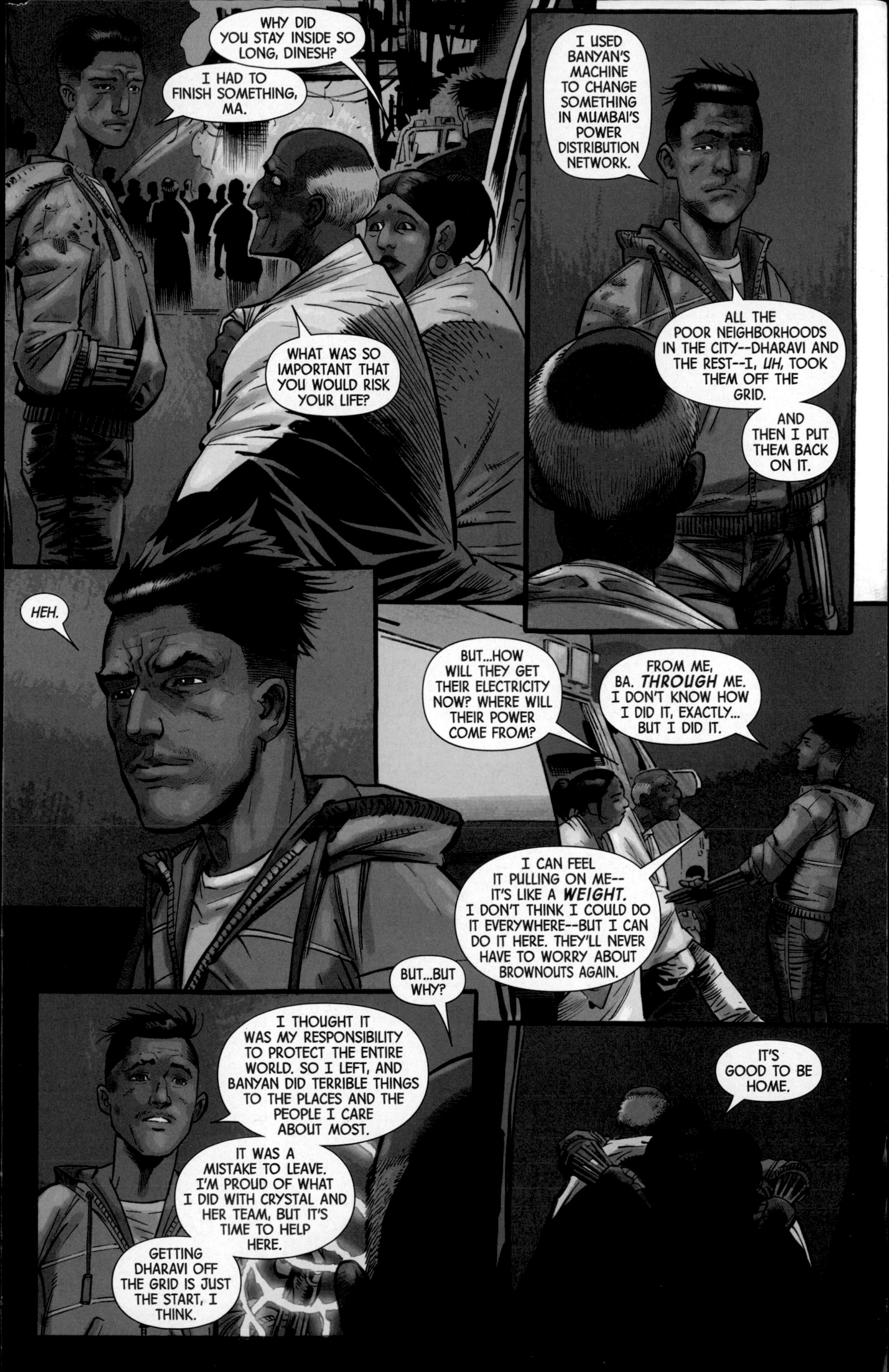
WHY DID YOU STAY INSIDE SO LONG, DINESH?
I HAD TO FINISH SOMETHING, MA.
WHAT WAS SO IMPORTANT THAT YOU WOULD RISK YOUR LIFE?
I USED BANYAN'S MACHINE TO CHANGE SOMETHING IN MUMBAI'S POWER DISTRIBUTION NETWORK.
ALL THE POOR NEIGHBORHOODS IN THE CITY--DHARAVI AND THE REST--I, *UH*, TOOK THEM OFF THE GRID.
AND THEN I PUT THEM BACK ON IT.
HEH.
BUT...HOW WILL THEY GET THEIR ELECTRICITY NOW? WHERE WILL THEIR POWER COME FROM?
FROM ME, BA. ***THROUGH*** ME. I DON'T KNOW HOW I DID IT, EXACTLY... BUT I DID IT.
I CAN FEEL IT PULLING ON ME--IT'S LIKE A ***WEIGHT.*** I DON'T THINK I COULD DO IT EVERYWHERE--BUT I CAN DO IT HERE. THEY'LL NEVER HAVE TO WORRY ABOUT BROWNOUTS AGAIN.
BUT...BUT WHY?
I THOUGHT IT WAS MY RESPONSIBILITY TO PROTECT THE ENTIRE WORLD. SO I LEFT, AND BANYAN DID TERRIBLE THINGS TO THE PLACES AND THE PEOPLE I CARE ABOUT MOST.
IT WAS A MISTAKE TO LEAVE. I'M PROUD OF WHAT I DID WITH CRYSTAL AND HER TEAM, BUT IT'S TIME TO HELP HERE.
GETTING DHARAVI OFF THE GRID IS JUST THE START, I THINK.
IT'S GOOD TO BE HOME.

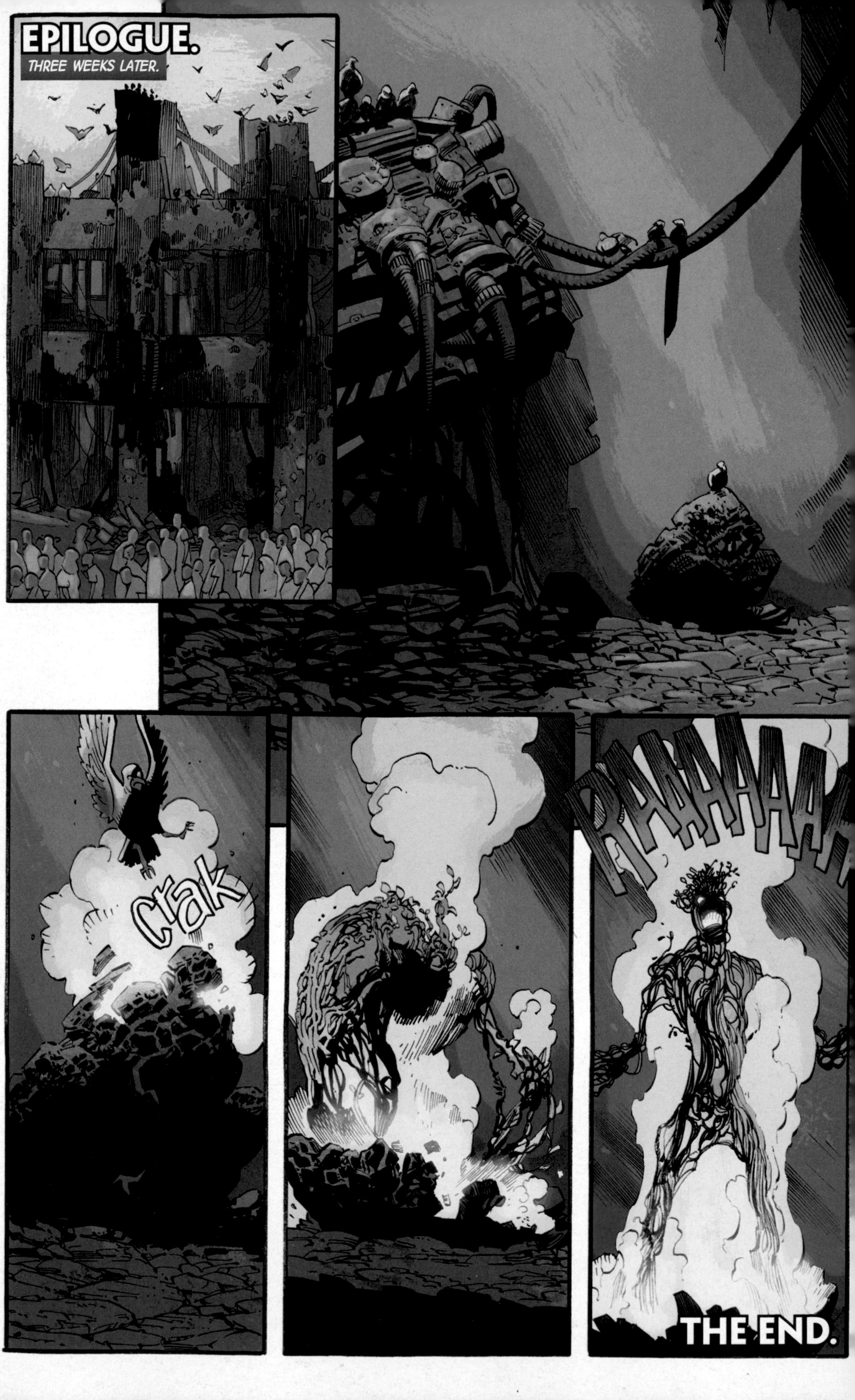
EPILOGUE.
THREE WEEKS LATER.
crak
RAAAAAAA
THE END.

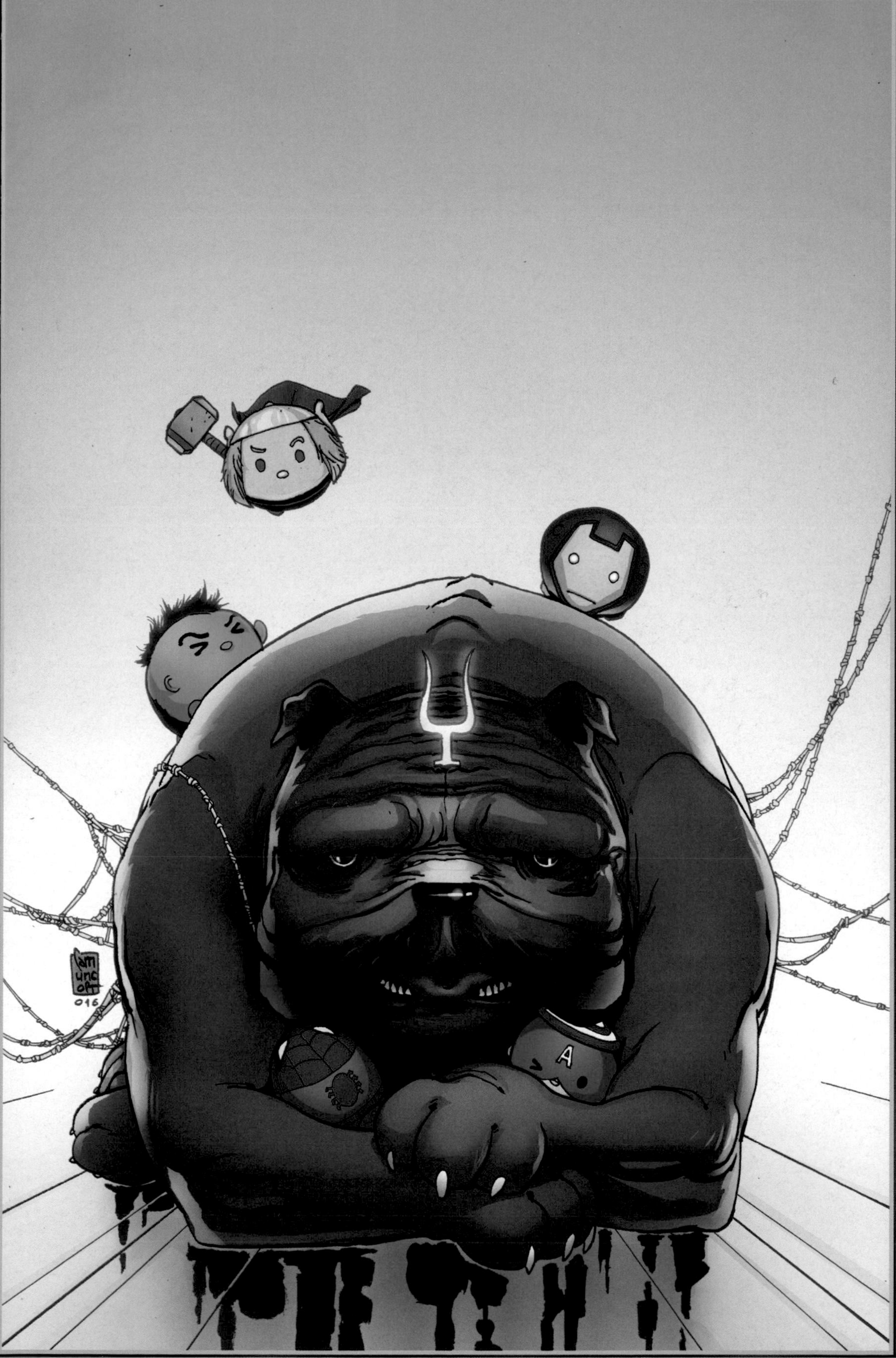

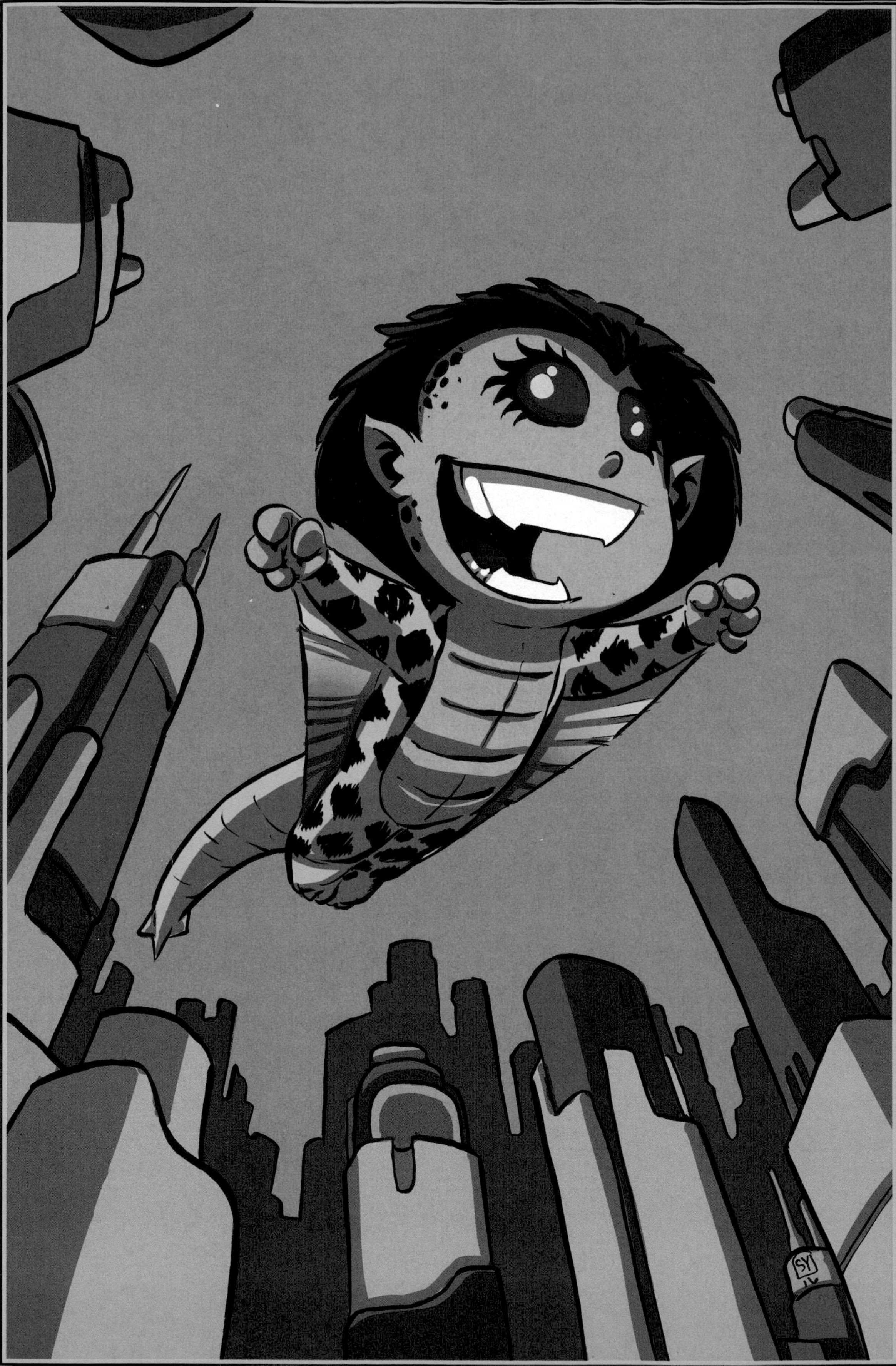

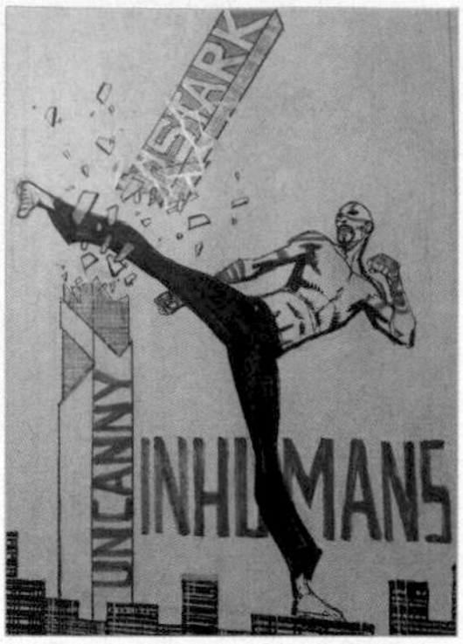
STARK
UNCANNY INHUMANS

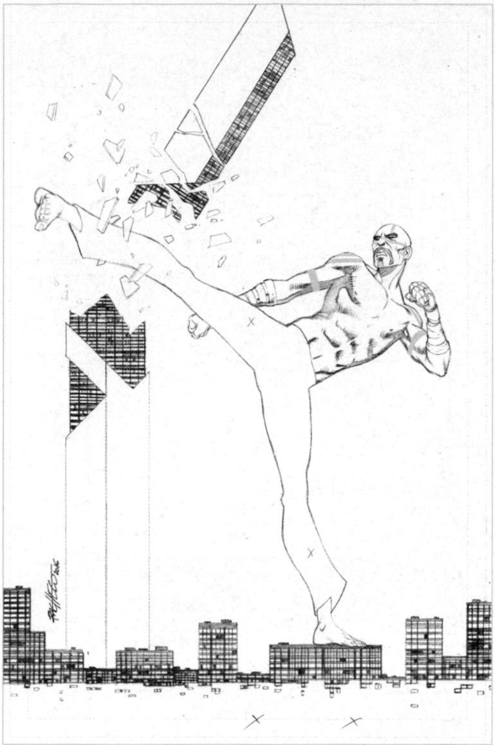

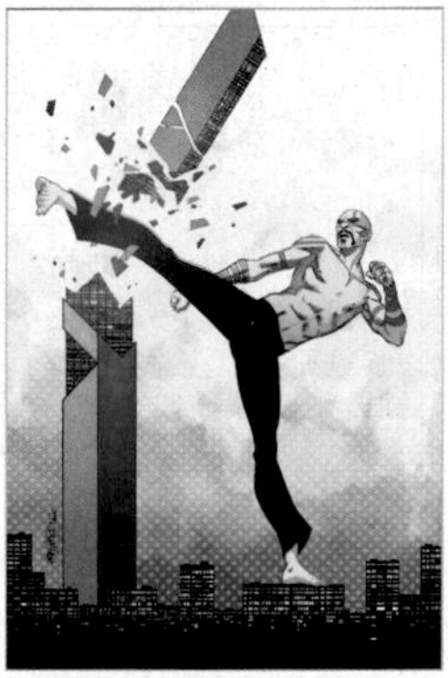

#11 COVER PROCESS BY CARLOS PACHECO & JAVA TARTAGLIA

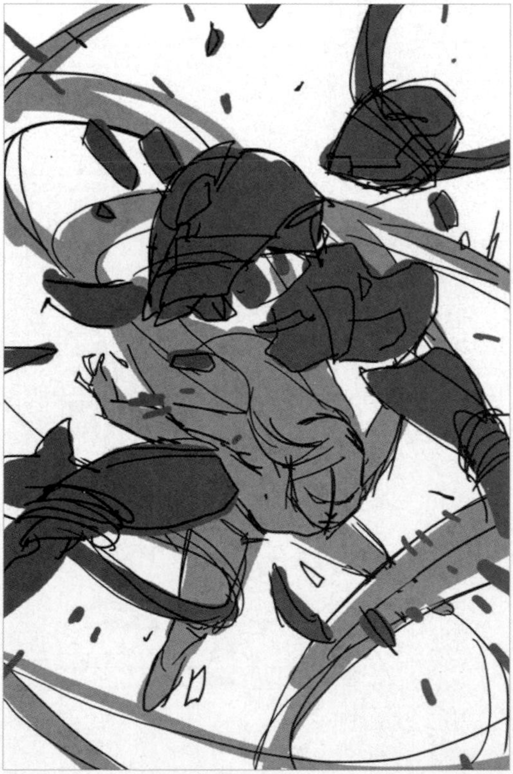

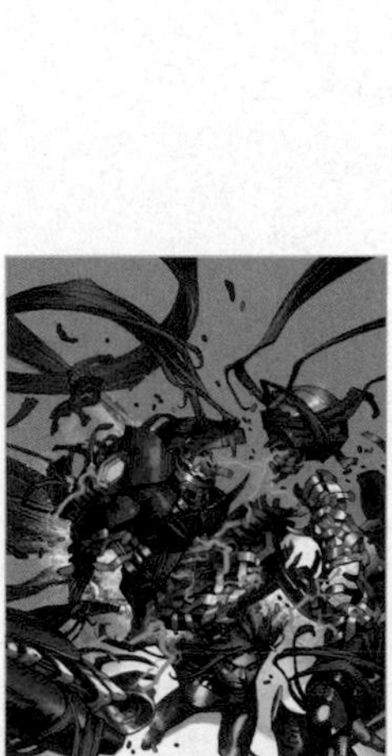

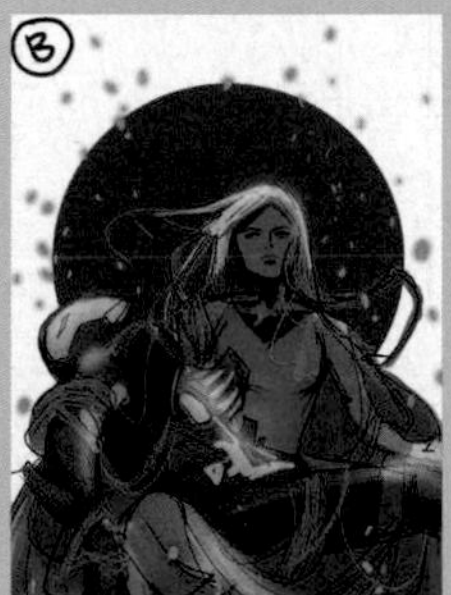
B

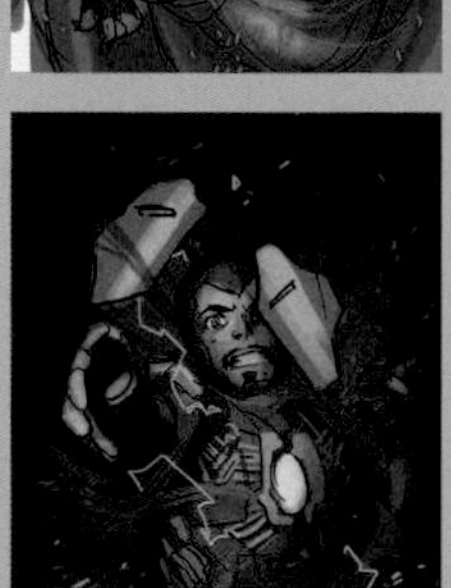
4

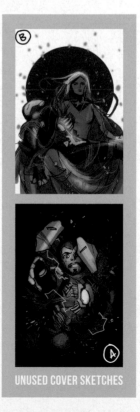

UNUSED COVER SKETCHES

#11 VARIANT COVER PROCESS BY YASMINE PUTRI

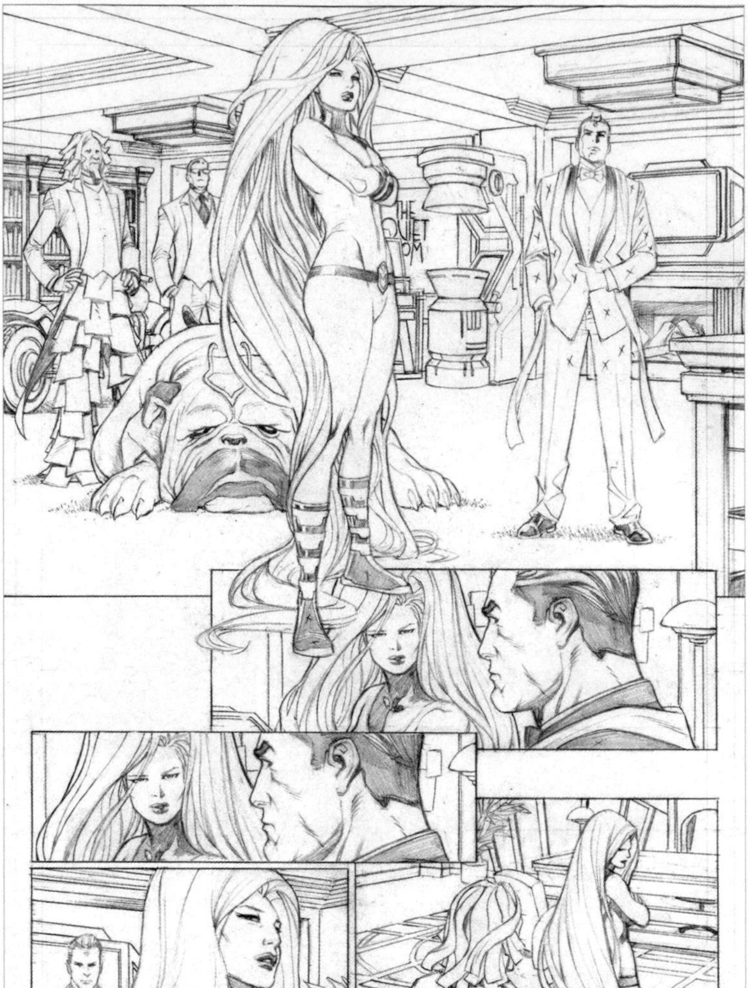
THE QUIET

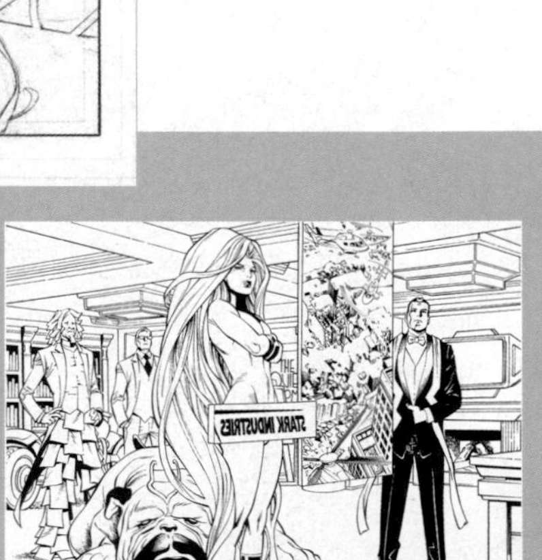
STARK INDUSTRIES

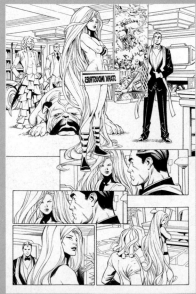

#12 PAGE 7 PENCILS BY CARLOS PACHECO;
INKS BY ANDY OWENS

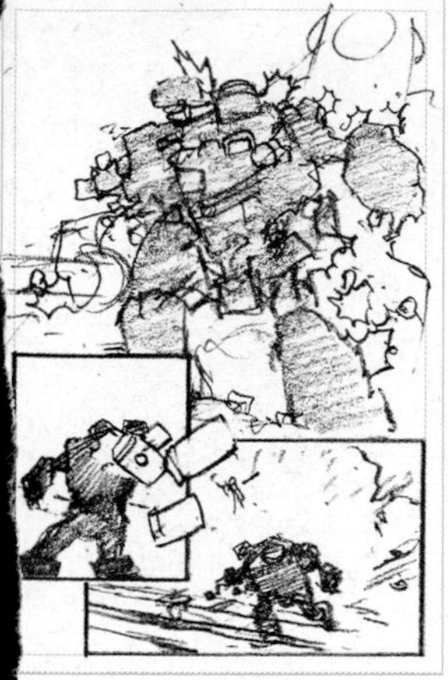

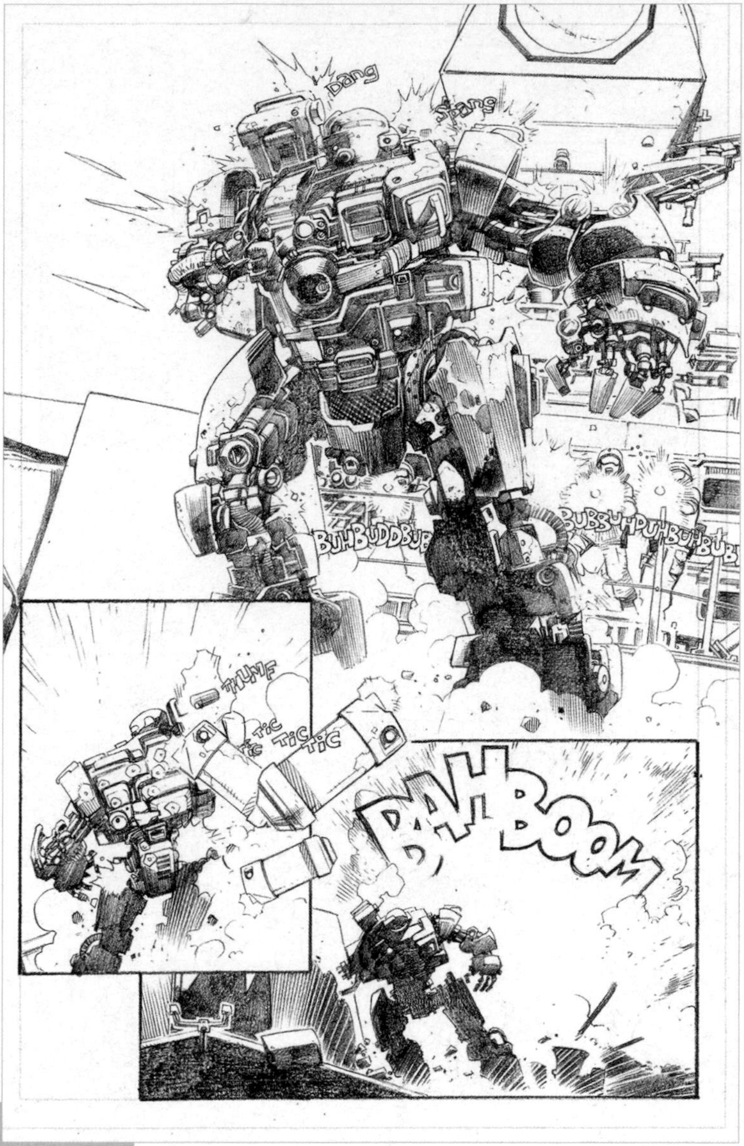
Dang
Spang
BUHBUDDBUB
BUBBUHPUHBUHBUB
THUMF
TIC
TIC
TIC
TIC
BAHBOOM

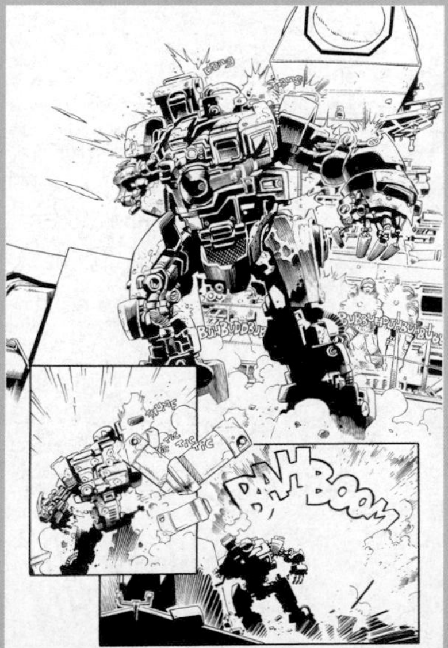
BAHBOOM

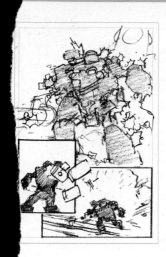

**ANNUAL #1 PAGE 1 LAYOUT & PENCILS BY KEV WALKER;
INKS BY SCOTT HANNA**

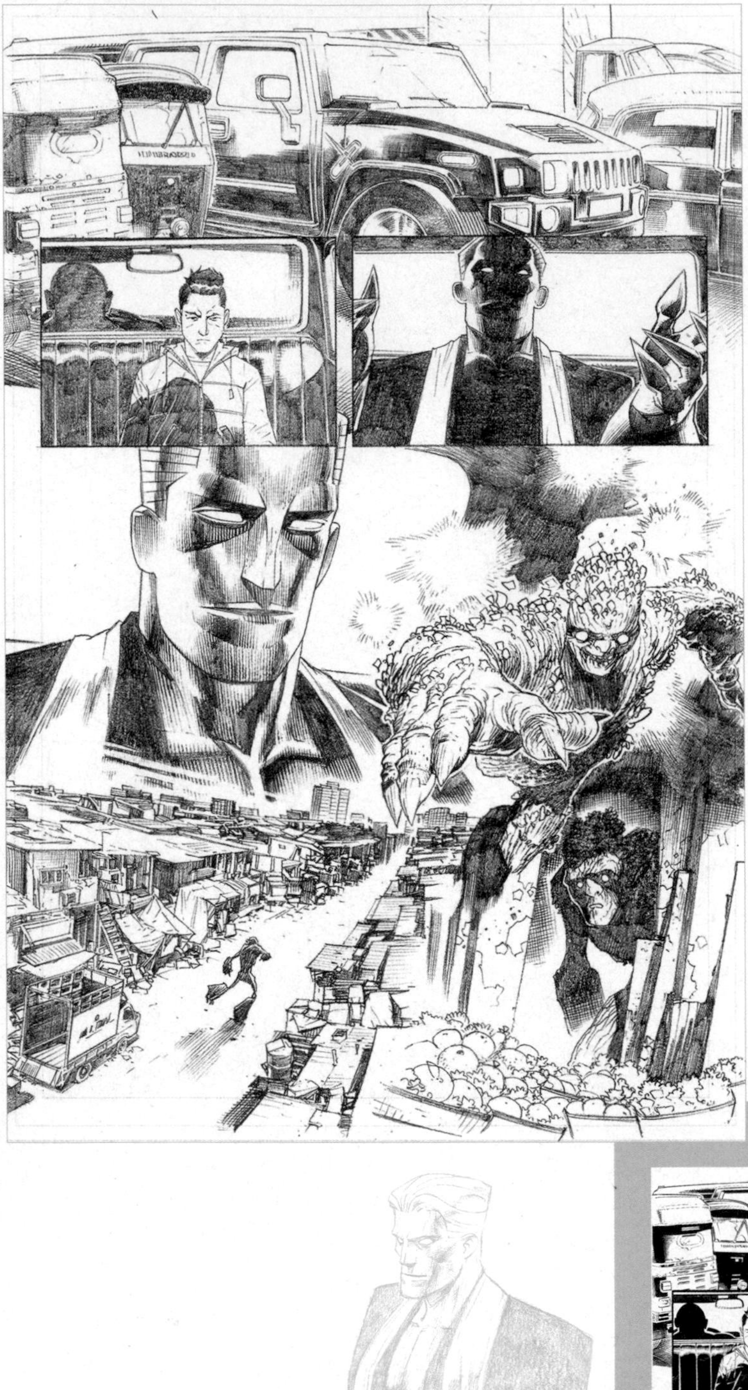

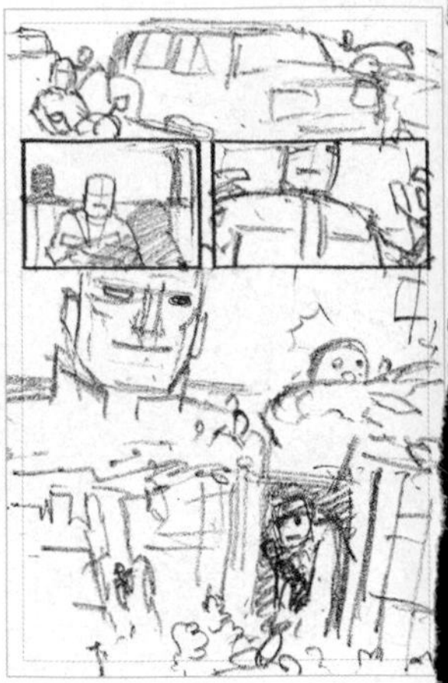

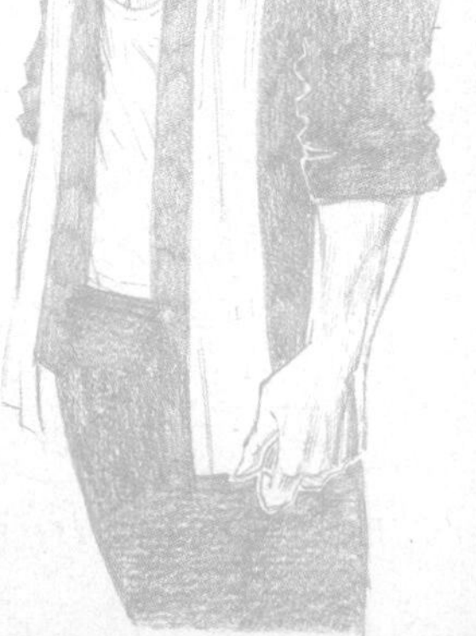

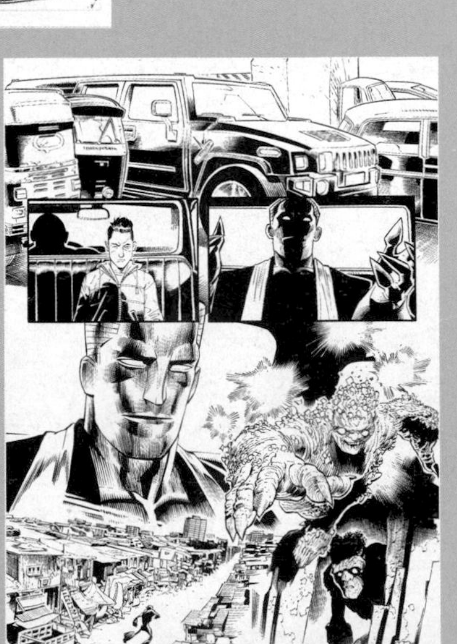

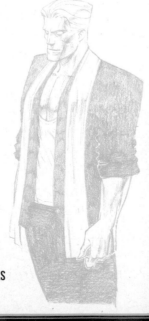

ANNUAL #1 PAGE 16 LAYOUT, PENCILS
& BANYAN SKETCH BY KEV WALKER